SWINBURNE

ALGERNON CHARLES SWINBURNE, *ÆTAT* 58

From the original drawing by Sir William Rothenstein
in the Municipal Gallery of Modern Art, Dublin

By permission of the Artist and of the Dublin Corporation

Photo T. F. Geoghegan

SWINBURNE

A LITERARY BIOGRAPHY

BY

GEORGES LAFOURCADE

NEW YORK / RUSSELL & RUSSELL

FIRST PUBLISHED IN 1932
REISSUED, 1967, BY RUSSELL & RUSSELL
A DIVISION OF ATHENEUM HOUSE INC.
BY ARRANGEMENT WITH G. BELL & SONS, LONDON
L. C. CATALOG CARD NO: 66−24720

PRINTED IN THE UNITED STATES OF AMERICA

TO
DENIS SAURAT

Above all, the noble evidence you have given that in his case, as in the case of any man not ignoble, the purest barest truth is best and safest for him as for us, demands all thanks from us all.

(Swinburne on **W. M** Rossetti's *Life of Shelley* – January 15, 1870)

CONTENTS

LIST OF ILLUSTRATIONS

FOREWORD

WRITING a life of Swinburne needs no justification : for, to set aside the importance of his work in the field of literature and the inevitable biographical connections, this life as such is interesting. It is indeed no small paradox that, comparatively uneventful as it was, it should compel to such an extent attention and even sympathy : to have known such people as Landor, Burton, Mazzini, Menken, Hugo, the Pre-Raphaelite painters, etc., is not in itself an exceptional experience ; a few short trips to France and Italy are common occurrences in the life of a man of letters ; Eton, Oxford and chambers in London form a very ordinary curriculum for a young aristocrat of literary proclivities. Yet these things acquire flavour and piquancy as soon as we know that Swinburne is concerned ; which is the test of personality. It is the sentimental force behind the man, his impulses and reactions, which give a new and unexpected significance to otherwise commonplace facts.

Interest in Swinburne was at its height between 1865 and 1880 : he aroused in friends or foes admiration, love, alarm, indignation, envy, hate, almost every feeling except indifference. To religious preachers as well as to undergraduates throughout the country he became a by-word and a symbol. He stood for revolt, for the justification of sin and for many other things. Famous artists, like G. F. Watts, accounted it a

ix

privilege to paint his portrait. Meredith, Goncourt and others introduced him as a character in their novels. His fame, or rather his personality, transcended the frontiers of his own country : my friend Mario Praz has explained with great skill and industry how he became abroad the type of the perverse Englishman of aesthetic tendencies.

Years passed. Swinburne's fame increased, but his popularity and magnetism were on the wane. It was discovered that this revolutionary poet held on some points distinctly conservative views ; that this great romantic preserved an eminently classical attitude as regards form and the canons of prosody ; that his boldest attempts were often a feat of consummate art ; that this lyrist and this pamphleteer was also a critic and a scholar. His way of life, which had at one time been wild and irregular, suddenly became deplorably quiet. He had retired to a ' dull suburban villa ' with a dull friend, and, being now stone-deaf, seemed sealed to all outward influences. Newspapermen and literary gossips, who had so often stated that the poet was at death's door, resented that he should live up to his seventy-third year. His lack of interest in the younger generation was manifest, and Oscar Wilde was an unwelcome guest at The Pines. The older generation, especially, among whom he had created such a sensation grew to dislike and even to hate him as one hates one's old illusions, enthusiasms or indignations. So the legend got about that Swinburne was stale and dull and old-fashioned. It is still current nowadays, and the exquisites of the modern school affect to see in him the last and perhaps the worst of the Victorians.

He was however essentially a modern. He is far

more akin to Proust and Gide,[1] Lawrence, Huxley or Joyce than either Tennyson, Browning, Leconte de Lisle, Zola, Meredith or Hardy. He sowed the seeds from which grew Pater, Wilde and the whole decadent school ; but he went further than these. In refusing to suppress some of the deepest sexual tendencies of his nature he was un-Victorian ; in the simple, straightforward manner in which he treats and records those impulses, he is as unlike Wilde as is possible. His political ideas are out of date ; but his sensibility is modern. And by the way in which he embodied this sensibility in perfect works of art he is the superior of most moderns. This rhetorician was in a sense truer and subtler than Meredith ; this romantic, more realistic than Hardy. The time will come when this much will be recognized as the truth concerning the author of *Lesbia Brandon, A Year's Letters, Poems and Ballads,* and *Solomon's Vision of Love.* And it will then be the turn of some of his most recent critics to look old-fashioned.[2]

But is there room for a *new* life of Swinburne ? Three men were particularly qualified to write such a biography : Theodore Watts-Dunton, Mr. Thomas James Wise and the late Sir Edmund Gosse. Watts-Dunton died in 1914 without even having attempted the task which he had promised the poet's sister, Isabel Swinburne, that he would undertake ; old age, ill-health and procrastination prevented him, as they had

---

[1] Gide's heroes read Swinburne more often than Tennyson or Hardy—Renée Vivien was of course steeped in Swinburne's poetry.

[2] It is striking that in the *Nouvelle Revue Française* for September 1930, M. Jean Paulhan speaks of the Marquis de Sade in practically the same terms as Swinburne (un écrivain qu'il faut sans doute placer parmi les plus grands—that illustrious artist and philosopher, etc.). Only Swinburne had his tongue in his cheek and M. Paulhan seems in dead earnest.

prevented his writing a life of Rossetti. His biography
of Swinburne would have been marked by many omissions and much reticence : but it would have been
accurate on most points, full of information, as he was
for over thirty years the poet's intimate friend ; he
knew nearly everything about Swinburne, and what he
would not have said he would have suppressed con-
sciously and deliberately. Mr. T. J. Wise, who from
1886 onwards has collected books, manuscripts, documents and information of all kinds on the poet, could
have given us a scientific and at the same time picturesque record of Swinburne ; his materials would
have been unusually extensive, his scruples infinite, his
method strict. But Mr. Wise chose another task for
himself ; by constituting, organizing and describing
the Ashley Library, he has become the bibliographer
of all that is most rare and curious in English Literature : in the ten-odd tomes of his catalogue he has
accumulated the matter of scores of volumes ; he has
discovered, selected and annotated hundreds of documents of absorbing interest ; his work can only be
paralleled in that of the great Renaissance Printers or
the eighteenth century Antiquaries.

    Edmund Gosse did write a *Life* of Swinburne in
1917, which was reprinted with a few alterations in
1927 : to its many qualities I have paid due homage
elsewhere ; what he liked and understood in Swinburne he has explained and analysed unsurpassably :
a master of style, and a great word-painter, his book
has the crowning merit of being a work of art. He
was qualified for his task as, beside being a great reader
of poetry, he had at a specially important period of
Swinburne's career been one of his close associates ;

and to this he added a deep knowledge and understanding of literary conditions and society from the
early seventies to the present day. It would not be
quite fair to make too much of the many inaccuracies
which occur in his narrative ; these were inevitable
in a work which was the first of its kind, and the extent of his information is in many other respects admirable ; in some instances he guessed with exquisite
sensitiveness what he did not know. But it should be
stated, first that he relied too much on the oral testimony of the poet's friends and contemporaries, whose
memory (or imagination) occasionally played them
false ; secondly, that he was often prejudiced by his
dislike of Watts-Dunton ; and lastly that he did
not see that ' modern ' side in Swinburne's nature
which I have just endeavoured to outline.

None of the many other books written on Swinburne
profess to be otherwise than secondarily biographical.
It seemed to me that a new biography, which would
make free use of the new material (published or unpublished) that has recently become accessible, which
would confront and compare the few biographical
opinions already expressed, and in many cases reinter-
pret the poet's personality in the light of his works,
was now called for. Whether the present writer was
qualified for this task remains to be seen. But he has
been fortunate in having had access to documents
of which full use has never been made before[1]—in

---

[1] In the course of the biographical narrative, it has not been thought advisable to
repeat in every instance where *letters* are concerned the precise source of the
original document, though in fact the dates and names of correspondents are
given in most cases. Most of the unpublished letters I have made use of are in
the private collection of Mr. T. J. Wise (letters to W. M. and D. G. Rossetti, to
Th. Watts, to C. A. Howell, etc.); the correspondence addressed to Powell is in
the National Library of Wales, Aberystwyth; the letters to Karl Blind are in the

particular the correspondence of Swinburne with Powell (Aberystwyth University) and the letters of Swinburne to W. M. Rossetti (in Mr. Wise's collection) which Edmund Gosse had not seen when he wrote the *Life*. My thanks are due to the authorities of the Welsh University and above all to Mr. Thomas James Wise, who placed at my disposal the documents of his Swinburne library and gave me, on all difficult points which I submitted, generous and valuable advice.

It would also be gross ingratitude on my part not to mention the help I have received at the hands of : the late Sir Edmund Gosse, Sir G. Young, Sir W. Rothenstein, Mrs. Clara Watts-Dunton, Mr. George Moore, Professor André Barbier, Mr. T. E. Welby, Dr. E. A. Baker, Professor H. J. C. Grierson, Mr. John Purves, MM. R. Galland and P. Berger, Messrs. G. Madan, Mario Praz, W. A. Roberts and E. B. Hall.

I am especially indebted to Messrs. Heinemann for allowing me to quote freely from the works of the poet.

British Museum. As for the unpublished works of Swinburne to which I refer or from which I quote, they are all in Mr. Wise's library, with the exception of *The Unhappy Revenge* and the *Temple of Janus* which were bequeathed to the British Museum by Isabel Swinburne. For this, as for all bibliographical matters relating to the first five chapters of this book, see my *Jeunesse de Swinburne*, 2 volumes, Paris, 1928.

Hertha

I am that which began.
Out of me the years roll;
Out of me God & man.
I am equal & whole.
God changes, & man, & the form of them bodily; I am the soul.

Before ever land was,
Before ever the sea,
Or soft-hair of the grass,
Or fair limbs of the tree,
Or the flesh-coloured fruit of my branches, I was, & thy soul was in me.

Reduced facsimile of the MS. of the first two stanzas of *Hertha*
Reproduced by courtesy of T. J. Wise, Esq.

CHAPTER I

SEMEL ET SEMPER

Swinburne—Ashburnham ! One seems to hear, on the threshold of the life of Swinburne, the sound of running brooks and the ' noise of many waters ' which echo through so many pages of his poetry :

> Bright and tawny, full of fun
> And storm and sunlight, taking change and chance
> With laugh on laugh of triumph—why, you know
> How they plunge, pause, chafe, chide across the rocks
> And chuckle along the rapids, till they breathe
> And rest and pant and build some bright deep bath
> For happy boys to dive in, and swim up,
> And match the water's laughter.

But those names do not merely sound as the course of a Sussex or Northumberland stream. They stand as the symbol of a close connection with the soil of age-old provinces. Let this be to us a warning : the poet who delighted in the ' limitless north-eastern ' and ' the strait south-western sea ', climbed their cliffs and galloped in the wind on their sounding strands, is not solely the sea-mews' wingless brother, some strange sea-god's changeling. A swimmer rather than a sailor, a lover of the billows breaking upon the shore, he is earth-born, and never disowned his mother. He knows the power of woods and hills, has learned from Proserpine as well as from Cymodoce, and is well up in the rites of Bacchus and of Pan. Let us not then wonder if, when he emerges from one of his prolonged ecstasies among the waves, we spy, firmly treading upon the rocks, the cloven foot of an Aegipan.

Ashburn, a small stream in Sussex, is mentioned in Drayton's *Polyolbion*.[1] As early as 1274 Allan de Swinburne had acquired from Sir Thomas de Fenwyke the castle of Capheaton, near Newcastle, which soon became the family seat in preference to the older castle of Swinburne. In spite of the poet's vague assertion that ' there *was* a Swinburne peerage dormant or forfeit since the 13th or 14th century ', definite information on this point is not forthcoming. Indeed the gene-alogy of the Swinburnes remains somewhat shadowy until the seventeenth century. The only member of the family before that date about whom something positive can here be said is one Thomas Swynbourne who lived at the end of the fourteenth century. After a voyage to the Holy Land, he received the Château de Guines from Richard II in 1396 and was eight years later appointed Mayor of Bordeaux. The French epitaph of this worthy predecessor of Montaigne can still be read in the church of Little Horkesley (Essex) :

Icy gist Monsr. Thomas Swynbourne . . . Mair de Bourdeux et capitaigne de Fronsak qe mourust dans la veile de Seint Laurence l'an de grace Mill CCCC XVe de qy Dieu eyt pitee et Mercye. Amen.

' Capitaigne de Fronsak'. This sets us dreaming and reminds us of Michelet's epigram about Guyenne under the English rule : ' The English, so as to be more certain of keeping it, treated it well, increased

---

[1] *Seventeenth Song :*
    As Ashburn undertakes to do the forests right
    (At Pevensey where she pours her soft and gentler flood).

its wealth, bought and drank its wines. Bordeaux could not reasonably hope to find masters who drank more. When the province became French again, it could only lose by it'.

The part played by the Swinburnes in the northern risings of 1568–69 in favour of Queen Mary seems, despite the poet's words and wishes, to have been obscure and unimportant. More conspicuous, however, must have been their services to Charles I during the Civil War, as these were rewarded by the granting, immediately after the Restoration, of a baronetcy to John Swinburne, ' the auld carle of Capheaton '. However much this distinction may have been deserved, the Swinburnes were, in those circumstances, eclipsed by the loyalty of the poet's maternal ancestor, John Ashburnham, Charles I's trusted companion.

But while the Ashburnhams came to regard the fate of the later Stuarts with growing unconcern, the Swinburnes displayed that blind enthusiasm for lost causes which rings in many pages of *Songs before Sunrise*, and their loyalty to the Stuarts continued unabated. It was for a long time a tradition with them to have one of their younger sons as a page at the Court of St-Germain. There could indeed have been no difficulty in keeping up this attendance, for the family showed, in those days, remarkable vitality : Henry Swinburne tells us that his grandmother, Isabella, ' walked in Newcastle with a mob after her on account of her having had thirty children. She was tall and very handsome, her husband swarthy and lame, and only came up to her elbow '.

Whether the Swinburnes had anything to do with the rising of 1715 is uncertain. It seems far more

probable, however, that some younger members of the
house were concerned with that of 1745. Swinburne
has been taxed with poetic exaggeration when he wrote
of

> Mine own twice-banished fathers' harbour-land,
> Their nursing-mother, France, the well beloved,

but it remains to be seen whether his statement concerning the double banishment of his ancestors is not
on the whole correct. A first period of exile may very
well have taken place during the Commonwealth. As
for the second, one may at least wonder if it did not
affect Sir John Swinburne's third son, Edward, the
poet's great-grandfather. Some documents in the
municipal records of Bordeaux seem to bear out this
view. The governor of Bordeaux wrote in 1756 that
among the English subjects who were allowed to stay
in the town during the hostilities was one ' Edw.
Swinburne du Northumberland, fils cadet du baronnet
John Swinburne, d'une famille catholique et zélée
pour les Stuarts '. Edward was still in Bordeaux in
1761 when he married Christina Dillon, connected
with the Irish family of the Dillons of Roscommon :
she was the ancestress to whom Swinburne so often
referred as being responsible for the ' Irish particles
in his blood ' ; her mother was Martha Newland of
Beckenham, Kent, and her father, Robert Dillon, took
as his second wife a Miss Disconson who in 1762 acted
as John Edward's god-mother ; this lady, who was a
daughter of the Governor of James II's eldest son at
St-Germain, seems to have had a somewhat remote
connection with the French House of Polignac. This
was enough for Swinburne to claim with typical
alacrity that he was descended from the Polignac

family. In his correspondence he often refers to the fact as absolutely beyond doubt, and, when travelling in Auvergne in 1869, it was with great emotion that he visited the ruins of the Castle of Polignac in the company of Burton who was no doubt much impressed. It can however be seen from what has been said above how utterly impossible was Swinburne's contention : he was repudiating the wholly uninteresting Miss Newland for the far more attractive step-mother of French extraction, boldly grafting upon the old Saxon stock a delightful, though unreal, Franco-Irish sprout.

Edward Swinburne was still residing in Bordeaux in 1764, as shown by the birth certificate of one of his sons.[1] He had inherited the title at the death of his brother in 1763, and it is strange to find him away from England at that date. When did he return to Northumberland ? Henry Swinburne, the traveller, who addressed to him most of his charming though dignified epistles, mentions that his brother was ' taken prisoner ' on board a ship coming from the Continent in 1779. One can scarcely believe that his ' exile ', if exile it ever was, lasted until then ; let us however notice that his brother Henry was educated in France ; that his sister Anne was a nun at Mont-argis ; and that his son John Edward, the poet's grandfather, born in the Paroisse St-Projet, Bordeaux,[2] was also educated in France. Whatever the reason, the ties of this old Jacobite Catholic house with the continent were at the end of the eighteenth century closer than ever.

[1] Henry. Archives Municipales de Bordeaux, Paroisse St-André—Registre G G 104 No. 1907.
[2] On March 6, 1762. Archives Municipales de Bordeaux, Paroisse St-André. Registre G G 103 No, 1450,

At the personality of Swinburne's grandfather it is necessary to pause for a while. The influence of heredity or even the more certain influence of direct intercourse is impossible to gauge. But Swinburne formed an idealized conception of his grandfather which haunted him throughout his life ; Sir John Edward became a kind of standard to whom Swinburne successively compared Landor, Mazzini and Hugo, when he met them personally. Nor is there much reason to believe that reality was far remote from his ideal. From his birth and upbringing in France John Edward had preserved, if not ' the appearance of a French nobleman ', at least all the urbanity of manners of the *ancien régime*. But he struck new and discordant notes on the keyboard of family tradition. First, he gave up the religion of his fathers and, with Sir Edward's approval, conformed without the slightest hesitation or regret. ' It was absurd ', he wrote, ' to sacrifice my consideration in my own country, my prospects in life, to condemn myself to eternal insignificance and oblivion for Tenets I did not believe, and Ceremonies I never practised '. This shows clearly that he was not prompted by religious scruples ; his decision arose from purely political considerations. Having discarded the Jacobite convictions of his house, he was returned for Parliament by the borough of Launceston, Cornwall, in 1788, as an ' ultra-liberal ' Swinburne informs us ; and, if we are to trust the same source, he did not spare the Prince of Wales in his Parliamentary speeches. Nor is this to be wondered at if, as seems to be the case, he had enjoyed the friendship of Mirabeau and Wilkes. His correspondence with Leigh Hunt tends to confirm all this :

SWINBURNE'S GRANDFATHER,
SIR JOHN EDWARD SWINBURNE.
6th BARONET, b. 1762, d. 1860.

From the portrait by Gainsborough in the
possession of Sir Hubert Swinburne.

CAPHEATON HALL
The home of Sir John Edward Swinburne.

Reproduced by courtesy of Sir Hubert Swinburne.

when Hunt was sentenced in 1814 for libelling the Regent, he wrote to him expressing his ' sorrow and indignation ', and offering ' from two to three hundred pounds ' towards the payment of the fine. He rejoiced at the formation of the Canning government in 1827. He had been Provincial Grand Master at the Masonic Festivals in 1817. Lastly, he combined this new religious and political attitude with literary and artistic tastes which had not so far been very conspicuous in the family. Sir John Edward had constituted at Capheaton a library of eighteenth century French literature in which Swinburne was steeped when he wrote *A Year's Letters* ; he was an admirer of Leigh Hunt ; Mulready, possibly Turner, had been his friends. When eighty-eight years old, we find him in London ' indulging ' his daughter, Julia Swinburne, ' in seeing pictures and works of art of which she is a very competent judge having attained no common skill in painting under the long and competent instruction of my valuable friend Mulready '. He was till 1837 President of the Literary and Philosophical Society of Newcastle-on-Tyne and had at one time been President of the Society of Antiquaries. These new and unexpected activities he combined with the traditional pastimes of his race, riding and hunting, and was also possessed of an uncommon vitality (' the Swinburnes have a tendency to live ' as Julia Swinburne would say) which enabled him to reach his ninety-ninth year and to survive being trepanned after a shooting accident ; this accident especially endeared his grandfather to Swinburne ; I am not sure that he was not as proud of the scar it left over the old man's eyebrow as of the alleged friendship with Mirabeau and Wilkes.

It is not enough to say that Sir John Edward was all
that Swinburne could have wished for a grandfather ;
one should rather take the view that, had it not been
for his grandfather, Swinburne's early development
might have been different from what it was.   The
influence of John Edward, although exerting itself
at rare and irregular intervals, must have been an
antidote to that of Charles Henry and the High Church
atmosphere of East Dene.   In fact it would perhaps
be unkind, but none the less true, to say that Swinburne's grandfather should have been his father and
his father, his grandfather ; one is almost tempted to
add that most of the misunderstandings which spoilt
Swinburne's early career were to a certain extent due
to that original misunderstanding on the part of the
Creator.   Sir John Edward had married in 1787
Emilia Elizabeth Bennet, of Beckenham, Kent, a niece
to the second duke of Northumberland.   Charles
Henry (1797–1877) was his younger son.   Owing to
the bar of their religious beliefs, the Swinburnes had
not so far been able to give many soldiers or sailors to
the crown, but now, with the conforming of the family,
things were going to change ; to quote Sir John
Edward's own words ' cela aplanissait beaucoup les
choses '.   A Thomas Swinburne was already serving
in the army and was to be killed at Waterloo.   It was
decided that Charles Henry should become a naval
officer ; he went up to the Royal Naval College in
1810, which makes it barely possible for him to have
served under Collingwood as his son asserted ; he was
probably concerned with the capture of the American
ship *Chesapeake* by the *Shannon* in 1813, but he seems
to have seen little actual fighting.   He was, however, a

widely travelled man, having sailed over 'all the seas in the world' and visited many lands ; he had even gone to St. Helena and seen Napoleon. He became a captain in 1835 and married one year later the fourth daughter of the Earl of Asburnham, Lady Jane Henrietta, who was her husband's second cousin, their maternal grandfathers being brothers. The Ashburnhams were a family of great antiquity, already established in England before the conquest ; but in spite of great services rendered to Charles I by John Ashburnham, it was not until 1689 that his son John received the title of Baron ; his grandson was created in 1730 Viscount St. Asaph and Earl of Ashburnham ; the family seat was Ashburnham Place, near Battle, in Sussex, from which the house had borrowed its name.

Lady Jane had a dignified yet attractive appearance ; it seems that she was partly brought up in France and Italy, and she certainly had a genuine taste for French and Italian literatures with which she was conversant, she may have had a liking for poetry ; but we must not assume that she was possessed of a very wide culture. In common with her, although perhaps chiefly through her influence, Charles Henry Swinburne entertained 'high' religious tendencies ; but in sharp contrast with her he seems to have been a strict disciplinarian, a man of more energy than humour, and of more humour than artistic sense.

However all seems at first sight idyllic in the relations between Swinburne and his parents : his mother taught him French and Italian, and 'got him' the Modern Language Prize at Eton ; she read Shakespeare, Scott and Dickens to him, and, while placing a temporary ban on Byron, she introduced him to the great foreign masters, Dante, Ariosto, Molière. As for the Admiral, although he may have at one time disagreed with his son about the choice of a career and worried over his academic record, he did not persist in thwarting Swinburne's literary proclivities, allowed him a small income, and went so far as to bear the cost of the publication of his first volumes ; on several occasions he went to London, in spite of his old age, to take care of his son who was lying dangerously ill ; he read Swinburne's works with pride if not with a deep sense of comfort, and his death caused the poet, as his letters and poems show, a deep and genuine grief. When W. M. Rossetti visited the Swinburnes at Holmwood in 1867 he found a loving and united family.

We are, however, forced to the conclusion that, whatever happened afterwards, during most of his childhood and adolescence there existed a strong antagonism between the poet and his father. There are, to support this view, two documents which cannot be overlooked. One is the following passage from an unpublished letter to W. M. Rossetti (15 January 1870) :

I think you are rather hard upon [Shelley] as to the filial relation. I have no more doubt that it may be said for Sir Timothy that his son was what Carlyle calls an 'afflictive phenomenon' than that I was the same to my father before, during, and since my Oxford time ; but I do not think you make allowance for the provocation given (as well as received) by a father who may be kindly and generous, to a boy or man between 17 or 21 or 30, with whom he has no deep or wide ground of sympathy beyond the animal relation or family tradition. You will allow me to say that I am sure you can never have felt at that age the irreparable, total and inevitable isolation from all that had once been closest to the mind and thought, and was still closest to the flesh and the memory, the solitude, into which one passes from separation to antagonism of spirit, without violent quarrel or open offence, but by pure logical necessity of consequences, the sense that where attraction gradually ends repulsion gradually begins, which many besides Shelley, and as affectionate and faithful by nature and temperament as he, *have* felt at that age.

The other is that terrible letter alleged to have been written by Captain Harewood to his son Reginald in *A Year's Letters*, the autobiographical novel which Swinburne composed in 1862, just when his relations with his father must have been most strained.

From childhood upwards, I must once for all remind you, you have thwarted my wishes and betrayed my trust. . . . Prayer, discipline, confidence, restraint, hourly vigilance, untiring attention, one after another failed to work upon you. . . . At school you were incessantly under punishment ; at home you were constantly in disgrace. Pain and degradation could not keep you right ; to disgrace the most frequent, to pain the most severe, you opposed a deadly strength of sloth and tacit vigour of rebellion. . . .

Thus wrote the indignant captain. It is hard to believe that Swinburne did not, at Oxford, receive letters in the same style. And, if the reader wants to know how he reacted to them, let him turn to the letters of Reginald.

Having said so much, one has to say more. In two of Swinburne's autobiographical narratives, *Lesbia Brandon* and the unfinished prose story which he composed before beginning *A Year's Letters*, we are confronted by the same situation : a boy (Reginald Harewood, Herbert Seyton), who is evidently Swinburne, torn between a feeling of resentment and hate for his father or his tutor (Mr. Harewood, Denham) who maliciously flogs and tortures him, and a mad

irrepressible love for his sister (Eleanor Ashburst,
Lady Wariston) for whom he would like to give his
life. Now it would be misleading to speak here of
an ' Oedipus complex '. I believe that this situation
was the creation of Swinburne's mind and perverse
sensibility. But the situation once given and the
characters sketched out, to what elements could Swinburne turn within the range of his limited experience
as capable of supplying the necessary material for the
realistic treatment of such a theme ? To this question I can supply, from my imperfect knowledge of
this part of Swinburne's life, only one answer : his
own relations with his father and mother. The fact
that later on Swinburne seemed to disclaim such an
identification of his parents and the characters in his
novels merely tends to show that he was struck by
the similarity of circumstances, that he deprecated an
interpretation which was only partly true and which
perhaps had never definitely occurred to him while
writing his books. If anyone has another interpretation to offer, I shall welcome it, as it cannot fail to add
new facts to our knowledge of Swinburne's early years.

We are here however in the quicksands of probability and inference, and it is a relief to rise to the
vantage ground of general considerations on the poet's
heredity. To be sure the track has been trodden more
than once before. The opposition between the northern and southern origin of Swinburne's ancestors, has
been rightly emphasized. Stress has also, although
perhaps less fortunately, been laid on the ' detachment
from letters ' of the houses of Swinburne and Ashburnham until they ' chose at last to produce a poet '.
Algernon Charles is indeed the only great man of

letters on record, but it does not follow that the poet's forefathers were averse to literature. Henry Swinburne, the traveller, reveals in his letters a delicate, refined and extremely sensitive personality ; he could even write French descriptive poetry of tolerable mediocrity. Sir William Ashburnham had published in 1770 a slender volume of poems ; the poet's great uncle, Edward Swinburne,[1] and his aunt, Julia, could draw and paint with distinction. Sir John Edward was, as we have seen, a patron of the arts and a man of enlightened taste. There was in some members of the Swinburne household an unusually keen love for music. Two facts however which should more particularly be borne in mind are the Swinburnes' loyalty to the Stuarts and the Catholic religion, and their close connection with France in the course of the eighteenth century. During the first half of his life Swinburne delighted in emphasizing those two features and even exaggerating them to the point of inventing a French genealogy. It remains that owing to their Jacobite sympathies the Swinburne house had for many years been subjected to continental influences ; it was only after the conforming of Sir John Edward, with the generation of Edward and Charles Henry, that a narrower and more insular outlook began to prevail.

It is said that in some of the preposterous novels of the seventeenth century, the author contrived to reach the twelfth chapter without even getting his hero born. For such an error there would, in a biography, be no excuse, and I hasten to state that Algernon Charles was born, the eldest of a family of six children, on April 5, 1837, at No. 7 Chester Street, Grosvenor Place,

[1] He was responsible for the illustrations in Hodgson's *History of Northumberland.*

London, where his parents were making a temporary visit. The motto on the Swinburnes' coat of arms was : *Semel et Semper*. It is indeed to be presumed that with the birth of such a poet the lyrical and artistic powers of the family are likely to have been exhausted until the name becomes extinct.

CHAPTER II

CHILDHOOD

WE know surprisingly little about the childhood of most great men. Only in exceptional cases do they provide genuine and precise information on their early years. It is not so much that memory is at fault as that school education with its intellectual discipline cuts them adrift from a world of instincts and sensations through which they find it difficult to retrace their steps. It was not, I think, until Rousseau that it became possible to read about a writer's childhood ; Rousseau had had practically no education, which made things easier for him ; yet he found the task hard and unpleasant enough at times. But Swinburne went through a long and strict academic career, although with somewhat disconcerting results ; and while refusing to submit himself regularly to any form of mental exercise, he carried on from the beginning an extensive reading in the five greatest literatures of the world. This is exactly why we turn all the more eagerly to his pre-Etonian days in the hope of reconstituting some of his experiences which were not derived from a literary source. If it can be proved that, before books began to speak to him, Swinburne was in a marked degree affected by the influences of nature, most of the charges of rhetoric and insincerity so commonly brought against his inspiration will run wide of the mark or fall short of it.

There is however but little information available—and that almost entirely of an external kind. External evidence, so valuable when it can be used to check and supplement the poet's own accounts of himself, is strangely inadequate when unconfirmed. The danger is that one finds oneself writing family history instead of biography, and has thus enlisted the reader's sympathies on false pretences ; than which there can be no more grievous sin.

When one has said that Swinburne's childhood was spent in the Isle of Wight, with visits to Sussex and Northumberland, one has not said much, and one is tempted to say more. There is honestly but little to add. Captain Swinburne had rented in Bonchurch a large house, East Dene ; the Isle of Wight, with which his mother's family was connected, had also the advantage of being the residence of Sir Henry Gordon (Capt. Swinburne's cousin) and of Lady Mary Gordon (the poet's maternal aunt). They lived a few miles from Bonchurch in their fine inland mansion of Northcourt, but were often staying at the home of Sir Henry's parents, The Orchard, Niton, on the loveliest part of the coast.

East Dene, The Orchard, Northcourt form a long narrow triangle with the undercliff for its base and Shorwell for its extreme point which supplies most of the background of Swinburne's childhood. Riding, swimming and rambles on the shore from the Landslip to Ventnor or Culver Cliff were with him daily occurrences ; he could use freely

> The sun to sport in and the cliffs to scale,
> The sea to clasp and wrestle with. . . .

Especially the sea, which spread literally at the foot of the house, now rough and grey as when it rose in wrath against the Armada, now blue like the Mediterranean —only concealed, in the ' garden walled about with woodland ', by a screen of ' trellised flowers ' and trees. Those scenes, and especially the terraced lawns of The Orchard, clung to Swinburne's memory in later years and passed into many a poem. He had, as we see, splendid opportunities for feeling and absorbing beauty. But what did he make of them ? Were his perceptions in any way clearer and keener than those of the children around him ? What guarantee can we have that in *Hesperia* or the *Triumph of Time*, when he writes that

> The sweet sea, mother of loves and hours,
> Shudders and shines as the grey winds gleam
> Turning her smile to a fugitive pain . .

the bright vision is a real aspect of the ever-changing Channel, and not a reflection of some lines in Virgil, or Aeschylus' ' innumerable laughter of the waves ' ? Even Mary Gordon, Sir Henry's daughter, that beloved kinswoman and lifelong friend of the poet, whom, in her eightieth year, I found as full of love and reverence as ever for her fairy cousin, has nothing to say to us. ' I do not remember anything of special note ' is the burden of her early recollections : walks across the Bonchurch down, her cousin's ' springy, dancing step ', his ' beautiful reading ' of the Bible at prayer-time, are among the most valuable traits in an otherwise worthless and oversentimental record.

About Swinburne's visits to Northumberland she has, as is natural, still less to say ; for the Swinburnes

spent only a few weeks in the north every year and the
Gordons would make but a brief stay there on their way
to Aberdeenshire.   The old restoration manor of
Capheaton and its surroundings were however likely
to make on the mind of the future poet an even keener
impression than the more familiar landscapes of the
Isle of Wight.   Here was indeed the land of his
ancestors, and those short visits, repeated every year,
to a country forming a sharp contrast with southern
England were bound to affect Swinburne more than a
prolonged stay would have done.   The grounds and
woodland round Capheaton and the shooting property
of Mounces, the ruined border castles, the hills, the
running brooks and above all the strong Northumbrian atmosphere with the silver grey sea shining in
the distance,

> the sweet grey-gleaming sky,
> And the lordly strand of Northumberland,
> And the goodly towers thereby—

all these became as familiar to the child as the sunlit
meadows of East Dene, without losing however any of
their rough mysterious charm.   One has to realize
that Northumberland and the Isle of Wight gradually
became the poles round which the child's sensibility
learned to revolve with something like astronomic
regularity.   His visits to Capheaton, in the late summer
and the autumn, emphasized and exaggerated in his
eyes the immutable course of the seasons.   Spring-
time in Ventnor, autumn-time in Northumberland are
not the same as any other spring or winter ; the
contrast was more marked and more deeply felt.   It lay
at the root of many of Swinburne's finest inspirations,

as the lyric impulse swayed him from regrets of the
north to desire of the south, the swing of the pen-
dulum increasing at times with enlarged experience
and reaching as far as Siena or Fiesole, Edinburgh and
Lochleven.   In *Chastelard*, in *Four Songs of Four
Seasons*, in *A Vision of Spring in Winter*, in the *Eve of
Revolution*, in the ' gleanings of a northern shore ' of
Ave atque Vale so skilfully contrasted with Baudelaire's
' glories of heavier suns in mightier skies ', the beats
of the same rhythm can be recognized.

It would of course be a serious misconception to
imagine the child as passively submitted to all these
external influences during protracted periods of inaction and solitude.   He was no Emile ; the record of
his early years would, if recounted, offer but the
slightest resemblance to the strange immortal pages at
the beginning of the *Mémoires d'Outre-Tombe*.   We
have already had occasion to introduce his cousin
Mary Gordon.   Nearer in blood, if not closer in
affection, were his sisters and brother : Alice, the
eldest, who took a keen interest in the literary career
of her brother, and to whom *Locrine* is dedicated ;
Edith, Swinburne's red-haired sister, who was to die
in 1863 just as he began *Atalanta* ; Charlotte, and
Isabel (the only member of the family to survive her
brother), whom W. M. Rossetti described in 1867 as
' evidently talented '.   With his brother Edward, the
youngest of the family, Swinburne's relations seem to
have been somewhat strained ; a lover of music and
a passionate admirer of Schumann and Wagner,
Edward seems to have had no special leaning to poetry,
at least his brother's (' my art is at a discount here '
Swinburne wrote, alluding to Edward's presence at

Holmwood) ; he is scarcely ever mentioned in the correspondence and W. M. Rossetti noted during his stay at Holmwood that ' the youngest son was unwell, and had not shown '. His health must have been frail : he died unexpectedly from heart-failure in 1891 ; on that occasion Swinburne disclosed his distress in a letter to Watts, referring with emotion to his brother's unfortunate marriage, but without implying anything beyond the grief inseparable from the loss of one so nearly related to him.

At Capheaton, Swinburne had no lack of playmates, as a large company of cousins never failed to gather there (Sir John Edward had no fewer than twenty-four grandchildren). There he met the sons of his uncle Edward, and it may have been then that he conceived for John, the future baronet, that strong childish dislike which did not disappear with the years. In the well known sketch drawn in 1843 by George Richmond we see the future poet at play with Alice and Edith ; no dreamy or melancholy expression can be traced on the round, receding face with the bulging forehead, any more than in the photograph taken about the same date, which rather emphasizes the mischievous and stubborn look in the eyes and reminds us of Swinburne's own description of himself at a slightly later date as a ' small but not usually good boy of nine or ten '. Riding and swimming were the chief occupation of the children ; to which they soon added more ambitious pastimes in the form of dramatic performances for the benefit of their elders. If we want to recapture something of this atmosphere, we must refer to the fourth act of *The Sisters* (which is nothing else than an interlude performed by a company of cousins at Clavering

Hall, Northumberland) and to the chapter in *Lesbia Brandon* in which Herbert-Algernon is introduced in fancy dress to Lesbia after a performance of *Lucrèce Borgia*.

We are thus inevitably drawn to the poet's works for additional information of a more intimate nature. These seem at first to yield but little : we find in his correspondence a vivid recollection of being ' held up naked in my father's arms . . . and shot like a stone from a sling through the air . . . head foremost into the coming wave ' ; in the *Prologue* to *A Year's Letters,* some not too pleasant scenes reminiscent of Eton ; in *Thalassius,* a florid and (for our purpose) useless allegory ; in *The Sisters* and in the dedicatory poem to Lady Mary Gordon, descriptions of Northumberland and The Orchard ; and, lastly, some scattered recollections in the poems, such as the charming piece entitled *In a Rosary,* buried in that dismal volume, *A Channel Passage.*

So much and no more till we come to *Lesbia Brandon* ; this fragment whose publication has, in spite of Mr. Wise's generous efforts, been unjustifiably delayed, contains in its opening pages what in my opinion more than makes up for the unpleasant and disappointing character of its later chapters. I wish Swinburne had postponed for another hundred pages the introduction of Denham and Lesbia and Mariani, and described at full length the growth of Herbert Seyton's mind and his relation to nature ; his novel might then well have been a masterpiece. Be that as it may, those first pages give us exactly what we want ; here we hear no more about the red hair and the dancing step of ' cousin Hadji ' or his kindness to animals ; we catch a glimpse

of the soul of the child. True, Bertie's childhood is
not exactly like Swinburne's ; he is described as more
solitary in his early years than the poet ever was ; true,
Ensdon fantastically combines the features of East
Dene, Ashburnham Place and Capheaton. But the
autobiographical element far outweighs the fiction.
Bertie's state of mind is exactly what at fifteen years'
distance, Swinburne, to the best of his belief, conceived
his own to have been. And, as he is dealing not with
facts, but with sentiments, there is little danger of his
being mistaken. For here we have not to do with a
few details of an external character, but with the most
spontaneous and almost animal reactions of a child's
soul. In fact we have here, though in too brief and
fragmentary a state, the whole structure of *Thalassius*
washed pure of its allegory. We seem to be given
a chance of finding whether, to a certain extent, Swinburne really was, as he claimed, what ' sun, and wind,
and waters made him ', or whether he was merely, as
many of his critics would have it, ' what verse, and plays
and novels made him '.

Like Herbert when he left Kirlowes for Ensdon,
Swinburne learned, during his early years, to ' live at
large and stray at will '. Apart from his mother's lessons, casual reading, and some private tuition at Brook
Rectory under the Rev. C. Foster Fenwick (who, by
the way, may very well be that ' parish clergyman, a
man meeker than Moses ' who looked after Herbert),
he had most of his time to himself and spent it in the
open air :

Well broken in to solitude and sensitive of all outward things,
he found life and pleasure enough in the gardens and woods,
the downs and the beach. Small sights and sounds excited and

satisfied him ; his mind was as yet more impressible than
capacious, his senses more retentive than his thoughts. Water
and wind and darkness and light made friends with him ; he
went among beautiful things without wonder or fear. For
months he lived and grew on like an animal or a fruit : and
things seemed to deal with him as with one of these ; earth set
herself to caress and amuse him ; air blew and rain fell and leaves
changed to his great delight ; he felt no want in life.

He was sensitive to the varied aspects of the land :
leaves, hills, streams :

For places rather than persons he had a violent and blind
affection. Small pools in the pausing streams roofed with
noiseless leaves out of the wind's way ; hot hollows of short
grass in the slanting down, shaped like cups for the sun to fill ;
higher places where the hill-streams began among patches of
reeds, extorting from the moist moorland a little life ; dry
corners of crag, whence light trees had sprung out of the lean
soil, shadowing narrow brown nooks and ledges of burnt up
turfs, slippery with the warm dust of arid lands—all these
attracted and retained him.

But these sensations cannot be compared with the
appeal the sea made to him. In his description of
Herbert's first meeting with ' the only sight of divine
and durable beauty in the world ', Swinburne has
condensed symbolically his own delight in the sight,
sounds and motion of the sea :

The water moved like tired tossing limbs of a goddess,
troubled with strength and vexed with love. Northward and
southward the grey glitter of remote foam flickered along the
extreme sea-line marking off the low sky so that water and cloud
were distinct. Nearer inshore the sea was an April field of sweet
and pale colour, filled with white and windy flowers. To this
the only sight of divine and durable beauty on which any eyes
can rest in the world, the boy's eyes first turned, and his heart
opened and ached with pleasure. His face trembled and changed,
his eyelids tingled, his limbs yearned all over : the colour and

savour of the sea seemed to pass in at his eyes and mouth—all his
nerves desired the divine touch of it, all his soul saluted it through
the senses. ' What on earth is the matter with him ?' said Lord
Wariston. ' Nothing on earth ', said his sister, ' it's the sea.'

He set to study the sea like a book and gave himself
up to her influence. He soon knew all her various
and changing aspects : the colour of the waves on
the beach :

In a few months' time he could have gone blindfold over
miles of beach. All the hollows of the cliffs and all the curves of
the sand-hills were friendly to his feet. The long reefs that
rang with returning waves and flashed with ebbing ripples ;
the smooth slopes of coloured rock full of small brilliant lakes
that fed and saved from sunburning their anchored fleet of
flowers, yellower lilies and redder roses of the sea.

all the many sounds of the water :

Here among the reefs he ran riot, skirting with light, quick
feet the edge of the running ripple, laughing with love when the
fleeter foam caught them up, skimming the mobile fringe that
murmured and fluttered and fell, gathering up with gladdened
ears all the fervent sighs and whispers of the tender water, all
delicate sounds of washing and wandering waves, all sweet and
suppressed semitones of light music struck out of shingle or sand
by the faint extended fingers of foam and tired eager lips of
yielding sea that touch the soft and mutable limits of their life, to
recede in extremity and exhaustion.

But he more often turned his eyes from the shore and
looked out to the open sea :

At other times he would set his face seaward and feed his eyes
for hours on the fruitless floating fields of wan green water,
fairer than all spring-meadows or summer-gardens, till the soul
of the sea entered him and filled him with fleshly pleasure and
the pride of life ; he felt the fierce gladness and glory of living
stroke and sting him all over as with soft hands and sharp lips :

and under their impulse he went as before a steady pace over sands and rocks blown and driven by the wind of his own delight, crying out to the sea betweenwhiles as to a mother that talked with him, throwing at it all the scraps of song that came upon his lips and by chance laughing and leaping, envious only of sea-birds who might stay longer between two waves.

This passive, observant attitude is often exchanged, at the more violent aspects of nature, for an active, almost Byronic sense of enjoyment :

In thunder that drowned his voice, wind that blew over his balance, and snow-storms of the flying or falling foam that blinded his eyes and salted his face, the boy took his pleasure to the full ; this travail and triumph of the married wind and sea filled him with a furious luxury of the senses, and that kindled all his nerves and exalted all his life. From these haunts he came back wet and rough, blown out of shape and beaten into colour, his ears full of music and his eyes of dreams ; all the sounds of the sea rang through him, all its airs and lights breathed and shone upon him : he felt land-sick when out of the sea's sight, and twice alive when hard by it.

It was however when bathing in a rough sea, ' got down ' by breakers and ' hurled back with thunder in his ears ' that the boy had his most intense experiences. But the rough caress of the waves, though painful, seemed desirable ; the stinging of salt water on the bruised flesh caused sensuous pleasure : ' It was rather desire than courage that attracted and attached him to the rough water '. ' The scourging of the surf made him red from the shoulder to the knees and sent him on shore whipped by the sea into a single blush of the whole skin '. Thus he learned to recognize two things : the blind cruelty of natural forces, and the element of pleasure which, in some circumstances, attaches to the infliction or the suffering of pain.

There can be little doubt that those experiences were to a degree those of Swinburne as a child. But, apart from the development of the senses, did they leave any deep impression on the boy's nature ? Should we admit that ' there was matter in him fit to mould into form and impregnate with colour ' ? that ' upon this life and nature were at work, having leisure and liberty to take their time ' ? Did those scattered sensations properly constitute an education ? And if so what did it exactly amount to ?

It seems indeed that some deep-seated tendencies in Swinburne's soul can be traced, at least in part, to that period. First among those is the sense of beauty in nature, the direct apprehension of the divinely beautiful aspect of things. As soon as he sees it Herbert *knows* that the sea is divine. With this realization of beauty goes a sense of the rhythm and power which are part of it. Poetry is but the rhythm of natural beauty translated into words. This is why the sounds, winds and motions of the sea never fail to prompt Herbert to shout whatever fragments of poetry he may happen to know, ' throwing at it all the scraps of song that came upon his lips '. However, beauty in the elements is combined with a power of blind destruction ; the merciless buffets of the waves on the body of the swimmer merely confirm what the boy already knew or guessed ; the sea is cruel, treacherous, violent :

The winter dangers of the coast were as yet mere rumours to him ; but the knowledge of how many lives went yearly to feed with blood the lovely lips of the sea-furies who had such songs and smiles for summer, and for winter the teeth and throats of ravening wolves or snakes untameable, the hard heavy hands that beat out their bruised life from sinking bodies of men, gave point to his pleasure and a sheathed edge of cruel sympathy to his love.   All cruelties and treacheries, all subtle appetites and violent secrets of the sea, were part of her divine nature, adorable and acceptable to her lovers.

Cruelty thus becomes an attribute almost inseparable from beauty ; the gods of nature are beautiful and cruel, and it is right that they should be so :

Why should the gods spare men ? or she, a sure and visible goddess, be merciful to meaner things ? why should any pity befall their unlovely children and ephemeral victims at the hands of the beautiful and eternal gods ?

It follows that the natural attitude corresponding to this conception is one of spontaneous self-accepted stoicism ; a belief that things cannot be other than they are, that life is subjected to limitations which are part of its essence, to a law that cannot be evaded :

These things he felt without thinking of them, like a child ; conscious all over of the beauty and the law of things about him, the manner and condition of their life.

This stoicism is all the more easily accepted because it is felt that pain is not unmixed with pleasure when suffered through and in the presence of beauty.   The unbending passivity of the stoic becomes a kind of glad and spontaneous surrender.

It has thus been found possible to perceive in Swinburne's experiences of nature as a child the root of many essential factors in his inspiration : love of beauty and rhythm, the identification of the divine with the beautiful aspects of nature, the cruelty of the gods, the necessity and the acceptance of pain.   One detail further tends to make us consider Swinburne's

autobiographical retrospect as genuine ; he is careful
to note that :

This present boy, whose training on the whole was duly
secular, had made himself, apart and not averse from the daily
religion taken and taught on trust, a new and credible mythology.
He was an example of infant faith and infant thought ; he was
very generally and admirably ignorant ; neither saint nor
genius, but a small satisfied pagan. The nature of things had
room to work in him, for the chief places in his mind were not
preoccupied by intrusive and unhealthy guests wheeled in and
kept up by machinery of teaching and preaching.

We are now able to realize how the religious instruction so strictly imparted at East Dene utterly
failed, although accepted without discussion, to outweigh the influences at work on one who was in daily
communion with nature.

It should not, of course, be believed that Swinburne's
sole masters were wind, sun and sea. Due note has
already been made that Herbert is depicted as more
solitary and neglected than Swinburne ever was in
his childhood. And even Herbert, although ' put
through no work ', managed to read surreptitiously
a good many books : ' The boy fell upon the Ensdon
library shelves with miscellaneous voracity, reading
various books desirable and otherwise, swallowing a
nameless quantity of English and French verse and
fiction '. We may be sure that Swinburne did the
same. Capheaton and Ashburnham Place boasted
two of the finest private libraries in the Kingdom, the
former being exceptionally rich in eighteenth century
French literature. Moreover those old family seats
were stocked with works of art, especially pictures, of
no mean value, which the boy could admire and study

at leisure : Ashburnham Place and Northcourt were
noted for their artistic treasures. Even in the more
modest household at East Dene his eyes could rest on
a landscape by Crome ' showing just a wild sad track
of shoreward brushwood and chill fen '. Swinburne's
artistic education had started long before the Pre-
raphaelite days at Oxford.

However, the only books and poems he read with
any regularity or knew at all intimately were not of such
a character as to affect his attitude to nature. He read
the Bible and no doubt delighted in the Oriental
metaphors and the fine rhythm of the style. But we
know that the ' daily religion taken and taught on
trust ' was something in a sphere apart, which the
boy would never associate with things within the field
of his own experience. Of a still less literary and
artificial character were the old ballads, genuine or
modernized, which he probably read out of Percy's
and Scott's Collections, but which certainly were on
some occasions sung in his presence either by servants
or peasants in the North, or at East Dene by members
of the household. The chapter of *Lesbia Brandon* in
which Lady Wariston sings some of these ' old faint
rhymes ' to her children in the nursery at dusk has an
autobiographical ring. Lastly we have Swinburne's
own statement that he had been ' studying Shakespeare
ever since he was six years old ', his mother having
early presented him with Bowdler's *Family Shakespeare*
' in which nothing is added to the original text, but
these words and expressions are omitted which cannot
with propriety be read aloud in a family '. But here
again the plots of most of Shakespeare's plays are so
extravagant and removed from a child's experience

that he is inclined to treat them as fairy tales—believing them to be true of course, but quite unable to connect them with the realities of everyday life.

We have therefore every reason to believe that when in April 1849 Swinburne, after a brief and not very intense coaching at the hands of Mr. Fenwick, went up to Eton, he answered fairly closely to the description of his own autobiographical hero, being ' an example of infant faith and infant thought . . . very generally and admirably ignorant, neither saint nor genius, but a small satisfied pagan '.

CHAPTER III

ETON

' Very generally and admirably ignorant ' ; if we accept this as an accurate description we must admit that during the four years he spent at school Swinburne achieved a complete transformation. When he left Eton in August 1853 he had attained to a fairly extensive knowledge of Greek and Latin poetry, a good acquaintance with some French and Italian classics and a truly remarkable reading in English Literature, and he had begun to write poetry of real merit, though purely imitative in character. From the academic point of view, he had a very fair record. In this light one is inclined to interpret the numerous good-humoured references to Eton in his works and correspondence and the *Ode* on the 450th anniversary of the College as tokens of a well-founded gratitude. We have however already had warnings that in writing a biography of Swinburne it is just as dangerous to paint the facts in too dark as in too rosy a hue. The purely idyllic or the cynical standpoint will never do. One must rather aim at striking a middle course, and the facts cannot too carefully be considered. What is the precise extent of Swinburne's debt to Eton ?

From an intellectual point of view he owed Eton something but not as much as might be expected. He no doubt benefited by the double education imparted on different lines according to the Master and Tutor system : the frequent change of the former combined

with continued supervision of the latter is one of the
most striking features of Etonian training and seems
to ensure a harmonious combination of variety and
permanence, a happy compromise between our modern
school-education and that of Emile and Pantagruel.
There can be no doubt that to this system was due the
boy's early proficiency in the classics.   That his
masters were on the whole pleased with him is shown
by the marks ' very well ' and ' very creditable ' which
occur on some of his school exercises preserved at the
British Museum, and by the fact that in 1852 he was
' sent up for good ' for a composition in Greek elegiacs.
He entered the Upper Remove of the fourth Form in
April 1849, and was in 1853 in the Middle Remove of
the fifth Form, a few places from the headmaster's
class, having in four years' time been in three forms and
nine ' removes ' and nearly overtaken his cousin
Bertram Mitford (Lord Redesdale) who had one or
two years' start of him : this must certainly constitute
a fair record in a school where the study of the classics
was all important, and one does not understand Lord
Redesdale's statement that ' he knew no more Greek
than any intelligent school-boy should ', an opinion
which is contradicted by another friend of Swinburne,
Sir George Young.   In a school-examination Swinburne ranked third, while Dr. Warre, the future headmaster, was only fourth.   Later on, the poet could
afford to write concerning Shelley : ' exquisite as his
scholarship was on the æsthetic side, he could mis-
spell Greek in a way the consequences of which at
Eton would have been tragical—not to say sadical '.
The inference is that Swinburne was liable to no such
consequences.

He read Greek and Latin poetry extensively : the official Eton anthology ' Poetae Graeci ' he had soon mastered, concentrating as we know on the passages from Theocritus, Callimachus, Sappho and Pindar rather than on the extracts from Homer and Hesiod. But he was also acquainted with Aristophanes and Euripides.[1] In Latin literature his reading was even wider ; but here again, and to a greater extent, he exercised a marked independence of taste which goes far to ruin the view that as a youth Swinburne was amenable to all influences, but later in life, to none : he disliked Virgil and especially Horace, who was however a favourite with his tutor, but delighted in Ovid and Catullus, to such an extent that he attempted a composition in that unorthodox metre, Galliambics, and the consequences, were, as we know, unpleasant.

Latin composition and translation into English were in those days essential elements of education at Eton ; no doubt Swinburne obtained by being put through this drill a free and early intercourse with some of the classics. But it should be noted how very romantic and probably uncritical this study of the classics was : the texts were translated at high speed (Oscar Browning, who ought to have known, mentions that a Book of the Iliad was read in two hours' time), especially during periods of tutorial work, and little time was allowed for historical or literary comments. Moreover the great importance attached to composition in Latin verse led to undue neglect of the study of prose writers. Swinburne's acquaintance with ancient historians and philosophers seems on the whole to have been slight.

[1] Of course he also must have read some Aeschylus and Sophocles.

It is however in other subjects than the humanities that the Etonian system of education in the forties strikes us as out of the common and worthy of notice : it is true that the teaching of modern languages was, as almost everywhere else at the time, casual and unmethodical. But French happened to be adequately taught at Eton by the Tarvers, who had undoubted literary ability : Henry Tarver reread the French classics with Swinburne and introduced him to Victor Hugo : this very broad-minded tutor actually placed in Swinburne's hands *Le Roi s'amuse*, *Notre-Dame* and *Lucrèce Borgia*. The latter excited Swinburne considerably, and he states in an unpublished letter that ' since then I have taken the deepest and most reverential interest in the Holy Family to which that illustrious lady belonged by right of birth—and something more '. Such lessons no doubt highly appealed to Swinburne, and although the French classes were not compulsory, he must have attended them regularly. Tarver might well, in a half-humorous, half-pathetic vein, describe himself as ' un simple objet de luxe ' ; he was a luxury of which Swinburne fully availed himself. In 1852 he won the Prince Consort's prize for Modern Languages.

Apart from Greek, Latin, French and Italian it seems that no subject was then taught at Eton in a regular way. We must more especially pause at two extraordinary gaps : one is the lack of any training in positive science. It was only in 1851 that Mathematics became part of the syllabus, and although Swinburne was certainly given sums to work out, he probably knew nothing of algebra and geometry. As for chemistry, physics and natural history, only a few

lectures of an occasional character were given every
year. In 1882, Swinburne, being concerned about the
illness of a friend, wrote in confidence to Watts asking
him in what part of the body the bladder was, as he had
never known and dared not ask his mother or sisters.

Thus Eton offered no scientific training such as
could counteract some of the effects of a purely literary
education, which consisted mainly of translation, reading or imitative exercises, and was scarcely analytical.
Moreover it presented a further incredible *lacuna* :
there was no teaching of English Literature. It was
commonly believed among the staff that the study of
English writers was both impossible and unnecessary.
The process through which this preposterous conception was reached was twofold, as is well seen in William
Johnson's pamphlet on *Eton Reform* (1861). It was
first assumed that, with the possible exception of Shakespeare, no English author could appeal to schoolboys
as much as the classics : ' You cannot get young
students to be permanently interested in Milton etc.
as much as they are in the best Greek and Latin books'.
As for the only Shakespeare, he was disposed of in an
unexpected manner ; it being admitted that he was
' the only English author available in the way of a
schoolbook ', it was promptly asserted that the best
way of studying Shakespeare's plays was to translate
them into Greek : ' More brainwork is bestowed upon
turning a passage of Shakespeare into Greek than in
any possible analysis of his plays without translation'.

Upon this system did Swinburne thrive : for while
English was not taught at Eton as a subject, private
reading was permitted and even encouraged. He became to himself his own tutor. One cannot lay too

much emphasis on the fact that, as far as the literature
of his own country was concerned, Swinburne was
practically self-taught. Hence his wide reading (one
has to read much before getting at the purple passages),
his strange dislikes and antipathies which are often the
consequences of a lack of background or an imperfect
sense of proportion, and above all those sudden outbursts of enthusiasm at the discovery of a ' new ' masterpiece. As a critic Swinburne was and always remained a ' discoverer '. He thus discovered (or even
invented) in succession : Blake, Baudelaire, Villon,
Charles Wells, FitzGerald, and many of the minor
Elizabethans—not to mention imaginary writers like
Ernest Wheldrake, Ernest Clouet and Félicien Cossu.
This attitude on the part of a critic is essentially a
romantic one, as opposed to the classical attitude, which
implies constant reading and rereading of passages of
approved beauty sooner or later to be transformed into
standards.

Lord Redesdale has described Swinburne sitting
' turk or tailor wise ' in a window of the boys' library
with ' a huge tome on his lap '. Sir George Young
remembers how he would recite or quote poetry in their
walks through Windsor forest. What was he reading
and reciting ? We have on this point, thanks to his
two contemporaries, some precise information. He
seems to have been above all attracted by the Elizabethans ; his early introduction to Shakespeare was
doubtless responsible for this. With the help of
Lamb's and Campbell's *Specimens* he soon tackled
' Dodsley's Great Old Plays ' which his Tutor consented to lend him and he thus began to lay the founda-
tions of his immense reading in the Elizabethan drama.

More than by the broad humour of the Comedies, he
was attracted by the horrible and the mysterious character of plays like *The Duchess of Malfy* and Ford's *'Tis
Pity* ; this love of terror remained for some time a
feature of Swinburne's mind, witness some of his early
works. From it also sprang his admiration for Tourneur's *Revenger's Tragedy*, a feeling as strange and as
unwarranted as, in a totally different direction, that experienced by Voltaire for Quinault. Soon these an-
thologies and selections were not enough. Swinburne
had at his disposal a great deal of pocket-money, and,
with the help of his mother, he soon bought the complete works of Marlowe, Massinger, Ford, Marston
and others, which were then being reprinted. His enthusiasm extended to the modern imitators of the Elizabethan drama : as well as Shelley's *Cenci*, he had begun
to read, at an early date, the works of Talfourd and
R. H. Horne.

More unexpected is the evidence of his reading in
eighteenth century poetry ; yet, apart from what he
could find in Campbell's *Specimens*, he had probably
bought, in Pickering's editions of the *Aldine Poets*, the
works of Burns, Collins, Cowper, Gray, Pope, Thomson, Young and even Falconer, in whose *Shipwreck* he
detected with great acumen two different manners of
style.

Among the moderns, he knew Wordsworth, Shelley
and Keats and was also much attracted by the ballads
of Southey—probably because he recognized in them
something of those buoyant metres which had charmed
his ears from early childhood. We can understand his
sudden enthusiasm for the novels of Dickens which,
in their serial form, circulated at East Dene from 1849

onwards. But his genuine enjoyment of Landor's *Idylls* and some of Matthew Arnold's poems such as *Empedocles* is far more remarkable and shows genuine taste as well as a true sense of rhythm.

As Montaigne found long ago, it is difficult to read much without being tempted to write a little. At Eton Swinburne was already writing mediocre original poetry, or rather imitative poetry of great merit. He was later on under the impression that he had burnt at the age of sixteen ' every scrap of manuscript he had in the world '. Two poems have escaped the holocaust, and adequately supply an instance of the two different directions in which he was endeavouring to exercise his style.

On June 4, 1851, Queen Victoria and the Prince Consort paid a visit to Eton. This ceremony was used for educational purposes and some of the classes were invited to write a record of the glorious day instead of the weekly Latin composition ; to such exceptional occasions was the teaching of English confined. But the demon of prosody was still haunting the mind of the masters and it was laid down that the composition must be in English heroic couplets. Swinburne handed in *The Triumph of Gloriana* and it is reported that he received due praise for it and even won some sort of unofficial prize. It is true that this ephemeral glory has been more than counterbalanced by the severity of later critics. Sir Edmund Gosse wrote that the poem as a whole was ' a dull mass of imitative correctness ' and most critics have endorsed this judgment. I must confess that such remarks strike me as absolutely pointless. *The Triumph of Gloriana*, one should not forget, was the work of a schoolboy of fourteen, rather

promising no doubt, but not exactly precocious. It was
a school exercise. It had to be in classical couplets :
one should no more quarrel with its style than with
the irregularities of a so-called Pindaric Ode. It displays great power of imitation and justifies Sir George
Young's opinion that Swinburne's poems at Eton
' flowed but did not sing ' ; it was already no small
merit that they flowed. All this might be argued for
Gloriana. But I can hardly understand that Edmund
Gosse, who mentions the poem half apologetically,
should not have had his sense of humour tickled by
the fact that we have in *Gloriana* a sort of anticipated
echo of the patriotic ' odes ' and ' songs ' which Swinburne, after a long evolution, was to write at the end
of his career. The style is of course different but, in
these few lines which I select for quotation, the inspiration is the same :

> Our new Miltiades [Wellington] of happier fate
> All ancient warriors strive in vain to emulate ;
> On high another Aristides [Chatham] stands
> The fate of nations balanced in his hands . . .
> And while he strives his liberty to save
> Finds in each British heart a glorious grave!

If we consider *Gloriana, Modern Hellenism* and *The
Death of Sir John Franklin* on the one hand, and such
poems as *A Word for the Navy* and *The Jubilee* on the
other, we can admit that at some thirty years' distance
Swinburne had almost exactly returned to the point
from which he started.

The Unhappy Revenge is a blood-curdling tragedy
composed by Swinburne about 1849 ; it offers interesting evidence of his early reading of Elizabethan dramatists—more particularly Tourneur, Massinger and

Webster. But it is less of a pastiche than Swinburne's Oxford tragedies, and is interesting to us as an instance of the violent and gruesome situations in which the child's romantic imagination exulted. This terrible story tells of the ' unhappy revenge ' of Eudoxia, a sister to the late Roman emperor, who, to avenge her honour which has been grievously damaged by the present emperor Maximus, betrays Rome into the hands of the Huns. The unfortunate Maximus seems however sufficiently punished as it is, though in a way more reminiscent of Molière than of Tourneur,—the shameless *liaison* of his wife Pulcheria with the villainous Dorax being in the present instance the instrument of divine retribution. The degradation of those characters is further enhanced by the figure of Eroclea, a Christian virgin, who with the help of bishop Pamphilius manages the arduous task of preserving her spotless purity until she becomes a martyr. This character is treated more earnestly than the others, and there is no doubt that Eroclea embodies the solid religious faith which Swinburne had brought with him from East Dene and which he was to retain until his Oxford days. Some of her speeches sound like an emotional child's prayer, precisely like those ' unaffected and unashamed ecstasies of adoration when receiving the sacrament ' which Swinburne has himself described :

> To Heaven I bear
> My soul a white transported sacrifice
> Wash'd pure in my own blood.

But all this pathetic innocence is unavailing ; Eroclea is duly martyred. It is true that Maximus,

Pulcheria and a few others will soon follow her to the grave. Swinburne, writing from memory in 1876, stated that, in his early tragedy which he thought was lost, he had 'contrived to pack twice as many rapes and about three times as many murders as are contained in the model [Tourneur's *Revenger's Tragedy*], which is not noticeably or exceptionally deficient in such incidents. It must have been a sweet work, and full of the tender and visionary innocence of childhood's unsullied fancy'. Swinburne was however exaggerating the merits of his play : Tourneur's tragedy contains three rapes, one public execution and a dozen murders ; Swinburne's can only boast one rape, one suicide, two murders by poison, and four executions. It must however in fairness be added that the *Unhappy Revenge* is unfinished.

Swinburne's taste for poetry and consciousness of his budding powers was no doubt encouraged by his interviews with two poets : Wordsworth and Rogers. It must be confessed that Wordsworth did all he could to quench the spark of inspiration in the boy's heart ; after informing Algernon's parents (the meeting took place at Rydal Mount during the Summer holiday of 1849) that he thought the boy would find nothing harmful in his poems, he proceeded to recite Gray's *Elegy*, a poem which ever since Swinburne cordially disliked. He went on to show the visitors round his house and displayed proudly some tokens of favour he had received from royalty—including no doubt the 'handful of silver' and the 'ribbon to stick in his coat'. He ended by asserting that Swinburne would never forget the interview in so dismal a voice that the boy burst into tears. Samuel Rogers, whom

Swinburne probably met in 1852, was also on the wane, but he had never been a very brilliant star in the heaven of poetry, and, in this instance at least, he rose to the occasion which the Fates were giving him. He smiled and said, laying his hand on the red hair of the child : ' I prophesy that you will be a poet too '. Thus Swinburne, before he was fifteen, had already collected the dying words and blessings of two famous poets.

From a human point of view Eton did, it seems, little for Swinburne. Contrary to what happened at Oxford he made very few friends. Only two names can be mentioned with certainty : Bertram Mitford (Lord Redesdale) and Sir George Young. The former has left us a picturesque record of the poet as a school-boy, more picturesque perhaps than it is precise ; he was able to supply graphic descriptions and images of his cousin at Eton but does not seem to have been on intimate terms with him. Mitford was slightly older and on his own admission saw very little of Swinburne after being sent to College ; it is not impossible that the domineering manners of the older Etonian may have produced an unfavourable impression on the newcomer. With Sir George Young the case was quite different. He was a day-boy and could share with his friends the comfort of a private home. Swinburne, who was to remember him later on as ' the best friend of his schoolboyhood', was introduced to him in October 1849, through the good offices of Joynes ; their friendship began at once but did not ripen until later, as Sir George Young left Eton shortly afterwards and did not return till 1851. They then became close friends and it is to Sir George Young's (still un-published) recollections that the biographer should turn for information of a precise nature. But even with Sir George Young Swinburne did not continue his acquaintance after he had left school. It was not until 1892 that he heard again from him through a common friend. Nobody else seems to have known Swinburne well at Eton, although some, like Oscar Browning, have without justification claimed his acquaintance. It should not be inferred that he was bullied or held in contempt : both Mitford and Sir George Young are definite on this point : ' none dreamt of interfering with him ', ' there was something a little formidable about him '. He simply kept apart, being content with his share in the life of the school, his books and his dreams. In the course of the latter, he must have more than once been haunted by a boyish shape who had also once walked the same fields and sat on the same forms : he had perhaps seen in a register similar to that in which he entered his own name on first coming to Eton, the signature of Shelley ; the parallel between their two careers was in later days to impress Swinburne to such an extent that the biographer is perhaps fairly close to reality and not indulging his romantic imagination when suggesting that the spirit of Shelley kept the lonely schoolboy company.

From his masters, Swinburne, eager to learn and inspired with that reverence for his elders which was a feature of his character, might have received a deeper impression. But this was apparently not the case. About Cookesley and Tarver he had nothing to say : he remembered that the latter had introduced him to Hugo, but gave the credit for his winning the Prince Consort's Prize to his mother entirely. Dr. Hawtrey

he scarcely ever saw ' for a boy not in the sixth never
sees the *head* master. . . . In fact, the Supreme Being of
an Etonian Olympus (or Purgatory) is a rite, a law,
a custom—not a man'.   It seems that William Johnson (Cory) whose fine æsthetic sense might have appealed to the boy was not even aware of his existence.
The man to whom we look for the possibility of a deep
lasting influence is James Leigh Joynes who, as his
tutor and housemaster, ought to have had his share in
shaping the character of his charge.   But here again
we are disappointed.   A. C. Benson, in *Memories and
Friends*, supplies us with an interesting memoir of the
Eton Master, which helps us to understand why.   Joynes
(' Jimmy ' for his pupils) was, it is true, an excellent
disciplinarian and had seldom to give punishment ;
which shows that Swinburne, in spite of the Galli-
ambic incident, did not feel the weight of his anger as
frequently as could be imagined.   But Joynes' teaching may not have been so good as his discipline : ' it
was sound old-fashioned Eton scholarship, which was
a curious little exotic bloom of culture, conventional
and narrow, and based upon a minute acquaintance
with two or three authors '.   To be precise, he insisted
on his scholars learning Horace by heart ; which made
Swinburne dislike Horace to the end of his days.
Physically he was ' short, broad, very strongly built,
his small and sturdy legs slightly bowed outwards . . .
he ran rather than walked, his big feet twinkling
along '.   One trait will help to determine his character : when Hawtrey retired and he was asked to stand
for the headship, he became ' panic-stricken ' and refused at once, as he had no ideas or theories of any
kind on education.   In fact he was sadly lacking in

personality. His wife, a German lady by birth, was
' modest and charming ' but 'very retiring', and ' took
little part in the social life of the College '. In brief,
despite Joynes' ' kind and fatherly manner ', his
' hardworking and conscientious nature ', despite Mrs.
Joynes ' who was so infinitely kind to [him] at the age
when [he] most needed kindness ', Swinburne found
the Joyneses very dull. He may have nursed no ill-
feeling towards them until the last days of his stay at
Eton, or even after. But he found them dull, and we
cannot blame him if he preferred his tutor's Dodsley
to his tutor's lectures.

It may be thought that the chief points connected
with Swinburne's stay at Eton have now been touched
upon, but the following sentence from a letter written
in 1867 comes as a reminder that some things cannot
go unsaid : ' I should like to see two things at Eton
again ', Swinburne writes, ' the river—and the
block'. As far as the river is concerned we can understand Swinburne's longing. Although he played no
games, he practised one sport, having brought with
him from the shores of the Channel and the North
Sea a passion for swimming. The Thames afforded
him opportunities which were eagerly embraced ; the
recollection of swimming parties at Cuckoo Weir was
for ever with him a cherished memory. He could
write in the course of one of the numerous parallels
which he liked to make between Shelley and himself :

I am more than ever amazed at Shelley's neglect of swimming . . . my one really and wholly delightful recollection of
the place and time being that of the swimming lessons and play
in the Thames. I would have wagered that Shelley of all
verse-writing men and Eton boys would have been the one at

least to match me in the passion for that pursuit. I suppose he took it out afterwards in boating—whereas I can never be *on* the water without wishing to be *in* it. But then he, like me, seems not to have gone in for boating at school.

Swinburne's second cause for regret—the flogging-block—is a matter more delicate to write about. If he does not already know it, the reader will realize as he proceeds that Swinburne's sensibility developed on abnormal lines which were to modify the whole of his sexual life : he had early tendencies towards masochism and sadism, and there can be no doubt that he indulged and confirmed those tendencies in his later life. But the danger here would be to say too much rather than not enough. Those tendencies existed in Swinburne but it is not clear at what time they began to assert themselves in a definite manner. It is true that the old-fashioned kind of corporal punishment in favour at Eton (flogging was then a common occurrence, and, in the lower classes, was inflicted publicly) may have created in the boy's mind indestructible associations. This would seem to be borne out by the numerous allusions made by Swinburne in his works and correspondence, not only to this feature of Etonian discipline but also to actual scenes in which he was supposed to play the main and passive part. *A Year's Letter*, *The Flogging-Block*, *The Whippingham Papers*, *Lesbia Brandon* recount at length the titanic flagellations inflicted by masters on their pupils. There exists a poem, *Eton : another Ode* (a strange counterpart to the well known *Ode* for the 450th anniversary) which records the very peculiar mood in which its author wrote it :

Dawn smiles on the fields of Eton, and wakes from slumber
    her youthful flock,
Lad by lad, whether good or bad : alas for those who at nine
    o'clock
Seek the room of disgraceful doom, to smart like fun on the
    flogging block.

Swish, swish, swish! O I wish, I wish I'd not been late for lock-
    up last night !
Swish, that mill I'm bruised from still (I couldn't help it—I
    had to fight)
Makes the beast (I suppose at least) who flogs me flog me with
    all his might.

' Tell me, S—e, does shame within burn as hot (Swish ! Swish !)
    as your stripes my lad,
Burn outside, have I tamed your pride ? I'm glad to see how
    it hurts you—glad—
Swish ! I wish it may cure you. Swish ! Get up '. By Jove,
    what a dose I've had.

The realistic and autobiographical character of such
recollections is hard to deny. But I want to emphasize
that we do not know at what time Swinburne began
to indulge and dwell on those early experiences. Some
scenes of his Oxford Elizabethan Tragedies were
certainly written from the masochist point of view
and show beyond doubt that Swinburne's sensibility
was rapidly evolving on the lines already indicated.
We have no such corroborating evidence for the Eton
period ; the *Unhappy Revenge* contains, it is true,
descriptions of tortures and of the martyrs' bliss in the
midst of their pangs :

Fetch more irons
Hotter than these that tear me ; pour fresh oils
On the flames that consume my flesh. . . .

These details (which were partly taken from Neale's
Lives of the Saints) tend to show that the connection

between pain and sensual pleasure was latent in Swinburne's sensibility ; but not that he had reached a clear understanding of the nature of what he felt. My impression is that Swinburne registered at Eton certain experiences, both in himself and in others, which were to have a great influence on his sexual development ; but that it was only at a later date that he began to analyse, describe and magnify those early experiences which then became a sort of obsession.

We have no picture or photograph of Swinburne at Eton ; this is all the more to be regretted as, partly owing to causes which have just been mentioned, the Etonian schoolboy became with the poet a sort of ideal which haunted him throughout his life. Eton represented for him a stage of his development which he never quite outgrew, and he felt obscurely that it was at Eton that his personality expressed itself in the most natural and spontaneous manner. However the description of Reginald in *A Year's Letters* will here stand very adequately as a mental photograph of what the author (with a few modifications and exaggerations) believed himself to have been :

The visitor was a splendid-looking fellow, lithe and lightly built, but of a good compact make, with a sunburnt oval face, and hair like unspun yellow silk in colour, but one mass of short rough curls ; eyebrows, eyes, and eyelashes all dark, showing quaintly enough against his golden hair and bright pale skin. His mouth, with a rather full red under-lip for a child, had a look of such impudent and wilful beauty as to suggest at once the frequent call for birch in such a boy's education. His eyes too had a defiant laugh latent under the lazy light in them. Rather well got-up for the rest and delicately costumed, though with a distinct school stamp on him, but by no means after the muscle-manful type.

We are told that Swinburne was happy at Eton ;
that he liked the chivalrous traditions of the place.
Without denying that his thought often went back to
the scenes of his schooldays and that he never disclaimed his connection with the school (as he was to do
with Oxford) one cannot help feeling that his interest
in Eton was not very human. He liked the natural
setting, the woods, the fields, the Thames ; he liked
swimming the river ('his one really and wholly
delightful recollection of the place and time') ; he
liked the library, the books ; he liked, perhaps, the
flogging-block. And that was all. For his masters
and their teaching, for his own housemaster he felt
little interest or affection. Sir George Young remarks
'as a scholar at school, he was always a rebel'. He
had learnt independence from his long intercourse
with sun, wind and waters, and, although this latent
spirit of rebellion never extended to matters of religion
or to school regulations in general, Swinburne passed
through Eton cold and unconcerned. In August
1853 it was unexpectedly decided that he would not
return to Eton.[1] Had he quarrelled with his tutor ?
It is quite possible, and A. C. Benson mentions that
when he applied to Joynes for reminiscences 'he
seemed to be able to recollect nothing except that
Swinburne had had red hair. When I mentioned his
poetry he changed the subject decisively with obvious
disapproval'. But the main reason was of course that
Swinburne did not want to stay and was no longer

---

[1] Swinburne's few friends, including Sir George Young, were greatly shocked at
the news that he was not coming back, and had to send instead of handing him,
the farewell gift usual in such circumstances—which in the present occurrence took
the form of the Dindorf collection 'Poetarum Scenicorum Graecorum' (a typical
choice).

interested in his life and studies at the College. He severed his connection with Eton abruptly and painlessly ; his schoolfellows never quite understood why he was not coming back. ' For places rather than persons he had a violent and blind affection '.

CHAPTER IV

OXFORD

Not only are we in the dark about the reason why Swinburne left Eton, but also about where he went. Some biographers state, not without exaggeration, that the years 1853–56 are, in Swinburne's life, ' almost a blank '. Others have conjectured that he spent those three years ' climbing and swimming '—a remarkable feat of endurance, even if we allow for some intervals of rest. Others there are who believe that he was from the first coached for Oxford. Sir George Young told me that, after so many years, he remembered having heard that Swinburne ' had gone to France with a tutor '. But the poet himself stated that he ' never was out of England till he was eighteen '. Moreover, had he been abroad he would have sent letters home, and it is probable that his very inaccurate but understanding and devoted editor, Mrs. Disney Leith, would have published some extracts from them. We must be content with what evidence there is, but we cannot afford, as many of our predecessors have, to reject or ignore any. A few facts emerge ; they will be briefly stated.

In October 1853 Swinburne did not return to Eton ; in October-November 1854, when the news of the Balaklava charge reached England, he was at East Dene, and still fostered hopes that he might be allowed to enter the army ; it was in the ' Christmas

holidays ' that a final decision was reached and that the
Admiral vetoed his son's schemes. The word ' holidays ', used by Swinburne himself in a letter, suggests
that the boy was still being regularly taught. It is
reasonable to infer that from October 1853 to the end
of 1854 he received some sort of private tuition which
might eventually have facilitated his obtaining a
commission in the army. But after the Christmas
holidays' fateful decision, and the consequent climbing
of Culver Cliff[1] (to prove to himself that he was not a
coward) the course of his studies naturally changed.
Oxford was seriously contemplated, probably with an
idea at the back of the parents' mind that the Church
might receive their son in its fold. It is easy now to
rail and wonder ; but their plans were eminently
reasonable : Algernon was not physically very strong ;
his religious faith was whole and perfect; he read aloud
beautifully with a fine sense of rhythm ; he revelled
in the Bible and the classics. To achieve their ambition, the best and almost the only possible means
was an (Arts) Honours Degree, to be followed later
by a degree in Divinity. Steps had to be taken in
order to pave the way for such a course ; it seems that
it was in Northumberland that Swinburne began or
rather resumed work. W. B. Scott, who came regularly
to those parts as early as 1854, remembered passing
him riding a small pony, with big tomes strapped to
his saddle, on his way from Capheaton to Cambo,
where the incumbent, the Rev. J. W. Wilkinson, had

----

[1] Swinburne, in a letter published by Mrs. D. Leith, recounted at great length
how at Christmas 1854 he made up his mind to climb the steeper and almost im-
pregnable slopes of Culver Cliff, some ten miles to the north-east of Bonchurch as a
means of ' testing his nerve in face of death '. It seems, from his coloured narrative,
that the attempt, which eventually was successful, proved at times extremely
dangerous (see *Boyhood* p. 13).

agreed to coach him—probably in history and the classics. Scott was then painting pictures for the decoration of Wallington Hall, and although he did not actually make Swinburne's acquaintance till four or five years later, there can be no doubt that the prospective undergraduate was a frequent visitor at the Hall. Sir W. Trevelyan, a compact of science and philanthropy, was no great attraction ; but his wife Pauline, intellectually not inferior to her husband, and much his superior in charm and artistic understanding, had soon taken a keen and possibly half-maternal interest in her young neighbour. She encouraged his visits and listened to his first poems. Her influence over him for several years is undoubted. In fact she was to him, what his mother never quite was, a friend and a confidante. But what is perhaps of more importance to us is that, at Wallington, Swinburne breathed an air faintly laden with Pre-Raphaelite incense. W. B. Scott was under the spell of the theories of the *Germ* ; Ruskin, a frequent visitor, presided over the decoration of the house. Lady Trevelyan had defended the new school in the *Scotsman* with courage and intelligence. Wallington was probably the first purely artistic circle which Swinburne entered. And to the appeal it made, he was keenly responsive.

The lessons given and received at Cambo were however insufficient and did not last longer than a summer holiday. When, probably in the course of 1854 or early in 1855, Swinburne's parents had recourse to James Russell Woodford, curate of St. Mark's, Easton, Bristol, the training became more systematic. The future bishop of Ely settled at East

Dene for a little while, but on being appointed to the living of Kempsford, Gloucestershire, he took his pupil with him. Mr. Thomas Snow, who shared in the coaching, remembers how Swinburne would ' declaim Greek poetry to a late hour of the night '. What is certain is that Woodford put Swinburne through most of the works of Juvenal to his pupil's keen enjoyment. This author was on the syllabus of the Oxford entrance examination ; so Woodford crammed him with Juvenal, little thinking that he thus helped to sharpen the arrows which were later to rain on the head of Napoleon III, alive and dead.

About the same time, or perhaps just a little later, Swinburne supplemented the instruction he was thus receiving in the fine art of invective by reading *Les Châtiments*, 'of which I used day after day to repeat pages to myself as I walked up and down alone on the beach between Bonchurch and Shanklin '.

In the summer of 1855, with Oxford looming large in the near distance, Swinburne accompanied his uncle, Colonel the Hon. Thomas Ashburnham, on a journey to Wiesbaden. It was the first time that Swinburne left England, and it was not a bad thing for the prospective undergraduate to have travelled a little. The Colonel, whose health was probably much shattered by a long stay in India, wanted to drink the waters of a German Spa, and his nephew jumped at the opportunity of a visit to the Continent. The few letters which he wrote to his family, although published in a fragmentary and mutilated form by Mrs. Disney Leith, make up a fresh and charming record of his experiences—remarkable both for a keen delight in art and for occasional touches of unaffected humour.

On the 16th of July the travellers slept at Calais. The following day was spent at Liège, Swinburne being especially attracted by the woodland scenery round the town ; what he could see of it from the railway called forth a comparison with Northumberland—no small praise, as his cousin remarks. Throughout his life Swinburne had thus standards of beauty by which to judge everything ; for scenery, it was at first Northumberland, then some parts of Italy ; in the last years, Wimbledon Common.

Aix-la-Chapelle ; Swinburne set foot on German soil, an experience which was not to be renewed. Early on the 18th uncle and nephew were in Cologne and at once visited, one dragging the other, the ' magnificent ' Cathedral and the Church of St. Ursula. Characteristically, the boy was struck and affected by the religious atmosphere as well as by the artistic beauty of the monuments ; the shrines, bones and relics impressed him deeply. And when the divine service began while the young tourist stood apart in a corner, a great sadness overcame him :

I felt quite miserable, it was such a wretched feeling that while they all were praying, old men and tiny children kneeling together, I was not one of them, I was shut out as it were. I could have sat down and cried, I was so unhappy. How I do trust that some day all will be able to worship together and no divisions and jealousies ' keep us any longer asunder '.

Swinburne, as we see, was still deeply attached to ' the daily religion taken and taught on trust '.

About the 24th or the 25th the party settled at Wiesbaden, after a fine journey by steamer down the Rhine and a night spent at Coblenz. Swinburne had taken quite a liking to this life of wanderings, but he had now to remain in Wiesbaden for three or four weeks. He soon got reconciled to the idea, especially as he lived in the same hotel as an officer who had fought at Balaklava, and made frequent trips round the town, visiting the ruins of Sauerburg, the cave of the Robber Luttweis and the cathedral of Mayence ; there the reckless English boy repeated on a minor scale the performance of Culver Cliff by climbing to an upper gallery ' much to the terror and alarm of the showman ' just as the great clock struck four, ' making a most awful noise that made the whole concern shake and rattle '. It was probably during this stay at Wiesbaden that Swinburne had an opportunity of attending a performance of Kleist's *Kätchen von Heilbronn*. Although he had had but a few lessons in German, he was much impressed by the play and carried away ' a chaste and delightful impression which will never vanish either from my heart or my mind '.

On August 13th they left Wiesbaden for Würtzburg, and went on to Nuremberg where they stayed until August 16th. This must have been the extreme point they reached, and the party soon after retraced their steps. During the night of August 23rd they crossed over from Ostend. But this final stage of the journey held yet one other experience in store for Swinburne : a violent storm broke on their ship with such fierce intensity that the tough old Colonel swore he had never seen anything like it outside the Tropics. As for Algernon, in direct contrast to his elder's obvious resentment, he delighted in the lightnings and the wind. In this memory he was to revel for at least fifty years. It is an interesting study of style to read descriptions of this storm in *The Times* of

August 25th, 1855, in the opening paragraph of *Essays and Studies*, and in *A Channel Passage*, and to see the same experience recorded first in dull journalese, then in fine rhythmical prose, lastly in ponderous anapaests.

On January 23rd, 1856, Swinburne went up to Balliol College. Edmund Gosse in the *Life* gave the impression that at first he led a solitary life, which induced a ' return ' of religious fervour, and this statement has been duly repeated and exaggerated by later critics. But there is not the slightest foundation for such an inference : Swinburne's ' faith ' was untouched when he reached Oxford as an extract from his German letters shows ; as for his alleged ' loneliness', biographers like to enlarge upon it for the simple reason that there is extremely little information about Swinburne's first months at Oxford. Why not then suppose that the freshman remained shut up in his rooms, reading the Bible and singing hymns ? And anyhow who could say he did not ? But little as we know of that period, we know enough to contradict this. The truth is that Swinburne early began to dislike the theological atmosphere of a University which had so recently been torn by the great quarrels of the Oxford Movement. On the other hand the staff of Balliol College (including the Master, Robert Scott, E. C. Woolcombe, J. Riddell, E. Palmer, J. G. Lonsdale, and even Jowett) were out of sympathy with him. Also such undergraduates as delighted in boating and outdoor games could not be greatly attracted to one who disliked all sports except swimming and riding. But there were others to whom Swinburne was soon bound by ties of close friendship. In May

1856, three months after his arrival, George Birkbeck Hill wrote that he had ' dined at the Observatory and met a Balliol friend of mine—Swinburne—with his father Captain Swinburne '. Now Hill, as a Pembroke undergraduate, was acquainted with Edwin Hatch and the members of the ' Birmingham set ' which included Morris and Burne-Jones ; the importance of his association with Swinburne at this early date cannot be overstated. The reference to the Observatory in Hill's letter reminds us that Swinburne had had through his father an introduction to Manuel John Johnson, keeper of the Radcliffe Observatory, and that he remained on friendly terms with the astronomer and his wife until the end of his stay at Oxford. Another acquaintance was, as W. B. Woodgate, the famous oarsman, informed Edmund Gosse, Walter Sewell, Warden of Radley, and brother to Elizabeth Sewell, the Bonchurch Schoolmistress. Swinburne seems to have been at one time a frequent visitor at Radley ; he was allowed to mix freely with the boys and probably enjoyed an atmosphere which was reminiscent of Eton. It is true that, after he had defended *Maud* at the School Debating Society, and after information had reached Sewell about his having developed 'theories of free thinking in religion', the doors of Radley were closed to him. But this certainly caused him little annoyance.

For he was by now (November 1856), as appears from the above reference to ' free-thinking ', closely connected with the set of undergraduates who were about to found the ' Old Mortality '. Much has been written about this institution. Copious extracts from the statutes have been printed and reprinted. It was in

the rooms of John Nichol that they were first drafted
in presence of the other five original members :
Swinburne, S. Grenfell, A. V. Dicey, Hill, G. R. Luke.
What was the object of the society ? : ' stimulating
and promoting the interchange of thought among the
members on the more general questions of literature,
philosophy, science as well as the diffusion of a correct
knowledge and critical appreciation of our standard
English authors '.   But where did the name come
from ?   ' From the consideration that every member
of the said society was or has lately been in so weak and
precarious a condition of bodily health as plainly
and manifestly to instance the great frailties and so
to speak mortality of this our human life and constitution '.   In fact, owing to an illness of Nichol's,
the first full sitting of the society had to be adjourned
till May of the following year, but several informal
meetings were held in his absence.   The above
extracts from the statutes suffice to show that the
members of the new society were averse to physical
exercises and given to intellectual pursuits, and that
their opinions on politics or religion were probably of
an advanced nature—an impression amply substanti-
ated by the minutes of the later sittings.   The Old
Mortality soon became an exclusive, aristocratic and
very unorthodox institution.   Hill noted with satisfaction that he belonged to ' one of the cleverest sets
in Oxford ' ; soon it was rumoured that ' they were a
revolutionary set and read Browning '.   And of this
set Swinburne in his first year at Oxford had managed
to become an important member. This was indeed no
small achievement on the part of one who, as some
would have us believe, was ' lonely ', ' very reserved

and sullen ' and who was just passing ' through a
recrudescence of Anglican ritualism '.

The significance of Swinburne's connection with
the Old Mortality lies almost entirely in his relations
with Nichol. He was never intimate with any of the
other members ; the views of the society were mostly
those held by Nichol ; in *Undergraduate Papers*, the
review which was for a brief spell the organ of the Old
Mortality, Swinburne chiefly published works of a
marked Pre-Raphaelite character which belong to
another sphere of influence.

As the chief events of Swinburne's life come to be
rightly understood, it will be seen that John Nichol
played an exceptional part in the development of his
genius ; a fact which Swinburne implicitly recognized
by keeping up his former intimacy with Nichol at a
time when the two men had but little left in common.
Nichol was able to gain Swinburne's attention and
confidence primarily owing to the fact that he gave the
impression of a remarkably strong personality. This
was perhaps more apparent than real : Nichol, under
the care of his father, had been at first a minor Admirable Crichton, coming up to the University of Glasgow
at the age of fifteen and distinguishing himself by
various prize-essays ; but when he left Scotland for
Oxford in 1855 he found himself considerably older
than most of the other undergraduates ; over the
members of the Old Mortality he had a seniority of
from three to five years. All this contributed to give
his fellow students the conviction that he had come up
to Oxford with ' his intellectual and moral capacities
fully developed ' and that he was possessed of ' the
power of influencing his friends and companions '.

One other hold he had over Swinburne : he helped
him considerably with his University work. Nichol
was a born ' coach ' and although he did not officially
act in that capacity until after taking his degree, he
was quite capable of being of help to a friend if he was
interested in him. It was in the study of logic—a
subject which Swinburne had to take until Easter
1858—that Nichol proved invaluable. He was thus
in a favourable position to exercise a deep influence
over his friend. In matters of religion there can be
little doubt that he was instrumental in destroying
Swinburne's orthodoxy ; although a dissenter by
education, he seems to have had no deep belief of a
fixed nature, and, as a dogmatic advocate of complete
tolerance, persisted in refusing to sign the tests at
Oxford, thus debarring himself from a fellowship.
But it was chiefly in politics that Nichol ' helped '
Swinburne, confirming him in tendencies which must
have so far been rather vague, in spite of the patriarch
of Capheaton. Through Nichol, the Old Mortality
was a Republican set. In Glasgow he was a member
of several radical societies. The works of J. S. Mill
were his Bible. He had met Mazzini and Kossuth,
whom his father had entertained in his own house on
the occasion of a lecture delivered at Glasgow. He
had followed with passionate interest the Italian and
Hungarian risings of 1848. Swinburne was too young
to feel the force of the revolutionary tide which then
swept over Europe ; but thanks to Nichol the fervid
enthusiasm of the men of 1848 was brought home to
him, and caused him to adopt an attitude which he was
to preserve throughout his life. This is well seen in
the *Ode to Mazzini,* which was read to Hill in March

1857 and had probably been composed or conceived in November 1856 when the friendship with Nichol was being formed. As far as the problem of abstract liberty and of foreign nationalities is concerned, Nichol was Swinburne's tutor—almost a prophet.

His influence in the literary field is far less certain and always of a superficial nature : Nichol was more interested in history and moral philosophy than in art. His appreciation—perhaps his understanding—of Greek literature was slight. It was from the intellectual side that he was attracted to Browning's works —which Swinburne had no difficulty in admiring with him. But to his panegyrics of Carlyle and Byron the younger undergraduate gave but a reluctant ear. In modern poetry Nichol could only recommend to his friend's admiration the poems of Alexander Smith and Sydney Dobell, and Swinburne politely but firmly declined to share his enthusiasm.

The difference between those two natures is best expressed in the poems written by Nichol and Swinburne for the Newdigate competition of March 1857 on the somewhat vague subject : *The Temple of Janus.* While Nichol's dull and correct composition is full of abstract ideas and historical or political allusions, such as to the Crimean war, Swinburne's is far nearer to the spirit of classical poetry and free from anachronism in thought or style ; moreover he appears as steeped in Shelleyan diction and, transcending Roman or Italian history, seems to go back to the Greek lyrists and dramatists for the rhythm and movement of his verse. Neither poem was successful, but Nichol, with editorial authority, printed his own contribution in *Undergraduate Papers* ; Swinburne's remained uncrowned and unpublished ; and he began to dislike Oxford a little more.[1]

However, Nichol's influence, which even throughout *The Temple of Janus* is discernible in the apology of Liberty and Tyrannicide, asserted itself as early as the Autumn of 1856 rather than in 1857 : from January to May the founder of the Old Mortality was away from Oxford, but Swinburne saw a great deal more of Nichol in the Summer, when he paid him a prolonged visit in the north which included a cruise, lasting a full week, to the solitudes of Skye. It was shortly after that Swinburne, staying at Capheaton on his way back from the north, was introduced to W. B. Scott by Lady Trevelyan.

He must have left Wallington with reluctance : the prospect of returning to Oxford was doubtless to him far less attractive than a year ago when, in spite of his reported ' isolation ', he was beginning to make a few choice friends who appreciated him. The charm of new acquaintances was beginning to wear out ; besides, several strangers had been or were on the point of being elected members of the society ; such were James Bryce and T. H. Green ' who preached Hegel with the accent of a puritan '. Swinburne found that his papers on Marlowe and the Brontës, or his readings from Dickens, were not as welcome to the society as essays on Wycliffe or Cicero contributed by others. The intellectual character of the Old

[1] Gosse states in the two editions of his *Life* that Swinburne competed again for the Newdigate in 1858, the subject being ' The discovery of the North West Passage '. This was contradicted, and it is now proved beyond doubt that Swinburne's *Death of Sir John Franklin* was written in 1860 for a totally different occasion (see page 76). Gosse's original mistake was natural and intelligible. But it is amusing to read that he received from Lord Bryce confirmation of his erroneous hypothesis : ' Lord Bryce recollects that the Old Mortality were indignant that the prize was awarded, not to Algernon but to Mr. F. L. Latham . . . ' (*Life*, p. 44).

Mortality was becoming exaggerated, its artistic proclivities, which had never been strong, were tending to
disappear altogether. Also the young poet had not
forgotten his unsuccessful attempt at the Newdigate
Prize, and he was faced by an unpleasant examination
at the beginning of the coming year. He was moreover disappointed in most of his tutors and professors
—including Matthew Arnold, whom he loved as a
poet, but whose lectures as Professor of Poetry had not
answered his expectations. He must have been inclined to view with misgiving his third year's residence
at Balliol and to dread hours of solitude and melancholy.
But his fears were groundless. For, when he came up
in the Autumn of 1857, the Pre-Raphaelite Brotherhood had been let loose in Oxford.

Pre-Raphaelitism indeed was past its days of *Sturm
und Drang*. Obloquy and blind abuse were no longer
poured on its works and principles as in 1850. Indignation had yielded to sympathy and contempt to
commissions. The danger now lay in the opposite
direction : with Ruskin as its blind prophet, Pre-
Raphaelitism was an accepted religion, at least a sect,
no longer a heresy. Together with its power to shock,
as in the days of Millais' ' Christ in the House of his
Parents', it had lost a great deal of its dynamic quality.
And now the Pre-Raphaelites had come to Oxford !
A dangerous consecration. True, Rossetti had not
been offered an honorary degree. The college authorities were not responsible for his visit. Everything
had been arranged with Benjamin Woodward, the
architect, with the Union Society and with its
treasurer. For this body, not for the University,
Rossetti and his friends were to work, their task being

to decorate in fresco the walls of the Debating Hall. Here was indeed a great opportunity for the new School to prove its worth : and it was understood that the painters would work for love, not for money. It was obvious that Rossetti could not rely on such full-fledged painters and expert technicians as Millais, Holman Hunt or even Madox-Brown. He brought with him two neophytes, Burne-Jones and William Morris (both Oxford men, as Woodward might plead to the Union authorities) and some artists of lesser reputation than the great Pre-Raphaelite pioneers ; these were Arthur Hughes, J. H. Pollen, Spencer Stanhope, Val Prinsep and Monroe.

Thus a second Pre-Raphaelite Brotherhood, partly composed of former members of the Birmingham set, had sprung into existence : it possessed over the former real advantages : it could boast of a greater unity, a stricter acceptance of the authority of a chief—Rossetti ; it could also bring to the task in hand more freshness and enthusiasm, and a deeper poetic understanding. But it was deficient in experience, skill, technique. The training of most of the artists, including Rossetti, was not complete. Of fresco painting they seem to have had but the faintest notions. Now that the attempt has proved a failure, and the paintings have almost completely disappeared, it is easy enough to criticize. But Rossetti's conception was grand : had he succeeded, had he not been mistaken in the kind of decoration he chose and the material he used, he would have left a standing and complete record of what his school could achieve. Rather than a few art galleries and private collections, the Union Debating Hall would be a fit temple of

Pre-Raphaelite art. But Rossetti ought to have known better ; even before the work was begun, even in the ranks of his disciples, serious misgivings were entertained. Spencer Stanhope wrote at the time : ' Rossetti has had the painting in Frescoe of the Oxford Museum entrusted to him. This is really a great mistake on the part of the managers '. Whether Stanhope meant that the ' great mistake ' lay in attempting fresco painting in a building like the Debating Hall, or in entrusting it to Rossetti, is not quite clear ; he probably meant both.

One thing soon became certain : the work was proceeding very slowly. The painters had arrived in August ; contrary to what had been hoped, the Hall was not ready in October for the students' return. The Pre-Raphaelites were still busy in November ; work went on in a sporadic manner, till well into 1858 ; the decoration was never properly completed. As the Union treasurer had agreed to pay the artists' expenses (including beer) we may well picture his state of mind. But, in spite of his regrets and repentance over the state of affairs, it is the strict duty of Swinburne's biographer to rejoice.

It was on November 1st that the fateful meeting occurred, at Birkbeck Hill's rooms. We know that Hill was a friend of both parties. Burne-Jones, Morris and probably Rossetti were present. Thanks to a mistake on the part of W. M. Rossetti in the *Memoir* of his brother we know the exact circumstances of the meeting ; William Michael had written that Swinburne had ' introduced himself ' to Rossetti at the Union. This drew from Putney the following typical protest :

I never (allow me to say) introduced myself to anybody, and certainly should not have done so in my nonage. An Oxford friend, Hill, who knew Jones and Morris and through them Gabriel, introduced me to them, and Gabriel almost instantly asked me to sit (or stand) to him—but the intended 'fresco' never was even begun.

Swinburne might well pour torrents of abuse on Ferdinand of Naples and Napoleon III, but he would never have ' introduced himself ' to anybody. Let us make a note of this and remember that, in the midst of his worst excesses, erotic, political or others, Swinburne's Muse will always preserve a vine-leaf of respectability.

Swinburne's appearance, as we see, impressed at once the Pre-Raphaelite painters (he had red hair and green eyes like Miss Siddal with whom Rossetti had been living for some years). To them Swinburne was at first a striking model, nothing more ; but to him they appeared as demi-gods : the magnificent manner and quiet authority of Rossetti, the boyish enthusiasm of Burne-Jones, the powerful exuberance of Morris were to him a source of wonder ; and when Morris read (as he did then or a few days later) *The Eve of Crecy*, *Blanche*, *The Haystack in the Flood* and *The Defence of Guinevere*, the intense inspiration concealed in the monotonous rugged lines burnt and dazzled him like a sudden blaze of beauty.

However deep and vivid may have been this first experience it was not until, soon afterwards, he entered the Debating Hall that Swinburne fully realized the originality and charm of Pre-Raphaelite art. Work was now well begun on the ten-odd large frescoes which were required to fill the blank space between the bookshelf and the dome on the upper portion of the walls : on that rough damp irregular surface the brush is being busily applied. The subjects are taken from the *Morte d'Arthur*. Tristan, Lancelot, Guinevere are everywhere ; on all sides, clad in medieval costumes, knights and ladies with strained keen faces assume heraldic attitudes. The very soul of Pre-Raphaelitism meets Swinburne's eye ; he remembers the conversations of the night before, and the poems of Morris ; he remembers also what Lady Trevelyan, Ruskin and W. B. Scott may have told him at Wallington ; he understands, he is delighted, he is one of them. Fortunately, he cannot paint. He can only sit for them, and write.

Rossetti is at work on the typical *motif* he has chosen for himself : ' Sir Lancelot prevented by his sin from entering the chapel of the Holy Grail '. Swinburne gazes, with admiration no doubt, also with interest and curiosity. In spite of Rossetti's deliberate calm and quiet authority, is there no painful secret lurking behind those beetling brows, the gloom of some unknown weakness or the cloud of a remorse ? Is he not a modern Lancelot or perhaps King Arthur himself surrounded by the whole Round Table ?

Certainly not ; for there is nothing ascetic or mystical in the atmosphere of this ungainly Oxford building, temporarily transformed into a Chelsea studio. From the scaffolding, from the ladders, from the platforms where models sit or stand, even from the roof where Morris plies his brush, puns are dropped, loud guffaws rise, jokes are good-naturedly bandied. ' What fun we had in that Union ! What jokes ! What roars of laughter ' wrote Val Prinsep. ' It was blue summer

then and always morning and the air sweet and full
of bells ' sighed Burne-Jones many years later. And
Pollen complained comically in a letter to his wife :
' There is such a rattle of talk from surrounding
worthies that I fear my wits will fail, Topsy and Rossetti giving vent to most startling opinions' .... Thus
is disclosed another ingredient of the Pre-Raphaelite
atmosphere : the free chaff, the outrageous exaggerations, the continuous interchange of jokes and para-
doxes in the course of which many pregnant suggestions were born and took shape.

In the whole history of English literature I can think
of no more picturesque scene than the meeting of Swinburne and the Pre-Raphaelites in the Union Hall. Let
this be my excuse for tarrying over it. There may
come a day when it will supply a most effective second
act to some dramatized version of Rossetti's or Swinburne's life. Meanwhile, even when inadequately
described as in the preceding lines, the mere thought
of it is a joy to the mind.

' Ah that such sweet things should be fleet——
Such fleet things sweet '. The scenes which make
such an appeal to our æsthetic sense of humour did
not last long. Rossetti had to leave for London before the end of November ; Burne-Jones did not return after Easter 1858 ; Morris, who stayed longest,
went to France early in the summer.

And, naturally enough, it was Morris who influenced
Swinburne most : in spite of a spontaneous admiration
for Rossetti, of a deeper affinity to the personality of
Burne-Jones, it so happened that Morris' work and
temperament were calculated to affect Swinburne in an
almost incredible manner at the stage he had then

reached. *The Defence of Guinevere* and many other poems not included in that volume caused Swinburne to alter completely his style, his themes and, partly, his inspiration. A few days, perhaps a few hours, after meeting Morris for the first time he began *Queen Yseult*. I have studied closely all the extant fragments of verse written by Swinburne in 1857–58 and reached the conclusion that they were for the most part attempts at reproducing Morris' style. Two things struck Swinburne in the rough pastiches of the poet-painter : the condensed sincerity of the sentiment, the monotonous simplicity of the style. He was led to give up his former models, Aeschylus, Landor, Shelley, Arnold and to study the medieval romances (French and English), Chaucer, the *Morte d'Arthur* ; in that new light he rediscovered Dante and found new charm in the Elizabethans of the earlier period. Here is not the place to analyse the range and purport of this remarkable change. Let us however note that the immediate result of Morris' influence was to persuade Swinburne of the imperative necessity of patient, disinterested work on the pattern of a definite model. The poet of *The Temple of Janus* and the *Ode to Mazzini* abandoned for the time being his attempts at poems of limited originality but of intrinsic interest and high literary finish ; he confined himself to an endless labour of reproduction and pastiche. Just as a painter is first given an object to copy accurately, even so Swinburne had to learn the art of verse over again by *copying* certain models. He sank his individuality in that of the authors he studied, or rather in the qualities of style he wished to master. Most of Swinburne's poetical works from 1858 to 1860 are a

long self-imposed grind, a series of prosodic exercises.
When he emerged from this trial, he had a style of his
own.   But he certainly had paid the price : by which
is meant, not that the price was too high, but that few
great poets would be willing to pay it.

While Swinburne was undergoing this evolution,
the three numbers of *Undergraduate Papers* were published. This review was the official organ of the Old
Mortality. Nichol's society had long been in want of a
magazine ; but it was only during the last weeks of
1857 that a publisher (W. Mansell) was found who was
willing not only to print and sell the paper, but also to
promise (if not to pay) a small fee to the contributors.
Out of Swinburne's three significant contributions to
the magazine (he was responsible for five in all) only
one (*Church Imperialism*) reflects the political views of
the Old Mortality ; the two others (*Queen Yseult*,
The Early English Dramatists) have a clear Pre-Raphaelite ring.   They ought to have been published in the
Oxford and Cambridge Magazine, not in *Undergraduate
Papers*. Swinburne in the midst of his Pre-Raphaelite
fervour used the paper to express conceptions which
were foreign to it ; the tendencies of the Old Mortality,
though not averse to Rossetti and his clan, lay in a
totally different direction.   So obvious was the clash
that Swinburne had to give up the idea of publishing
the last Cantos of *Queen Yseult* : ' I think it is better
not to hazard too much in the poetical way of business '
he wrote to Nichol, ' Canto I stands well enough as a
separate ballad . . . Pray do not think it necessary
to make any difficulty about dropping me for the
present '. Had *Undergraduate Papers* appeared a year
earlier, Swinburne would have printed in it *The Temple*

of Janus and the *Ode to Mazzini* instead of *Queen Yseult*. Although the publication of the latter was discontinued the sacrifice was not enough to save the Magazine ; *Undergraduate Papers* died in April 1858, within five months of the date of its birth and ' baptism ' at Nichol's rooms on December 1st, 1857.

After the departure of the Pre-Raphaelites at Easter, the end of the year could only come as an anticlimax : Nichol's return in April 1858 was no adequate compensation. The Old Mortality, which had managed to ' keep afloat ' during its founder's absence, had lost much of its attraction. Swinburne preferred to withdraw from the dull academic world into a world of dreams and secret poetic ambitions : he steeped himself in Browning and the *Revue des Deux Mondes*, he read and re-read *The Defence of Guinevere* ; he also went on writing ' original ' poetry if such a word can be used for the close pastiches he was drilling himself to write : a prose translation from the *Decameron*, a set of poems on Jaufré Rudel, an Elizabethan play entitled *The Laws of Corinth*. A first version of *Rosamond* was also completed about the same time and only serves to show that Swinburne could command a more independent style, and that the ' grinds ' (the word is his) he went through were gratuitous and self-imposed. But he knew what he wanted, and with a definite end in view, the task was probably not irksome, perhaps pleasant. What is extraordinary is that, with all this unacademic work on his hands, Swinburne managed to do so well in his June Examinations, winning the Taylorian Scholarship for French and Italian and a Second Class in Moderations. He probably reaped the fruit of the regular work he had put in until the beginning of 1858 ; moreover most of his subjects, French, Italian, Latin and Greek, were to him familiar and congenial.

One of Swinburne's chief connections with the Old Mortality was his residence at Balliol, where the society had originated. This came to an end when, some time in May or June 1859, Swinburne, in accordance with the regulations (he had now had over twelve terms' residence at College), took up lodgings in town. One other link had been his keen interest in international events and the struggle of foreign nationalities. But, with Nichol again away in Glasgow, and the enrolling of new members such as J. A. Symonds and Pater (whose acquaintance Swinburne in later years always disclaimed or minimized) the character of the debates changed and became more hermetic ; moreover Swinburne's concern in anything outside the sphere of art in which the Pre-Raphaelites lived was beginning to lessen. He knew now that

> between death and life are hours
> To flush with love and hide in flowers.

Those flowers were *Rosamond*, pastiches of Keats and Milton, revised versions of the old Northumbrian Ballads, and an ' Elizabethan ' play full of learning and quaint imitation as usual, but also remarkable for its warm, disconcerting sensuality. Evidence of his sympathy for the Italian cause, or of his hatred of Napoleon III, is however to be found in his ballad *The Ride from Milan* and in the addresses on tyrannicide which he is reported to have given, with Dicey's approval, not at the meetings of the Old Mortality, but—a choice typical in itself—in the Union Debating Hall whose walls Rossetti had so magnificently failed to decorate. One serious consequence of his drifting away from the Old Mortality was an increased neglect of academic studies on his part : after all the society, in spite of its advanced views, seems to have had a steadying and beneficial influence on its members ; the meetings proved an intellectual tonic, an incentive to work. Those young men were reading for the same examinations, and the minutes prove (as also the three numbers of *Undergraduate Papers*) that the essays and debates were often on points connected with the syllabus. Instead, Swinburne became more and more engrossed in his literary work, wrote lines for Burne-Jones' pictures, and read the works of Balzac, Stendhal, Michelet and Dumas at the Taylorian Library. It has also been asserted that he drank, kept irregular hours, incurred the displeasure of his landlady, and neglected to appear at chapel in the morning. The college authorities with whom he had never been on the best terms eyed him with growing disfavour. Jowett who was now his tutor and knew him to be a friend of Nichol, a favourite disciple of his, watched him with an attention which was perhaps sympathetic and certainly critical. When, in November 1859, Swinburne failed in his pass examination in classics, Jowett very firmly hinted that the best course for him was to go and read quietly in the country under that remarkable scholar and budding historical authority, William Stubbs, curate of Navestock.

It is not perhaps here out of place to say a few words on Swinburne's relations with Jowett which will contradict the general belief that the two men were, in those early days, on intimate and affectionate terms. Of Jowett's attitude to Swinburne until 1859 we know nothing ; but the editor of Stubbs' *Letters and Papers*, W. H. Hutton, who had access to the correspondence exchanged on this occasion between the curate of Navestock on the one hand, Captain Swinburne and Jowett on the other, has a truly edifying page which I find worth transcription :

Occasionally he [W. Stubbs] took pupils. The most distinguished of these was Mr. Algernon Swinburne. He came at the end of 1859, to read Modern History especially, during the last part of his time as an undergraduate at Balliol. He was a pupil of Mr. Jowett (' who is not the tutor I had selected for him, and hoped he would have been with ', wrote his father, Admiral Swinburne) who described him as ' in some respects the most singular young man I have ever known ', and was apparently much distressed in the presence of genius to which he was unaccustomed. ' He has extraordinary powers of imitation in writing ', he declared, ' and he composes (as I am told) Latin mediaeval hymns, French vaudevilles, as well as endless English poems, with the greatest facility '. Mr. Jowett deplored the influence of the Pre-Raphaelite artists, and considered that no good—scholastically—would come of him ' unless he can be hindered from writing poetry '.

After other observations, which sufficiently displayed his want of sympathy, Mr. Jowett concluded with the following 'sentiment '—

' I incline to believe that the greatest power that older persons have over the young is sympathy with them, especially as they grow up towards manhood. If we don't allow enough for the strange varieties of character, and often for their extreme, almost unintelligible unlikeness to ourselves, we lose influence over them, and they become alienated from fancying that they are not understood '.

It is obvious from the above passage, first that the Swinburnes did not altogether approve of Jowett as a tutor, and also that Jowett was incapable of understanding the poet's mentality ; indeed the two men

were wide as the poles asunder and what is surprising
is not their present lack of sympathy, but their future
friendship. What happened was this : Jowett, though
always firm and ' academic ', preserved with Swinburne
in those trying circumstances the greatest tact and
urbanity ; later on when Swinburne became famous
(which, L. A. Tollemache assures us, caused Jowett
' quite a shock ') the Master of Balliol made to the
poet repeated and gratifying advances [1] ; the poet
was flattered and yielded.   Swinburne wrote in his
Reminiscences that ' Jowett was a close friend of his,
but the Master of Balliol officially a stranger ' ; it
might perhaps be equally true to say that to Jowett,
while the author of *Atalanta* was a dear, frequent and
honoured guest, Mr. Swinburne, failed B.A., had been
little more than a stranger.

There are many pleasing anecdotes connected with
Swinburne's stay at Navestock ; he got on very well
with his host, who understood him much better than
Jowett.   Gosse has narrated with a skill which is perhaps only too exquisite to be convincing two delightful
incidents which, we must hope, have not been ' improved '.   It was the present writer's good fortune to
confirm or rather elucidate the circumstances in which
the *Death of Sir John Franklin* (the first poem in which
Swinburne struck a really original style) was composed.
On the 8th of February, 1860, as Swinburne was
reading the *Guardian*, he chanced upon the following
passage in the columns of the supplement :

The Vice-Chancellor of Oxford has received from ' a non-
resident member of the University much attached to her

---

[1] The first reference to Jowett in Swinburne's correspondence occurs in a letter
to Nichol of July 22, 1868. By then they were already on cordial terms as Jowett
offers him ' pecuniary help if needed '.

interests ' the sum of £50, for a prize to be awarded to the writer
of the best English poem on ' The Life, the Character and the
Death of the heroic seaman Sir John Franklin, with special
reference to the time, place, and discovery of his death '.   The
poem to be in rhymed verse to be recited during the meeting of
the British Association at the time and in the place which the
vice-chancellor may appoint. All members of the University
whatsoever to be at liberty to compete the prize.   The compositions to be sent to the Registrar of the University on or before
the 1st of June, 1860, the usual course for concealing the name
of the writer and distinguishing the compositions being followed.
The judges are to be the Vice-Chancellor, the Dean of Christ
Church, and Lord Ashburton, of Christ Church '.

This was enough to strike fire from the flint of Swinburne's inspiration, and with Stubbs' benevolent permission he spent two mornings writing off his fine and
in some ways miraculous contribution to the Poetry
Competition.   The result was lamentable, but less for
Swinburne than for others.   On July 2nd the prize
was solemnly awarded to Mr. Owen Alexander Vidal,
whose poem is not only worthless but reads to our
modern eyes as almost intolerable burlesque.   Retribution is not always a vain word, even in this world.
Posterity will set up a new tribunal at which the Vice-
Chancellor, the Dean of Christ Church and Lord Ashburton must attend ; but this time they will not be
the judges.

Meanwhile Swinburne had left Navestock in the
course of April with, it seems, a fair chance of passing
his Examination in June.   How were those two months
spent at Oxford ?   Did the ' general irregularities '
recommence ?   What is certain is that within a few
days of his examination Swinburne found time to work
at his poems and to read *La Lorgnette Littéraire* and
Les Gloires du Romantisme which had no connection

with his studies. Towards the end of May a riding accident laid him up for over a week. He was still in hopes of ' getting enough reading done ' to attempt the test with the chance of a ' decent place on the list '. But probably Jowett intervened and, judging from past experiments, very gently hinted that Swinburne had better not insist and force matters to an unpleasant conclusion. It seems that Swinburne gave up everything in despair and left Oxford for good about the middle of June. Gosse asserts in his revised *Life* (on what authority he does not state) that he did not finally go until November 21st. But we know from a letter written in September that he had made up his mind not to return and was contemplating a stay in Mentone in the autumn. If he went back to Oxford, it was only to pack up his things and take a more or less formal leave.

This vexed problem (the date of his departure from Oxford) which proved a pitfall even to Gosse, raises the whole question of Swinburne's academic record : no trifling point of mere erudition, but one which throws light on the poet's intellectual and psychological development. A few facts are now fairly certain, but much still remains in the dark : when Swinburne first came up to Oxford in January 1856 he had (as every undergraduate) to pass ' Responsions ', an entrance examination of rather a perfunctory nature bearing on Greek and Latin authors, Latin composition and grammar and elementary mathematics. His intention was to read for the degree of B.A. with Honours, which required a residence of at least sixteen terms, with the ulterior thought of making a career in the Church or perhaps at the Bar. On June 5, 1858

(the exact date was supplied by Gosse who had in his
possession the original certificate which the poet treasured to the end of his life) Swinburne took an inter-
mediate examination, ' Moderations ', which included
Greek, Latin and logic ; he seemed fully confident in
his powers, as he went in for Honours (which Nichol
dared not do in 1857) and obtained a second ; he also
won a few days later the Taylorian Scholarship for
French and Italian : his early knowledge of those two
languages stood him in good stead.   To us the chief
interest of this distinction is that it implies on the part
of Swinburne regular attendance at the lectures of
Aurelio Saffi,[1] Mazzini's trusted friend and president
of the *Societa degli Amici d'Italia*, and a free use of the
volumes in the Taylorian Library.   But after those
creditable achievements Swinburne's studies did not
run smoothly.   He had now to look forward to his
second public examination which was to be taken in
two Schools, and he chose to attempt a ' pass ' in the
first School (Litterae Humaniores,—which implied
the study of Greek, Latin, Ancient Philosophy and
Divinity) and Honours in the fourth School (Law and
Modern History, with a general study of English and
International Law and a special knowledge of the life
of Louis XI, the reign of Charles I, and the origin of
equitable juristry in Chancery to the Revolution).   We
are at a loss to understand why Swinburne did not
elect to take Honours in Litterae Humaniores, whose
syllabus was far more suited to his tastes than legal

[1] On the relations between Swinburne and Saffi, see two letters from Mr. John
Purves and the Signora Galimberti in the issues of *The Times Literary Supplement*
for September 24, and November 5, 1931. Saffi's statement (in his *Note* published
by *La Patria* in 1884) that he introduced Swinburne to Mazzini must be received
with caution.

studies ; he was probably disinclined to adopt this
course from the consideration that he would have had
to study more Logic and Divinity if he had taken
Honours in that school, while reading medieval history may have had a delusive charm for the newly converted Pre-Raphaelite. Swinburne's dislike for logic,
metaphysics and the law, and his inability to master
any of those subjects must be duly noted as a clue to
his mental development. Be that as it may, Swinburne
failed in his ' little examination ' (the pass in classics)
in November 1859 ; but in April or May 1860, after
a beneficial stay at Navestock, he attempted the same
examination with success, and Lady Trevelyan wrote
to a friend ' I have not heard lately from Algernon,
but what I have heard from him is good. He has
passed for his degree '. However the Great Examination (Honours in Law and History) was now but
a few weeks distant, and Swinburne had very little time
in which to complete the reading begun at Navestock.
His riding accident at the beginning of June only made
matters a little worse. He was sorely tempted to give
up everything. But here uncertainty prevails : did
Swinburne attempt his last examination and fail ? or
did he simply, on Jowett's tactful but forcible hint,
withdraw from a hopeless enterprise ? Let us hope
that one day this point will be settled. But if, as is
generally believed, Swinburne ' left without taking
a degree ' why should he write of his autobiographical
hero, Reginald Harewood, in a passage of *A Year's
Letters* which occurs in the manuscript alone, that ' he
had got himself *twice* plucked and once rusticated ' ?
Why should he repeatedly have stated that he had been
' rusticated *and* all but expelled ' ? What warranted

such an unusual step on the part of the authorities just when he was going to wind up his career as a student ? Why did Swinburne come back to Oxford in November 1860, as Gosse asserts and as a letter of February 1877 seems to confirm ? Lastly why did he renew his caution money every year till 1878 thus ensuring that his name would remain on the list of undergraduates ? We know that it is a biographer's business to solve, not ask questions. But in this case the biographer humbly confesses that he is puzzled. No enlightenment can now come from Swinburne ; is it too much to hope that it may one day come from Oxford ?

Whatever be the precise circumstances which attended Swinburne's departure, it is certain that he had failed to meet the intellectual requirements of his tutors. Taking his whole record at Oxford into consideration there can be little doubt that this was due to the influence of the Pre-Raphaelites. Although he fared tolerably well in his examinations of June 1858 it was a little later that the disturbing influence of this new factor in his life began to tell. The poems of Morris, the paintings of Rossetti and Burne-Jones, the conversations heard at the Union and elsewhere drew Swinburne's thoughts out of the intellectual circle to which they had been confined into a warmer sphere of art and sensuous beauty. ' In days past at Oxford ', he comically exclaimed to Rossetti several years later, ' when we first met, you fellows might have respected my spotless adolescence—I don't say that you did!'. His dreams, his imaginative power took another direction, and he exchanged his old ideals for new ones, Balaklava and Mazzini for Mary Stuart and Imperia. This last-named lady is the unedifying

heroine of *Laugh and Lie Down*, the Elizabethan
pastiche scribbled by Swinburne in the course of
1858–1859, and her relation to her page-boy Frank,
whom she in turns cajoles and has whipped to death,
throws a great deal of light on the direction in which
Swinburne's sexual sensibility was fast moving—never
to return to less exotic fields ; witness the following
fragment of a scene which is well worth quoting if one
wishes to understand the poet's personality now and
later :

IMPERIA :
   Come, come, you are not old enough.
FRANK :
   I have bled for your sake some twenty times a month,
   Some twenty drops each time ; are these no services ?
IMPERIA :
   I tell you, if you use me lovingly,
   I shall have you whipt again, most pitifully whipt,
   You little piece of love.
FRANK :
                    God knows I care not
   So I may stand and play to you, and you kiss me
   As you used to kiss me, tender little side-touches
   Of your lip's edge i' the neck.
IMPERIA :
                    By my hand's hope,
   Which is the neck of my Lord Galeas,
   I'll love your beard one day ; get you a beard, Frank ;
   I were as well now love a maid as you
   With such child's cheeks.
FRANK :
   Madam, you have pleasant hands,
   What sweet and kissing colour goes in them
   Running like blood !
IMPERIA :
   Ay, child, last year in Rome
   I held the Pope six minutes kissing them
   Before his eyes had grown up to my lips.
   Alas !

FRANK :
    What makes you sigh still ?   You are now
    So kind the sweetness in you stabs mine eyes
    With sharp tears through.   I would so fain be hurt
    But really hurt, hurt deadly, to do good
    To your most sudden fancy.

Those lines constitute the earliest clear instance of the
tendencies which cannot any longer be ignored in Swinburne, since they coloured and shaped his inspiration
and personality.   It seems that it is to that particular
year 1858 that we can trace their first unchecked expression.   It is not difficult to understand how the great
change Swinburne was then undergoing both mentally
and physically contributed to divert him from the line
of work he had so far followed with tolerable application.
In the course of his talks with some intimate friends—
more particularly Burne-Jones—he must have followed
unreservedly the impulses which were at work in his
nature.   These things rapidly become known.   It is
not impossible that such ' irregularities ' together with
rumours concerning his bacchic excesses and republican
fervour, coupled with the unsatisfactory character of
his work, may have influenced the authorities in the
decision they seem to have finally reached about him.
    One thing however is certain : when, in the summer
or the autumn of 1860, Swinburne and Oxford parted
company, they were equally dissatisfied with each other.
But, like gentlemen, they parted without public
scandal or open breach, with the result that we are
still in the dark about the real nature of their quarrel.
When Swinburne became famous Oxford was not long
in relenting and making unofficial, then official,
advances.   But Swinburne at heart never forgave.

CHAPTER V

BALLADS AND POEMS
(1860–1866)

AMONG many other consequences, Swinburne's in-glorious ' exit ' from Oxford made the relations with his father rather strained. There is no proof that Swinburne, instead of joining his family in London, thought it wiser, as has been stated, to take shelter with his grandfather at Capheaton, and from that sanctuary to break the news to the Admiral and open negotiations with him. But we may well believe the poet when he states that, in those days, he was an ' afflictive phenomenon ' to his father, and the reader should study carefully some of the pages of *A Year's Letters*, written about twelve months afterwards, if he cares to recapture the atmosphere of the family circle at that time. However, the Admiral's attitude must have been one of passive despair rather than active recrimination, for on September 18 we find that his son was again an inmate at East Dene, where he repaired after joining the family in London early in the Summer. There he had fallen ' under medical hands ' as he still felt the effects of his accident. But he had now quite recovered and the family was con-templating an early departure for Mentone where the Winter would be spent. At the idea of being within easy reach of Venice, Rome and Naples Swin-burne's political enthusiasm burst into flame ; the prospect of witnessing possible insurrections delighted

him. Nothing could be more conclusive as to the fact
that in his mind his University career was definitely
ended.

But a few days later came from Capheaton the news
of the sudden death of Sir John Swinburne, who was
now in his ninety-ninth year. He had been greatly
depressed by the death of his friend, Sir Henry Ward,
once governor of Madras, but his end was unexpected
and he preserved to the last his exceptional vitality.
The journey to the Riviera was of course postponed.
It is probable that, after a prolonged stay in the North
to settle the succession, the Swinburnes returned to
East Dene towards the end of October.

A note to Richard Monckton Milnes published in
the two-volume collection of the poet's letters under the
date 15th October, 1860, has led many to believe that
Swinburne was already living in lodgings at Grafton
Street, London in the Autumn of that year. I have no
doubt that the date has been misread on the original,
or that it was perhaps conjecturally supplied by the
editors, and that the letter was written on 15 October,
1861.

The intended journey to the Riviera did not material-
ize until the first days of 1861. Swinburne's time was
partly occupied by correcting the proofs of *Rosamond
and the Queen Mother* and seeing the book through
the press. The Admiral had been prevailed upon to
finance the enterprise—a proof that his resentment at
his son's recent failure was mild, and the firm of Pickering, a ' reasonable and friendly Jew thus far ', had
agreed to publish the plays. However, it is probable
that the Jew did not continue ' reasonable and friendly '
for we find that in the Autumn when the sheets of the

two hundred and fifty copies of the book were all printed, Swinburne transferred the volume to Moxon. Owing, possibly, to this unusual course, the cost of publication rose to £50, which the Admiral had to disburse.

Needless to say this £50 was irretrievably lost. *The Queen Mother* was totally ignored by the Press. The only review of it which I could discover (a few lines in the *Athenaeum*) was deadly : the reviewer simply refused to read the book through. Swinburne accepted the fact with typical courage and philosophy, and soon *The Queen Mother* became a standing-joke among the poet's friends and was constantly referred to as the symbol of unqualified failure. But in the course of January 1861, when Swinburne was on his way to Mentone and the book was just out of the press, he carried away with him many illusions and probably nursed the hope that on his return from the sunny south his book would have won him fame and money in his own land. He appears, in a charming and youthful letter he then sent to Lady Trevelyan, as full of schemes and optimism : if his book sells he will not only publish a volume of verse translations, songs and ballads, but a collection of prose short stories. He has worked hard and everything is nearly ready. But those expectations were not fulfilled. Most of the songs and ballads had to wait until 1866 to find their way into print, and the prose collection, which was never completed, is still unpublished.[1] It is extremely probable that, had Swinburne found means to place those two new books on the market in 1861 they would

---

[1] A few tales from the unfinished *Triameron* have been privately printed by Mr. Wise.

have attracted even less notice than the ill-fated *Queen Mother*.   No reader would have discerned in that dull shapeless mass of pastiches a bright vein of purer metal.

Literary ambition and consequent work did not prevent Swinburne from making the most of his journey abroad : we recognize in his letters the same tireless schoolboy who, five years earlier, had dragged a reluctant and rheumatic uncle through most of the museums and churches of the Rhineland ; only, the friend of Jones and Rossetti has now gained a wider artistic experience and some useful prejudices.   While crossing Paris, on his way to Mentone, he found means to visit the Louvre and compare some of Rossetti's rhymed descriptions of the Italian masters with the originals.   And now that he is so close to the promised land he cannot endure to remain too long at Maison Laurenti.   The Riviera coast has no charm for him ; at the beginning of February he sets out on a trip through the main towns of northern Italy.   He visits Genoa, Turin, Milan (where he seems to have stayed longest), Brescia, Verona, Vicenza, Padua and Venice. He is chiefly attracted by the pictures and monuments, revelling in the early masters and ignoring the ' sugared ' painting of Raphaël.   But the colour and picturesqueness of Italian atmosphere also make a strong appeal to his senses.   He feels the beauty of this land and realizes for the first time perhaps that there are finer scenes than the charming leas of the Isle of Wight or the hills of Northumberland,—that

> There the utter sky is holier, there
> More pure the intense white height of air,
> More clear men's eyes that mine would meet,
> And the sweet springs of things more sweet.

He forgets a little about art and poetry, he forgets about calling on Browning at Florence and laying his admiration at his feet, he forgets about his political fervour and his wish to hang the King of Naples. He begins to look at women and finds them beautiful :

> As to women, I saw at Venice (fourteen years ago) one of the three most beautiful I ever saw. The other two were at Genoa and Ventimiglia (Riviera). By her gaze I thought I might address her, but did not, considering that we could not have understood each other (verbally at least) ; so caution and chastity, or *mauvaise honte* and sense of embarrassment prevailed.

We might wish that Swinburne had stayed longer and looked longer, and that *mauvaise honte* had not prevailed.

In the course of March or April, he was back in England. What was he now to do ? Until the return from Mentone, uncertainty had prevailed. To Lady Trevelyan's friendly objurgations, he made the following answer : ' What *is* one to do ? I can't go to the bar : and much good I should do if I did. You know there is really no profession one can take up with and go on working. Item—Poetry is quite work enough for any one man '. We may feel sure that the same argument was repeated over and over again to the Admiral—though in a less playful form, so as not to tax his sense of humour He finally agreed to allow his son to follow a literary career, probably because he could think of no other that would suit him. He consented to let him have a small personal allowance, and in the early Spring of 1861 Swinburne had settled in London, at 16 Grafton Street.

He could thus work in the British Museum near by;

he could also visit his friends and get introductions
into the literary world ; with the Pre-Raphaelites he
had since 1857–58 remained on the most cordial
terms. Morris, Burne-Jones, Rossetti had all recently
married, and Swinburne was in the fortunate position
of the homeless bachelor who is privileged to call when
he likes. At Red House, Upton, he was a frequent
guest and paid the tribute of an equal admiration to
the art of Morris and the beauty of his wife. With
Burne-Jones, a kind of boisterous intimacy prevailed
and Swinburne called at Russell Place, a few yards from
his own address, two or three times a day to read a new
poem or impart a new joke ; Lady Burne-Jones has
left us a brilliant description of those unforgettable
visits. With Rossetti matters were slightly different :
in 1858 and 1859 Swinburne had often come to town
from Oxford and spent the day at Chatham Place. In
the course of long conversations, what had been only
a feeling of artistic curiosity on the one hand, and a
genuine but respectful admiration on the other, ripened
into a grave and earnest friendship : Rossetti was not
long in feeling the genius of Swinburne, and with this
discovery came a sense of responsibility ; he wanted
to foster and control the versatile inspiration of the
poet, to help him of course, and chiefly to defend him
from others and from himself. To this attitude of
affectionate authority, which could not but in time become irksome, Swinburne responded at first with gratefulness, and made a free gift to Rossetti of his friendship and admiration. His feelings took a typical form :
loyalty ; he was loyal to Rossetti and his art, just as
later on he was loyal to Mazzini and his ideals ; he
was ready to admire and love him in spite of his

enemies, in spite of his own faults. The difference in
the relation between the two men cannot be over-
emphasized : Swinburne was Rossetti's friend and
yet looked up to him ; he was ready to love and follow
him without restrictions of any kind ; Rossetti appreciated Swinburne's personality, but with many restrictions ; he wanted to be of use to him by his remarks,
encouragements or criticisms ; whether praising or
disagreeing, he was always passing judgment on him,
ever ready to strike the balance between what he admired and disapproved of. This difference did not
alter with the years, and a moment came when the ties
of the strongest friendship could no longer sustain the
intolerable strain they had to bear.

But in 1860–61 the relations between the two men
were of the closest, and there is no doubt that Swinburne greatly benefited by them. A warmer touch of
cordiality was of course supplied by Elizabeth Siddal,
Rossetti's model and future wife. Her real talent and
fine artistic sense, her keen humour and playful disposition, even her physical appearance created between
her and the poet a deep affinity. Rossetti's hours of
gloom and depression were brightened by the laughter
and childish games of ' Lizzie ' and his friend, and
his mature self-conscious genius experienced an uncommon pleasure and pride at the thought of the hold
he possessed over these two talents of a more spontaneous and more irresponsible nature. It was then
that Swinburne would read to Lizzie Beaumont and
Fletcher or Dickens by the hour. It is not certain that
Rossetti enjoyed those performances quite as much.
But he was often out. When he came back he
would himself read aloud to Swinburne some of his

discoveries, passages from rare, unknown, out of
the way works, which Swinburne in the course of
his classical and academic training had never come
across or heard of. These were Meinhold's *Sidonia
von Bork*, Blake's Poems, FitzGerald's *Rubáiyát*, Wells'
Joseph and his Brethren. And Swinburne would listen
in an ecstasy of admiration and pride to the voice which
revealed so many unsuspected treasures ; to him as to
others his friend must often have seemed not a Vic-
torian painter, but Merlin or Haroun al Raschid, a
magician from the *Morte d'Arthur* or the *Arabian
Nights*.

Swinburne was not content with confirming old
friendships ; he endeavoured to enlarge the circle of
his acquaintances, conscious as he was that he had a
career to make in the world of letters. Rossetti and
his friends were of course the means of many new introductions : William Michael and Christina Rossetti
made the acquaintance of the poet in the course of
1861, with the result that he formed a cordial and lasting friendship with the brother, and entertained feelings of respect and admiration for the sister. He was
also taken to the house of Madox Brown, whom he
had met at Oxford in 1858, and found there, much to
his satisfaction, a bracing atmosphere of political activities and Italian agitation : radicals from all over Europe
congregated at Brown's, and Swinburne, though engrossed by new artistic theories, remembered with pleasure the lectures of Aurelio Saffi and the meetings of
the Old Mortality.

But it is not certain that it was through the Pre-
Raphaelites that he met Monckton Milnes. We are
told that their first interview took place in London on

the 5th of May, 1861,[1] 'in reply to a formal summons' on the part of Milnes. But what was the original cause of the summons? Certainly not the fame of *The Queen Mother*. Gosse suggests an introduction from the Signora Fronduti, who read Italian to the poet in 1853 but does not appear to have preserved very close relations with him. I have noted elsewhere that Monckton Milnes and Swinburne had both been elected 'non artistic members' of the Hogarth Club, an institution of marked Pre-Raphaelite tendencies, in 1858. Be that as it may Milnes and Swinburne were soon on intimate terms. Of course Milnes' position and influence gave him some ascendency over his young *protégé*; but how different it all was from the oppressive and almost paternal supervision of Rossetti.

Richard Monckton Milnes introduced Swinburne to the works of the Marquis de Sade whose books, and perhaps name, seem, until 1861, to have been unknown to the poet. How deep and lasting was to be the impression left by Sade on the mind of Swinburne is now established, but it was not until a little later that Milnes lent him the novels. For the time being, Swinburne had to be content with the 'promise that I am yet to live and look upon the mystic pages of the martyred Marquis de Sade, ever since which the vision of that illustrious and ill-requited benefactor of humanity has hovered by night before my eyes'.[2]

---

[1] Not 1860, as Gosse prints in the *Life*. I have had occasion to point out the origin of the misunderstanding: when the *Life* was written, Gosse was under the impression that Swinburne had left Oxford in 1859 and accordingly misdated several documents: he failed to make all the necessary changes throughout the book when the original error was corrected in the Bonchurch reprint of his biography (1927).

[2] Letter to Monckton Milnes, October 15, 1861. For further details about the relations between Milnes and Swinburne, see my *Jeunesse de Swinburne*, I, pp. 176–9; and, about the circle of Swinburne's friends at the time, W. Hardman's *Papers* (1930) ed. by E. M. Ellis, pp. 91, 164–167, 191–192, 209–210, 320, 322–331.

But it should not be inferred that Milnes' influence exerted itself in that direction only. He is neither the 'amiable man' of Gosse's biography, nor the villainous tempter denounced by some ill-advised reviewers of my *Jeunesse de Swinburne*. I have no doubt that he was immensely useful to the poet, that he helped him in discerning the original character of his inspiration, that he encouraged him to emphasize the essential features of a personality which had been too long in crystallizing, that he gave him strength, and boldness and confidence. Swinburne felt all this and was attracted to Milnes, and grateful. I doubt whether there ever was anything like affection or real cordiality between them. Milnes' interest in Swinburne was mainly artistic and intellectual, but impersonal, and the poet realized it. But among the many hints of a practical nature which Milnes gave Swinburne regarding his future as a poet were two invaluable ones : he must at once give up writing medieval pastiches in which no one was interested and which no one would read ; he must apply his faculties to literary criticism and prose as well as to poetry. It is partly owing to Milnes' influence that we find Swinburne writing in 1861 an article on Charles Wells' *Joseph*, and a burlesque French novel *La Fille du Policeman*.

Milnes was not long in inviting Swinburne to his country residence, Fryston Hall, in Yorkshire. It is well known that he delighted in bringing together in this lonely mansion personalities that had been carefully chosen so as to form a sharp contrast with each other. He was thus able to watch at leisure, for the space of a week-end, select scenes from the everchanging comedy of mankind. Swinburne was a welcome addition to his collection of guests and would be sure to differ from almost anyone. But the idea of making him meet Richard Burton was an inspiration, its realization a work of art. It was in the summer of 1861, before Burton had left for Fernando-Pô towards the end of August, that Swinburne, attracted by the prospect of being introduced to *Justine* as well as by the hospitality of an influential friend, paid a visit to Fryston. With what a smile of sarcastic pride must Milnes have watched the Herculean explorer shaking hands with the frail Pre-Raphaelite model ! What thoughts must have passed through the mind of the keeper of this ' inn of strange meetings ' ! But to his great surprise he found that he had overshot the mark ; if he expected mutual disapproval, or at least bewilderment, on the part of those two creatures, he was disappointed. Swinburne and Burton struck up at once a fast and enduring friendship : the same indomitable courage lived in the heart of the man of action and the man of dreams ; both admired what the other possessed and he himself lacked : Burton, the faultless technique of a great artist-poet, Swinburne the fearless vitality of an Elizabethan sailor.

It was about the same time that Meredith who had recently been admitted into Rossetti's friendship made the acquaintance of Swinburne. His experience of journalism and literature as well as his wit and, to those who knew him, undoubted talent made him a valuable companion. He gave Swinburne useful advice and introduced him to a somewhat obscure magazine, *Once a Week*, which he ' occasionally propped up with fragments of his own '. Swinburne's contributions, at least two of them, were accepted, and

Once a Week has now the honour of having published *The Fratricide* and *Dead Love* ; the honour is strictly posthumous ; if the magazine failed to spread the reputation of the author of *The Queen Mother* much further, Swinburne's Pre-Raphaelite pastiches did nothing to promote the circulation of *Once a Week*. But Meredith's intention was excellent ; he was then taking a genuine interest in the young poet, so warmly recommended by Rossetti, and he could not yet experience the feelings of ill-suppressed envy which certainly found their way into his heart after the success of *Atalanta*. He took pleasure in advising and helping Swinburne. Only, like Rossetti, he was a little too prone to adopt an attitude of wisdom and higher common sense, to mix criticism with every praise, to defend Swinburne against some of the deepest impulses of his own nature. But, unlike Rossetti, he lacked the tact and dignity, the keen artistic sense, the almost tragic intensity of sentiment which alone could justify such an attitude—at least for a time. It is doubtful whether the friendship between Meredith and Swinburne, which was to last until 1867, ever approached a deep and real intimacy.

In December 1861 Meredith brought his friend W. Hardman to Chatham Place, and there he met Swinburne; the muscular Hardman immediately adopted to Swinburne the attitude which Milnes perhaps expected Burton to take up : the feeling of dislike and contempt of the athlete for the man who plays no games. His account is interesting because it reflects in a distorted form some of Meredith's own reactions to his friend. It is worth quoting as relating to a period about which documents are sadly lacking :

Swinburne is a strange fellow, young and beardless, with a shock head of red hair ; his parents were of two nations, the father Welsh, the mother French, and this mixture of blood has produced a singular result. Swinburne is strongly sensual ; although almost a boy, he upholds the Marquis de Sade as the acme and apostle of perfection, without (as he says) having read a word of his works. The assembled company evidently received Swinburne's tirades with ill-concealed disgust, but they behaved to him like to a spoiled child. He has a curious kind of nervous twitching, resembling or approaching St. Vitus Dance. [1]

Although the fact has never been fully emphasized, 1862 was the crucial year in Swinburne's early life. It is now possible to discern that some deep far-reaching changes took place within him during those short twelve months. This has been partly concealed, because those changes were not immediately reflected in Swinburne's publications, as he had but few outlets for his literary work—a fact which rather favoured the rise of the strong lyrical inspiration which was to last for over three years. At the beginning of 1862, he had only written medieval and Renaissance pastiches, some worthless, others of high technical order, but none of independent literary value. D. G. Rossetti in a letter to Theodore Martin in January, while giving warm praise to the poet, mentions that he has ' poems and tales *à placer* '—the stiff cold stories of the *Triameron*—and recognizes that ' he has his way to make '. By the beginning of 1863 we find that Swinburne has composed *Laus Veneris*, the *Hymn to Proserpine*, *Ilicet*, *A Match*, the *Ballad of Burdens*, *Les Noyades*, *Faustine*, *A Year's Letters*, *The Triumph of Time* and a large number of critical essays of high merit. It was this year which saw the end of a perhaps too long literary

[1] *The Letters and Memoirs of Sir W. Hardman*, ed. by E. M. Ellis, 1923.

ÆTAT 22

From the drawing by William Bell Scott reproduced from his 'Autobiographical Notes' *by permission of Messrs. Harper & Brothers*

ALGERNON CHARLES SWINBURNE

ÆTAT 31

Photo Elliott & Fry

apprenticeship, and the rise in English Literature of the strongest lyrical inspiration since Shelley.

It is possible for the biographer to account for this at least in part. New experiences crowded Swinburne's life in 1862. First, and not least, he became intimately acquainted with three great books of poetry : Baudelaire's *Fleurs du Mal*, FitzGerald's *Rubáiyát*, Whitman's *Leaves of Grass* ; this, coupled with a close study of the works of Villon and William Blake, contributed in no small way to lift him from the lower plane of Pre-Raphaelite imitation into the high regions of lyrical excellence. Most helpful and stimulating was also the influence of Milnes ; he would have no more Border Ballads or translations from Boccaccio, and the result was that Swinburne wrote *Faustine*, which a little later made even Ruskin ' all hot—like pies with the devil's finger in them ' (whatever he may have meant by this, the sentence is certainly descriptive of intense excitement!). Moreover Milnes added to his counsels the incentive of publication in an important review : the *Spectator*, at his express request, accepted from Swinburne signed poems and unsigned reviews which were published in the course of 1862. Lastly Milnes, whenever the audience was suitable, arranged private readings of Swinburne's poems : Lady Ritchie told Edmund Gosse how *Les Noyades* and *The Leper* were thus inflicted at Fryston on her father (Thackeray) and the Archbishop of York in the early summer of 1862.[1]

But earlier in the same year a tragical event had left its mark on the poet's sensibility : Elizabeth Siddal

---

[1] In June, 1863, Swinburne was again at Fryston, and Milnes introduced him to Matthew Arnold on that occasion. (See *Life*—Personal characteristics).

Rossetti, his close friend, one could almost write ' his playmate ', died on February 11. It was not so much her death (which owing to her state of health had been apprehended for a long time) which caused Swinburne such a shock, as the circumstances of her death. These have often been described, although the mystery which surrounds them has not been cleared up. Swinburne, as he wrote to his mother, had been ' almost the last person who saw her ' ; he was ' almost the first ' to hear of the tragedy in the morning. Others are more competent than I am to relate how Mrs. Rossetti was discovered unconscious after taking an overdose of laudanum. Recently the possibility of suicide, which had never been denied, has been reasserted with authority.[1] Swinburne knew, as we now know, that after taking his wife home Rossetti had gone out again. We cannot help believing that the possibility of Mrs. Rossetti's committing suicide on discovering that her husband had left the house—a fresh proof after perhaps many others—must have struck Swinburne even more vividly than it strikes us. And yet, in spite of his genuine love for ' poor Lizzie ', his attitude was quite remarkable : he remained loyal to Rossetti ; he attended the inquest and answered as best he could ; he said nothing to his grief-stricken friend which might have sounded like a reproach or even a question ; he agreed to come and live with him and help him to forget ; so great was his admiration for genius, so high his conception of friendship. But he also remained loyal to the memory of Lizzie, often referring to her in terms of brotherly affection which

---

[1] See Hall Caine's *Recollections of Rossetti*, 1928, pp. 38–41 and 197–99. Hall Caine's version is that, after taking his wife home, Rossetti ' went out again, apparently to walk '.

in time probably grew intolerable to the remorseful soul of Rossetti.   More certain still than all this is the inference that this tragic experience brought home to Swinburne the deep heart-rending realities underlying human love.

Elizabeth Rossetti was to Swinburne a dear friend, more than a sister in many ways, yet only a friend ; now that she had died in circumstances that cast a strange solemnity on their boyish affection, he felt more than ever the need of a companionship even closer and more intimate.   There is reason to believe that this young iconoclast and rejector of accepted morality —who professed to follow the canons of Baudelaire, Blake and Sade—felt at times strangely embarrassed and disconcerted in the presence of women.   We know that a year before, in Venice, he had, when confronted with a perfect image of Italian beauty, allowed ' mauvaise honte ' to prevail.   This consciousness was increased by a growing awareness on his part of a deficiency in his moral and physical life ; some of the jokes or allusions of Rossetti must have been precise and pointed enough to make him realize all this acutely.   Faustine and Lucrèce Borgia were all very well, but he knew what lay behind those fictions. Having spoken and written so much in praise of ' that much misused and belied thing, the purely sensuous and outward side of love ', he sometimes felt an urge, arising probably more from the intellect than the senses, to practise what he had preached, and taste the delights he had extolled.   When in the early summer of 1862 he composed under Meredith's roof at Copsham some of the stanzas of *Laus Veneris*, he might have identified himself with the knight of Venus who

Sang of love, too, knowing nought thereof . . .

I deeply regret that, while we know much about
Swinburne's aberrations and vices, so few facts have
been supplied about the episode in his sentimental life,
slight in itself, but far-reaching in its consequences,
which seems to have taken place about this time. The
only evidence concerning what was perhaps a turning-
point in the life of Swinburne is to be found in that
powerful but mysterious poem, *The Triumph of Time*,
in the reticent account given in the *Life*, in a few
allusions contained in the correspondence with Gosse,
and in three graceful stanzas, *To Boo*, unearthed by
Mr. Wise, whose connection with the main event is
doubtful. If we piece those scanty fragments together
and apply the glue of common sense mixed with
imagination, we can reconstruct the following story :
in the course of 1862 Swinburne came to know Dr.
John Simon and his wife, who were friends of Ruskin
and great admirers of the Pre-Raphaelite movement.
At their house he met a girl who was Dr. Simon's niece
and adopted daughter, Jane Faulkner ; this is practically all that is so far known about her ; her personality,
her charm or beauty, her past and future life, even her
age remain a sealed book and imagination is left with
nothing but her pet name—Boo—to play with. If we
admit the evidence of the stanzas *To Boo*, she and
Swinburne were on intimate terms in the summer of
1862. It is clear from the *Triumph of Time* that she
gave him roses and sang to him. What broke up a
friendship which might have gone on for ever ?
Gosse—who obviously discussed the subject with
Swinburne—hints at an impetuous proposal which was

greeted with laughter to the complete and permanent disgust of the poet. The story is not however complete, as is shown by four lines from the original draft of the *Triumph of Time* :

> But now you are cloven in twain, rent,
> Flesh of his flesh, but heart of my heart,
> And deep in *me* is the bitter root
> And sweet for *him* is the lifelong flower. (Italics mine)

Swinburne was obviously rejected in favour of another suitor. Hence the fine indignation which swells the poem and burns out self-pity and regret. But for all this angry note, the *Triumph of Time* which was composed in 1863 some months after the rupture it records is an intensely moving poem—more heart-rending in some of its cadences than the finest flights of Donne, Shakespeare, Meredith or Musset. This arises first from the picture of the violent hopes and aspirations aroused in Swinburne by his love :

> We had grown as gods, as the gods above
> O love, my love, had you loved but me !

The man who wrote those lines experienced no passing disappointment at the baffling of a casual desire; love meant to him more than to most others ; he had nerved himself up to seize the cup and taste the wine with the conviction that it would work in him some powerful and more than Circean change. Thus part of the poem expresses the strain of a great effort and the sense of an irreparable failure. The latter chiefly provides a magnificent theme ; the consciousness of all that has been lost—purity, happiness :

> I had grown pure as the dawn and the dew . . .
> I, too, might have stood with the souls that stand
> In the sun's sight, clothed with the light of the sun.

Then comes a distressing feeling, rarely expressed by
Swinburne, an almost Baudelairian feeling of impo-
tence and self-disgust—the realization that one cannot
escape one's nature or break the chains of instinct :

> As I have been, I know I shall surely be . . .
> For the worst is this after all : if they knew me
> Not a soul upon earth would pity me.

It may be that we are overstating the influence of what
was after all a very brief and early incident in Swinburne's life ; but the poet who wrote those lines had
just passed through nerve-racking experiences and
been a prey to merciless introspection and soul-
destroying doubt.

The Triumph of Time was not written on the spur of
the moment ; a few months must have elapsed between
its composition and Swinburne's great disappointment.
I have shown that there were in it signs of intense self-
analysis ; that the poem retains such fire and indignation is the proof of a keen sensibility, which Swinburne
shared perhaps with Musset alone, though to a lesser
extent.   Gosse tells us that *The Triumph of Time* was
written in Northumberland.   This may not be true
literally, as Swinburne seems to have been back in
London by January 8, 1863, and an early manuscript
of the poem is watermarked 1863.   But it is quite
probable that it was conceived and even partly written
there.   For Swinburne, who in the course of 1862 had
moved from Grafton Street to Newman Street, was now
giving up his rooms once more and preparing to share

Rossetti's new residence, Tudor House, Chelsea. It is however to be noticed that, although the removal took place on October 24th, Swinburne does not seem to have lived at Tudor House at once, but went to his parents' town house in Grosvenor Place : it was one thing to visit Rossetti at certain chosen hours of the day, and quite another to sleep under his roof, as not only Swinburne, but also Meredith, soon found out. Moreover Swinburne had decided to accompany Monckton Milnes to Fryston early in November on a somewhat prolonged visit. This trip to Yorkshire has a symbolic importance : in the frame of mind which the *Triumph of Time* allows us to imagine, Swinburne was glad to turn back to his old topics, jokes and conversations. Henry Adams, in his *Education*, has left us a brilliant and vivid picture of the poet on that occasion : what he tells us of Swinburne's flow of conversation, his paradoxical opinions on literature, his chaotic recitations from Sophocles, Villon and Landor, as well as from his own poems both lyrical, dramatic and burlesque, bears witness to the state of nervous strain and mental excitation in which he now found himself. It was on this occasion that Milnes redeemed his old promise and placed in Swinburne's hands the works of Sade—*Justine* and, probably, *Juliette* and *La Philosophie dans le Boudoir*. Swinburne was intensely amused and genuinely impressed [1] : the exasperation of Sade's style appealed to his sense of the burlesque, and the realistic descriptions to another sense in him, while the materialistic

---

[1] He was at first somewhat disconcerted by the inartistic form of the novels and their ' insane exaggeration '. But Monckton Milnes had no difficulty in pointing out the ' intelligence of the book ' and the merits of the characters—in particular the Comte de Rodin. Swinburne was easily converted.

manifestoes found an echo in Swinburne's mind. The
poet experienced a satisfaction in steeping himself in
the works of the ' arch-unmentionable ' after his recent sentimental failure. He yielded to the wildest
impulses of his nature, for ' as he had been, he knew
he would surely be '. And vice was an obvious remedy
to his grief. He felt, in his own words, that

> I would find a sin to do ere I die
> Sure to dissolve and destroy me all through . . .

In a mood half of sympathy, half of intellectual revolt,
he deciphered autograph letters of Sade and told W.
M. Rossetti how he ' flattered himself with thinking '
that his own handwriting was not unlike that of the
great man. Henceforth his letters are full of allusions
to and quotations from Sade, and testify to an incredibly
wide and close reading of the works of the illustrious
madman.

There is a light side to this interest of Swinburne
in Sade : by means of allusions to the forbidden novels,
his genius for parody often found expression, and the
perusal of the correspondence of the poet is not in-
frequently highly amusing. But there is also a serious
side to it : Swinburne was genuinely fond of the
Marquis' prose, and there is no doubt that he took
delight in books which, to me as to most others, are
frankly unreadable. Obviously he was not attracted to
them as an artist, and the faults of style and plot in
Sade's novels were as obvious to Swinburne as the
mistakes in spelling of his autograph letters. His
interest was therefore a psychological one ; it was the
feelings described and analysed by Juliette or Dolmancé which arrested his attention, as well as the

everlasting and revolting episodes of a chaotic story.
Not that Sade taught Swinburne anything ; one of
the most 'sadistic' passages in Swinburne's works
occurs in a comedy written at Oxford when Sade was
merely a name to him.   But the novels had a deeper
and subtler influence : they confirmed Swinburne in
his instincts.   He learnt from them not to be afraid
or ashamed at the tendencies of his own nature.[1]   He
relished the rhetoric of Dolmancé which proclaims
that nothing can be 'unnatural' and frankly des-
cribes his most perverse desires : 'Unnatural is it ?
Nature forbid this thing or that ?   Nay, could we
thwart nature, then might crime become possible
and sin an actual thing etc.' ; such are Swinburne's
own words when paraphrasing his model.   And he
was quite in earnest when he wrote to a friend : ' I
think your remarks on *Justine* the most sensible I ever
heard.   They quite give my own feeling, with which
I never found anyone to agree before ; usually that
work is either a stimulant for an old beast or an emetic
for a young man, instead of a valuable study to rational
curiosity '.

' A valuable study to rational curiosity ' ;   these
words afford a clue to Swinburne's inner nature.   Sade's
works were a mirror in which he spied the wildly distorted reflection of one side of his own nature.   Thanks
to Sade Swinburne reached a full conscience of his
personality, and was no longer disconcerted at his own
feelings.   While remaining an artist, and scarcely ever
indulging in too realistic or too frank an expression of

---

[1] The two lines :
> On n'est point criminel pour faire la peinture
> Des bizarres penchants qu'inspire la nature

serve as epigraph to Sade's works.

his feelings, he fed his inspiration from the live springs
of his own experience ; instead of *Laugh and Lie Down*
and *Tebaldeo Tebaldei* he wrote *Anactoria* and *Lesbia
Brandon*. He was resolutely himself. It is in that
sense that Swinburne is truly a modern ; in a cautious
and always artistic manner his verse enlarges the province of psychology ; he too is ' a valuable study to
rational curiosity '. In the bright classical metaphors
of *Atalanta*, in the turgid rhetoric of his prose, there
lurks a modernity of inspiration which reveals him as
akin to masters like Proust or Lawrence.

At Fryston Swinburne remained for nearly a month.
Towards the end of November the party was joined
by W. M. Rossetti who was anxious to examine the
Blake books and manuscripts in the possession of
Monckton Milnes. Swinburne was also by now keenly
interested in the works of the mystic : since the
death of Gilchrist in 1861 he had been helping
the Rossettis in arranging his unfinished *Life* for
publication and had even been requested to supply
the missing chapters. But in October 1862 he definitely declined to work for ' the chaste Macmillan '
and resolved to prepare on his own behalf ' a distinct
small commentary of a running kind '. This was the
origin of the *Essay* which did not appear till 1867.

In that winter of 1862 the whole Pre-Raphaelite
Brotherhood seems to have congregated in the north.
When Swinburne left Fryston early in December,
Rossetti was at Newcastle with W. B. Scott ; Swin-
burne spent a fortnight with them, staying at the Turf
Hotel, and declaimed to his friends in the course of
a walk along the shore *Laus Veneris* and *The Hymn to
Proserpine*—two fresh instances of the originality and

passion which his inspiration was gradually acquiring. After a short stay at Wallington, he was back in London at the beginning of January.

The year 1863 comes as an anti-climax after the many events and intense literary activity of the months that preceded.   Apart from the *Triumph of Time*, it seems that Swinburne set himself as his chief task during the first half of the year to complete and give some sort of definite shape to the much-modified and rewritten *Chastelard*.   On the other hand his connection with the *Spectator* had abruptly come to an end ; on the 21st of January he informed Milnes that he did not want to write any more for the *Spectator*, explaining that he was shocked at the meanness of the editor, who insisted on review copies being returned by the reviewer.   This was indeed most uncommon, but there were other reasons beside these.   An acute conflict had arisen between Swinburne and R. H. Hutton, the well-known editor and critic, in the following circumstances : Swinburne had submitted for publication two articles which purported to be reviews of alleged contemporary French writers, Félicien Cossu and Ernest Clouet ; the imaginary works of these ultra-Baudelairian[1] writers were denounced and blamed by the indignant reviewer, but amply quoted. Did Hutton suspect Swinburne's forgery ?   An extract from a letter printed by Mr. Wise points to a different conclusion.   But Hutton had probably been struck and greatly shocked at the attitude of contempt

---

[1] As far as we can judge, Clouet's ' Works ' are not unlike Petrus Borel's ' Contes Immoraux '.

and hostility which Swinburne had assumed in several articles to journalists and reviewers, and the Press in general. This was already obvious in his defence of *Modern Love* which the *Spectator* had however printed in June 1862 ; the same note was struck in the review of *Les Fleurs du Mal.* In Clouet and Cossu as well as in other articles such as *M. Prudhomme, Théophile, Father Garasse* which were probably offered and rejected in the same way the attack on the ' libellers, liars and prurient pastors of the press ' was renewed with a violence which is surprising if one considers that so far Swinburne had not had to suffer directly at the hands of the critics. Hutton could no longer remain blind to the fact that it was the profession as a whole which his reviewer involved in his blame, and that some of his staff answered perfectly the descriptions he supplied. He felt hurt and indignant. Swinburne was given to understand that his contributions were no longer desired and the two men must have parted on the worst of terms. Hutton's resentment was strong and lasting. From 1865 the reviews of Swinburne's works which appeared in the *Spectator* were conspicuous for their unfavourable character.

It can even be contended that, from the point of view of his literary fame, Swinburne's brief interlude as a reviewer on the *Spectator's* staff was more harmful than beneficial : while it seems doubtful whether the few signed contributions he published attracted any attention, the hostility of the *Spectator* was a factor in the hue and cry so artificially raised by the Press round *Poems and Ballads* in 1866. But Swinburne's prose contributions, though anonymous, had gained for him the friendship and recognition of two great poets :

Hugo, whether of his own accord or because they had been sent to him, had taken the trouble to write to Hutton in order to trace the author of the articles on *Les Misérables* and had congratulated him personally on his ' interest in philanthropic questions ' (?). Swinburne clinched the matter by asking Hugo to accept the dedication of the forthcoming *Chastelard* ; but, as he wrote (in French) to Milnes, ' Si j'eusse su qu'il devait lire [ces articles] j'aurais craint de lui avoir déplu en m'attaquant aux philosophes ; j'ai aussi un peu nargué en passant la vertu publique, la démocratie vertueuse ' ; the young critic had indeed had a narrow escape, and, little expecting that his prose would be read by the master, had made some very neat points in the true Baudelairian vein against the most preposterous tendencies of *Les Misérables*. But, as had been the case with Baudelaire, Hugo revealed himself magnanimous and truly Olympian ; he was all the more impervious to Swinburne's respectful criticism, since he could not read English and had probably been supplied with but a casual oral translation of the *Spectator's* five articles.

The ' friendship ' with Baudelaire was not so sudden or so definite ; its chief manifestations were limited to the exchange of two pamphlets : Swinburne's review of *Les Fleurs du Mal* incited Baudelaire to send him his *Wagner and Tannhäuser* at the end of 1863. True, Baudelaire wrote to Swinburne a letter which Nadar ought to have delivered in London ; but it never reached the addressee. This, though regrettable, does not matter much : even if Baudelaire and Swinburne had met, the former was no longer in a position either to exercise or undergo any influence. What matters is that, just before death intervened, fate had willed it that Swinburne and Baudelaire should hail and recognize each other. No letter passed between them,[1] only a few dedicated pamphlets and articles, a few oral ' messages and courtesies ' ; but their minds had met. This is no empty rhetoric : this article on *Les Fleurs du Mal* to which Baudelaire refers in a letter to his mother of June 1863, this pamphlet of Baudelaire's with its insignificant dedication—' Bon souvenir et mille remerciements '—are witness to posterity that their minds had met.

The ' messages and courtesies ' were conveyed from one poet to another by two men who had been quite recently introduced to Swinburne and whose possible influence on his development as an artist should be carefully noted. James McNeill Whistler and his friend Alphonse Legros probably came over from Paris in the middle of 1862 ; the former settled in Queen's Road, Chelsea. A letter of 21 August 1862, printed in the *Rossetti Papers*, shows that at that early date Dante Gabriel was already acquainted with Whistler. I incline to believe that it was in the early months of 1863, when he first came to live at Tudor House, that Swinburne met Whistler, who was probably not long in introducing Legros. For Whistler had been instrumental in persuading his French friend to try his fortune in London, and was doing what he could to make him known. The interest attaching to Swinburne's acquaintance with Legros, is that the painter was a personal friend of Baudelaire (they had both sat for a picture by Fantin-Latour) and that in the course of

---

[1] ' A thousand thanks for the return of poor Baudelaire's pamphlet, which I naturally value as my only memorial of a much admired though personally unknown friend '. (Unpublished letter to Karl Blind, 17th September, 1877.)

his frequent trips to Paris he must have more than once conveyed the aforesaid ' messages and courtesies '. When the artistic influences at work across the Channel during the end of the nineteenth century come to be closely studied, critics will not fail to notice two groups including Swinburne, Rossetti, Morris on the one hand, Baudelaire, Gautier, Fantin, Manet on the other, with Whistler and Legros as the bright painted butterflies who carried the pollen from one flower into the other.

In March 1863 Swinburne visited Paris with Whistler ; he was taken round the artistic circles in which the American painter was highly popular ; the poet himself later described to Mallarmé how he came to know Manet : ' C'était au printemps de 1863 que je fus conduit chez M. Manet par mes amis MM. Whistler et Fantin ; lui sans doute ne s'en souvient pas, mais moi alors très jeune et tout à fait inconnu (sinon de quelques amis intimes) comme poète ou du moins comme aspirant à ce nom, vous pensez bien que ce fut pour moi un souvenir qui ne s'envolerait pas facilement.' This visit to the Parisian *ateliers* is well worth remembering : Swinburne met Manet and Fantin, in whose studio he could see a sketch of Tannhäuser at the Venusberg drawn at the time of the failure of Wagner's opera—just when the poet was composing at Copsham the first verses of *Laus Veneris*; he visited the Louvre and composed about the statue of *Hermaphroditus* four sonnets which reveal him as steeped in the ethics of Théophile Gautier.

This is also the time when Swinburne wrote the central part of his *Essay on Blake* in which he embodied, in an extreme form, most of his views on art.   The

truth is that he had now adopted with few modifications the French theory of Art for Art's sake as laid
down by Gautier, Baudelaire and Poe. He had discovered the works of those writers some years before,
probably at Oxford. But it was only gradually that he
fell under their spell, that from admiration of their art
he passed to an unqualified acceptance of their ideas.
Rossetti had perhaps led the way, and added to his own
early Pre-Raphaelite mysticism much of the calm, thick
sensuousness of Théophile. But this does not alter the
fact that Swinburne had gradually drifted from the
principles expressed by the *Germ* ; he no longer
believed that ardent sincerity and close realism were
the only essential qualities in a work of art, beauty
being but a secondary matter ; he would no longer
submit himself to the imitation of a cramped and
primitive style. When he came back from his stay in
Paris in the spring of 1863 he was under the influence
of the theories which were current at that time in the
literary and artistic circles of the French capital. He
was now aware of the sovereign importance of beauty,
or rather his ideal of beauty had changed to a certain
extent : it had become something heavy, calm,
majestic, impassible, like Baudelaire's 'dream carved
in stone'. It had in it much of what later came to
be known as the 'Parnassian' style. And it was
precisely at this time that, having wound up his
Penelopian task, *Chastelard*, he sat down to write
Atalanta.

For, while most of his friends recognized his genius,
they were averse to his publishing what he had so far
written—either *Chastelard* or his poems. Ruskin, who
had been consulted, replied on July 5, 1863, that ' he

would be sorry if he published these poems for they
would win him a dark reputation '. Rossetti and
Meredith were equally apprehensive. This is why,
with the unpublished manuscript of a play and a
volume of verse in his drawer, Swinburne, though
eager to conquer a fame which had been too long
deferred, decided to turn to a new work which would
have to be a masterpiece.

How did he think of *Atalanta* ? How did it occur
to him to write a Greek tragedy, and one on the legend
of Meleager ? I should not be surprised if Monckton
Milnes were here entitled to our praise : Swinburne
had for several years drifted away from his classical
studies : since he had left Oxford, he had been steeped
in a Pre-Raphaelite atmosphere, and most of his friends
—Meredith, Rossetti, Scott—were not exactly classical
scholars. Milnes on the other hand had studied the
humanities. Swinburne had shown him the Greek
elegiacs he composed at Eton. Moreover he realized,
with his great experience, that the curb of a classical
form was exactly what Swinburne's genius required
at the moment, in order to produce a work which would
be acceptable to the public. What seems to point in
this direction, is the keen interest he took in Swinburne's masterpiece almost from the beginning. Be
that as it may, when early in July Swinburne left
Tudor House, where he had been staying for some
time, to go on a summer visit to East Dene, the tragedy
must have begun to take shape in his mind. In a
letter of August 5th he complained to W. M. Rossetti
of the preaching attitude assumed by Ruskin and
disclosed a keen interest in Blake and the story of the
Borgias ; but, of *Atalanta*, not the slightest mention

was made. The scheme was not sufficiently advanced in his mind for him to discuss it with a friend. However it matured in the course of the month of August which Swinburne probably spent in the Isle of Wight.[1] On September 25th Swinburne's sister, Edith, died at Bournemouth after a long illness which for some months had left very little hope. It seems that the very great grief (Edith was his favourite sister) which he then experienced, hastened within him the development of a new inspiration : in a state of mind which partook of deep and almost rebellious sorrow on the one hand, and of blank resignation to the inevitable on the other, he wrote the first lines of *Atalanta*. The tragedy was already begun when, in the first days of October, he left East Dene for his uncle's residence, Northcourt.

It seems that Swinburne's prolonged stay at Northcourt was due to the sudden departure of his family on a tour to the continent, probably owing to a desire for a complete change after the painful months which had preceded Edith's death. Why the poet did not accompany them is less clear. He was probably prompted by the same instinct which urged him not to go back to Tudor House (where, however, he was paying rent), and to leave his rooms unoccupied : having by now sat down to write *Atalanta*, he realized that the calm though stimulating influence of Northcourt was most conducive to a speedy completion of his work : and with this object in view he lingered there

---

[1] Swinburne did not go to Cornwall as is mistakenly stated by Gosse. The trip with Inchbold took place in 1864, that with Jowett several years later. In August, Swinburne was at East Dene. The rest of the summer till Edith's death he spent at Bournemouth (' several of the last hopeless months of my dear sister's illness were spent there by us all in weary expectation of the end '.—To W. M. Rossetti, November 5, 1875).

until the beginning of 1864, heedless of the objurgations of Rossetti, who was clamouring for his tenant and for his rent.   Work became to him rapid and pleasant as sometimes happens under the influence of deep grief.   Mary Gordon too had a beneficent and quickening effect on his inspiration : ' My greatest pleasure just now is when Mary practises Handel on the organ ; but I can hardly *behave* for delight at some of the choruses.   It crams me and crowds me with old and new verses, half-remembered and half-made, which new ones will hardly come straight afterwards ; but under their influence I have done some more of my *Atalanta* which will be among my great doings if it keeps up with its own last [sic] scenes throughout'. This passage from a letter of 31 December, 1863, contains the first reference to *Atalanta* in Swinburne's correspondence.   It was also to Mary Gordon that the opening chorus ' When the hounds of spring ' was recited for the first time during a horse-ride between Newport and Shorwell.   The atmosphere at Northcourt was truly tonic ; when not actually at work on his tragedy or on some cognate poems such as *Ilicet* and *Anactoria*, Swinburne was adding some pages to his ever-growing 'running commentary' on Blake's works, or supplying for a story which his cousin was writing an accomplished pastiche of the old Interludes, *The Pilgrimage of Pleasure*.   This is a most interesting and finished piece of work : it can be considered as a farewell on the part of Swinburne to the kind of poems he had so long been practising in which the element of imitation was allowed to outweigh the writer's originality.   But even here, in what is professedly a copy of such models as *Everyman* or *Lusty*

Juventus, the poet's inspiration breaks the fetters of a slavish erudition, and achieves without effort some of the grand rhythmical effects which he was later on to use for independent poems of a more serious character. This short fragmentary play, so long buried in a child-ish novel, makes finer reading from a strictly poetical point of view than either *The Queen Mother* or *Rosamond.* In some of the incidents in the novel, and in particular flagellation scenes, the hand of Swinburne is recogniz-able ; this was confirmed to me by Mrs. Disney Leith herself a few months before she died.

Thus the blue foolscap sheets were accumulating on the big library table of Northcourt. Swinburne had come to stay for two or three weeks ; he was to remain nearly three months. When he tore himself away from the charms of the Isle of Wight in the first days of February 1864, *Atalanta* was beginning to take shape, and an important portion of the text had been written out ; enough at least to impress Landor, and to Landor he went with all speed.

To be quite precise, and although Swinburne had resolved to go to Italy, he was called to London in the first days of February 1864 by Rossetti's urgent representations. The tenantship at Tudor House had not been a success ; Swinburne had not used his rooms very long or very regularly : he stayed at Tudor House perhaps in the first months of 1863, certainly in the early summer of the same year. But those brief experiments had been enough : it may be that Swin-burne's presence proved too noisy and hindered Rossetti in his work ; it may be that the poet, who still cherished Elizabeth's memory, eyed with disfavour Fanny Schott, Rossetti's model and housekeeper.

At any rate, there can be no doubt that in February 1864 Rossetti told Swinburne that he would
have to find other lodgings ; in a manuscript note,
rather inadequately entitled 'A Record of Friendship', Swinburne many years after set down his own
version of the facts :

It was not without surprise that after a separation of many
months spent by me in the country [at Northcourt] I received
from my friend D. G. Rossetti a letter . . . intimating with all
possible apology that he wished to have the house at Chelsea to
himself. . . . My reply was brief and clear, to the effect that I
observed with his usual frankness and his usual rectitude that
I had not understood our common agreement to be so termin-
able at the caprice of either party that one could desire the other
to give place to him without further reason alleged than his own
will and pleasure ; but the ultimate result could only be an amicable separation.

About this separation which may have been ' amicable ', but was a separation none the less, and in which
we can recognize the first rift which, some eight years
later, led to a complete severance of their friendship,
I am able to give some further details obtained from
the unpublished correspondence between Swinburne
and William Michael Rossetti. It seems that, as is so
often the case, a question of money was at the root of
the matter. On October 11th, 1863, Swinburne was
contemplating a prompt return to Tudor House and
had no idea of moving, for he wrote : ' When I return to Chelsea I shall enrich the house with curious
glories of Chinese origin fit to swamp Fenchurch
Street for ever '. But before December 13th he received from Dante Gabriel a stern letter reminding
him that not only had his presence at Chelsea been
most irregular, but he had failed to pay his rent, which

had proved a great inconvenience. Swinburne sent a cheque by return, apologizing for his prolonged absence, explaining that ' having settled down here for quiet with no company but some of my nearest relations and oldest intimates I have shrunk from moving week after week, *perhaps not wisely*. [Italics mine.] But I think after being hit hard one is more afraid of any change than any monotony : and so I let myself be kept '. That Rossetti's words had a serious implication and referred to long pent up grievances is shown by the following sentence from the same letter : ' We must look up matters honestly when I come to London which will be I think in a week or two'. In fact, some weeks later (January 31, 1864) Swinburne announced that he would be in London by the end of the week, and begged William Michael ' to let them know at Chelsea that I may be expected by Saturday or Monday at the latest '. He *was* indeed expected ; matters were probably ' honestly looked up ', and Rossetti having given Swinburne a straight hint that he had rented the house for his friends and himself in order to secure their company and cut down the expenses, but that, as he seemed to derive neither advantage from the arrangement, he might as well have the house to himself, there was nothing left for Swinburne to do but look for new rooms, and, perhaps, new friendships.

In the course of February he crossed over to France seemingly in the company of Monckton Milnes (now Lord Houghton). At any rate he saw him in Paris and they both had tea with Charles MacCarthy, a friend of Lord Houghton. The latter, having now become very proud of Swinburne's rising genius

which he had been one of the first to discern, insisted
that his friend should read some of his poems and
' his recitations so excited MacCarthy that he had
quite a bad night. He thought them wonderful, and
they quite haunted him '. Lord Houghton supplied
Swinburne with several letters of introduction to people
in Florence including Landor. So, leaving his noble
friend either in Paris, or at Hyères, to which he was
bound, the poet proceeded to Italy, his haste increasing
as he neared his goal ; he simply passed through
Genoa. In the first days of March he was in Florence.
Landor represented two things in his eyes : pagan
rebellion and pagan art. *Atalanta* could be dedicated
to him only. He rushed to see him, armed with
Lord Houghton's introduction. The story of their
two meetings has been told before and well told. On
the second occasion Swinburne had the long intimate
conversation which he sought : his Greek verse met
with approval, his dedication was accepted. With
that however he had to be content, for a short note
soon came from Landor : ' So totally am I exhausted
that I can hardly hold my pen to express my vexation
that I shall be unable to converse with you again.
Eyes and intellect fail me '. Swinburne's visit had
been only too successful : he had found the great
man ' as ardent and brilliant . . . as twenty years
since ' ; he had, with his youthful genius, revived
for one short spell the waning faculties of Landor,
even to the point of exhaustion ; no one else perhaps
could have achieved such a result at that time. But
Swinburne knew how to collect the blessings and dying
words of great poets and laureates : just as he had
visited Wordsworth and Samuel Rogers, just as he was

to visit Hugo in 1882 in Paris, he had now become, through that one symbolic interview, sole inheritor of the art and inspiration of Walter Savage Landor.

Having thus, to use the jargon of the age, indulged his great Landor complex, Swinburne was at liberty to enjoy Florence, and he made full use of Lord Houghton's introductions, visiting the town in the company of J. T. Leader, Isa Blagden, J. L. Graham, and notably Seymour Stocker Kirkup, the friend of Blake, Landor, Keats and Shelley, with whom Swinburne struck up quite a friendship which is reflected in their pleasant correspondence about Blake. But Swinburne was determined to go further south : he soon left Florence, and, apparently without any companion, visited Fiesole, Majano, Siena, Pisa, and San Gimignano. He was not merely sensitive to the art treasures of museums, churches and palazzios ; the full oppressive beauty of an exceptionally hot Italian spring overwhelmed him ; he heard the clamour of ' tempestuous nightingales ', saw the ' strange-shapen mountains ' round Siena and the ' sheer streets ' of the city, and, in spite of historical associations and republican enthusiasm, managed to draw with a faultless hand some impressive cameos of true Pre-Raphaelite accuracy :

> For the outer land is sad, and wears
>   A raiment of a flaming fire ;
> And the fierce fruitless mountain stairs
>   Climb, yet seem wroth and loth to aspire,
> Climb, and break, and are broken down,
> And through their clefts and crests the town
> Looks west and sees the dead sun lie,
> In sanguine death that stains the sky
> With angry dye.

His memory thus registered, in the glare of the Italian sun, the bright contrast of the 'fresh clear gloom' with the 'ardent air aloof' and the 'weight of the violent sky'. It was indeed his last chance, and to this experience he was to turn many and many a time in later years, either from the 'old green-girt sweet-hearted earth' of the fields round Holmwood, or from the more suburban beauties of Wimbledon Common.

But all that heat and bare splendour, much as he was impressed by them, were to him exotic and over-whelming ; the northern strain in his physical and moral self rebelled against the sun and the ' dolorous tideless midland sea ' ; moreover he was alone in a foreign land ; the enchantment lasted nearly two months, but, having reaped and garnered a rich harvest of beauty, he now returned to London which he reached on the 21st of May ; as he explained two days later in a letter to Nichol he had been ' beaten back by the Italian sun and starved out by the want of companionship '.

Being back in London, Swinburne was beset by the problem of finding new lodgings—a difficulty which ever since he took up residence in town at Oxford recurred periodically. He first stayed at an address in Bedford Street, and then went back to live at the family house in Grosvenor Place. Towards the end of July he moved to 124 Mount Street where he was not to stay more than a few months. All those changes were extremely irksome to him and in the ' horror and bustle ' of a first day in his new quarters he wrote to Nichol comically describing himself as ' unpacking, blaspheming, arranging etc., with my choicest books

ruined and endless things lost '. ' But for to-day's experience ', he added ' I might have begun to doubt my
theory of the diabolic government of this worst of all
possible worlds—even perhaps to believe in a beneficent supervision which rewards virtue '.

Meanwhile *Atalanta* was in abeyance. It is hard to
believe that much work was done either in Tuscany
or in London from May to August. Swinburne had
gathered in those busy months sufficient stimulus
and colour for his inspiration ; he now wanted calm
and meditation. That is why he accepted, towards
the end of August, his friend J. W. Inchbold's invitation to come and stay with him at Tintagel. The
tragedy, which had been begun by the sea-side, was to
be finished under the influence of the sea.

The open air life began anew : Swinburne and his
friend swam ' the subterranean inlets of the sea ',
climbed up the crags, rode the horses of a neighbouring farmer. But they both had time and taste for
work. While Inchbold patiently painted Swinburne
was winding up his tragedy with ease and confidence.
The poet was already in Cornwall when the news of
Landor's death, which occurred on September 23rd,
reached him and cast a shadow over his rambles along
the shore :

> By this white wandering waste of sea,
>   Far north, I hear
> One face shall never turn to me
>   As once this year.

The news caused Swinburne not only genuine grief
but also a keen intellectual disappointment ; Landor
had accepted his dedication : but he would never

read *Atalanta*, never seize the pen to thank the author and write, even in a few lines, how perfectly Greek it all sounded to him. However, the tragedy was nearly finished, and although the ' funereal circumstances ' might ' deepen the fatalism ', they had no power to dry up the inspiration of the poem. By the end of October 1864, Swinburne had completed *Atalanta*.

Towards the middle of November full arrangements had been made for its publication. If J. B. Payne, acting for the firm of Moxon and Co., accepted the play, it was not because of Swinburne's growing fame, although the poet was certainly better known than in 1860 ; in the eyes of his publishers, the total failure of his former book precluded all optimism. The Admiral having, however, undertaken to pay the cost of publication (this, Swinburne tells us, ran up to considerably more than £100—' not a farthing of which was ever repaid ') all possible objections were removed. It is only fair to add that Payne seems to have done all he could to make the book an attractive one, and that the type, paper and binding (with gold ornaments by Rossetti) were exquisitely executed. The Oxford University Press have done themselves honour in producing an exact facsimile of this fine edition of one of the most remarkable books of English poetry—probably the best classical tragedy in the English language. But all this minute care in the presentation, which delayed the publication for a few weeks, suggests that no great store was set by the poetical merits of the play. Anticipating modern methods, the cunning Payne had relied on the extrinsic value of the book to make it a commercial success. Few copies, perhaps not more than one hundred, were printed. However, Swinburne's genius upset all the calculations and forecasts of publishers.

Success came, sudden, violent. Nobody seems to have expected it, not even Swinburne who had grown sceptical since the utter failure of *The Queen Mother* and the abrupt termination of his connection with the *Spectator* in 1862. This is precisely why success came : Lord Houghton had been circulating *The Queen Mother* among his guests at Fryston ; he had got Swinburne to recite his poems before select friends ; he was endeavouring to create an impression that Swinburne was a genius, as yet totally ignored, whom he with unfailing judgment had distinguished. Rossetti too had been trying to obtain some recognition for his friend : in 1864, he was urging John Skelton to write an article about Swinburne, stating that ' in private he has made so large a circle of ardent admirers, that I cannot doubt his public reception would eventually be a most enthusiastic one ' (13th November, 1864). All those efforts had apparently been in vain. But there existed in literary circles a feeling that genius was there, unknown, and that bare justice had been done to it yet. The fire-wood of interest and sympathy had been accumulating slowly ; a brighter spark from Swinburne's genius was enough to set it alight.

Swinburne was still revising proofs early in February 1865 ; the first copies of the book were out soon afterwards, by which date Lady Trevelyan was already possessed of one. In the course of March a few copies were sent to the Press. Five reviews appeared in April, all of a most laudatory nature : the *Athenaeum* (1st April) proclaimed that there had been no such poet since Keats ; the *London Review* (8 April) recognized

in the book the ' finest constituents of poetry ' ; the
Morning Herald (27 April), true to its name, announced
that ' a scholar and a poet had come amongst us '.
The tone was maintained in May. It rose considerably in June with the first summer heat and *The Times*
(6 June) declared that Swinburne was endowed ' with
no small portion of the Divine Fire '. Meanwhile
Payne's limited issue had been sold out and he hurriedly
printed a second edition for which Swinburne corrected
proofs in June or July from Ashburnham Place. A
large number of copies was now sent to the Press.
From July to December the enthusiasm was maintained. Lord Houghton in the *Edinburgh Review*
(July) praised the work of his *protégé*, though with no
small admixture of gall. *Albion* (11 November)
found in the tragedy ' everything to praise and nothing
to censure '. The *Sunday Times* concluded (31
December) that Swinburne was ' permanently enrolled
among our great English poets '. A few discordant
notes (*Spectator*, 15 April ; *Frazer's Magazine*, June)
were lost in a chorus of praise.

From friends and strangers alike Swinburne received private marks of admiration : Ruskin, Burne-
Jones, Lady Trevelyan, even Christina Rossetti
expressed their enthusiasm directly or indirectly ; a
young Welsh Squire, George Powell, wrote to Swinburne asking him to accept the dedication of a forthcoming volume of Scandinavian ballads, thus laying
the foundation of what proved to be one of the poet's
closest friendships ; Philip Bourke Marston, the blind
poet, later confided to Swinburne how in the spring of
1865 he ' used to comfort his solitude with the choruses
of *Atalanta* and the servants fancied him in a religious

ecstasy '. Two omissions however cast their shadow on Swinburne's triumph : Mazzini failed to acknowledge *Atalanta*, and instead of the half-paternal half-kingly epistle he had once hoped to receive from Landor, he had to be content with the following note from H. Landor to whom he had had the book sent :

Mr. H. Landor acknowledges receipt of *Atalanta* and will be obliged to know the price of the book.

Swinburne's fame which, however sudden, had long been desired and was thoroughly merited, brought fruitful consequences : Payne was now ready to publish further volumes without any subsidy from the Admiral, which was a fresh stimulus to the poet's truly remarkable strength of inspiration. He at once set out to revise *Chastelard*, collect and complete his lyrical poems, and bring the *Essay on Blake* to an end, not to mention minor enterprises in the way of literary criticism. The success of *Atalanta* gave Swinburne just that extra touch of confidence which he needed to create his style and determine his manner.

It may be that it gave him a little too much of that good thing ; we find in the letters of his friends at the time commentaries which point to an excess of self-assertion, something like arrogance on his part ; it is difficult however to know how much should be discounted on the score of unconscious jealousy at seeing the triumph of one younger than themselves. What is however certain is that Swinburne's ways of life changed, and not for the good. When the sun of glory began to dawn on him, he was staying with his family at 36 Wilton Crescent, and, to quote his own words on a later occasion, 'all was innocence and purity' : the Admiral had sold East Dene and purchased a large country-house, Holmwood, in Oxfordshire, but the residence was not ready until the middle of April, and the whole family had taken up temporary quarters in town. But after they had gone Swinburne, who soon moved into those lodgings of Dorset Street in which he was to live for the next three years, was left to the excitement of his new existence as the most famous English poet of the younger generation. Must we ascribe the change that overcame him to the fumes of celebrity, to a reaction from the intense mental strain to which his work then submitted him, or to the development of inborn tendencies ? Is it not fair also to remember that his intimacy with some of his former friends, Rossetti and Meredith, had, through no fault of his, relaxed, and that he had to find new companions ? What is certain is that those companions he did find, and that their influence over him was not of the healthiest ; he was now probably fairly intimate with the young Jewish painter Simeon Solomon whom he may have met as early as 1860 through Burne-Jones. Solomon was ready to share in the wildest eccentricities of his now famous friend, as part of their correspondence, preserved in the collection of Mr. Wise, shows only too well ; he was violently attracted to his genius and responsive to all his moods. Quite different was Charles Augustus Howell : although no full account of this extraordinary and, in some respects, sinister personality has yet appeared, it is well known that Howell, chiefly through his connections in the world of art dealers and critics, was admitted into the intimacy of the Pre-Raphaelite circles ; after an exile of five years in Portugal, due perhaps to his having mixed in the Orsini conspiracy, he returned to London in 1864 ; Swinburne met this splendid parasite and liar of genius at Chelsea ; he had heard wild rumours about him ; doubtless the poet was interested in him for many reasons : for his democratic leanings, his fine artistic taste, his incomparable picturesqueness. But in his friendship Swinburne sought chiefly a satisfaction of the senses : the ever ready wit of Howell soon found out the way of amusing Swinburne in the fashion in which he best liked to be amused. As an entertainer, as a guide, as an intermediary Howell had no rivals : he soon became the indispensable companion of Swinburne's hours of leisure. Whenever the poet came to town, he sent for Howell. If he stayed for any length of time, he must plead for Howell's company at least once a week ; when in exile at Holmwood, Howell's letters, and their enclosures, alone had power to divert him. His attitude, as shown in the letters which Mr. Wise acquired from Watts-Dunton, is one of prayer and supplication ; he begs for Howell's presence as a favour, and Howell, as often as not, disappoints him ; this low parasite is not always prepared to vouchsafe his company to the author of *Atalanta*. The implication is not of course that Swinburne has a blind affection for Howell or ignores his faults, his bragging, his occasional vulgarity. But he likes Howell because his own pleasure depends upon his company ; he urges him to visit or write to him with boyish impatience, almost as a child crying for his milk—and little caring from what goat-footed creatures the savoury beverage has been obtained.

To make matters worse, Burton was now on leave in London, having arrived in the course of March. The close friendship between the two men has already been described, and Swinburne joined in the round of parties and orgies into which Burton plunged like a sailor on shore. It was about this date that Swinburne was introduced through his friend's good offices to the Cannibal Club. What was the logical connection between this institution and the Anthropological Society founded in 1863 by Dr. James Hunt, is not, I confess, clear to me, in spite of Mr. Wise's detailed comment in his Bibliography ; but how club-dinners, over which presided a mace representing a negro gnawing a thigh bone, appealed to Swinburne and Burton is easy enough to understand : anthropophagy was quite an article of faith with the English explorer, as well as with Dolmancé. Too much importance should not be accorded to those exhibitions of a somewhat childish humour. What is more significant is that the ' chaplain ' of the club was that Thomas Bendyshe, senior Fellow of King's College, Cambridge, editor of the *Reader* and translator of the Mahabharata who seems to have exercised no small influence over Swinburne's ' religious ' opinions ; the poet also met at the club-dinners Charles Bradlaugh, to whom he gave the manuscript of his *Cannibal Catechism*, a burlesque hymn in the manner of Burns. There is no doubt that Swinburne found in the tribal feasts with his fellow Cannibals an atmosphere which proved singularly congenial to the development of his own pagan and atheistic tendencies.

Flushed by *Atalanta*'s success—the book was beginning to pay, a novel experience for Swinburne—

encouraged and misled by the tone prevailing in the conversations of his new friends, the poet would not hear of delaying the publication of *Chastelard* any further. The manuscript underwent a final revision and was sent to press, so that some advance volumes were ready as early as the beginning of August, when Victor Hugo received his. Review copies were sent off in the course of November.

On the conception of love and the moral standard exhibited in the play, Edmund Gosse has an extraordinary sentence ; he writes : ' This was the exact morality of those who dwelt in Tendre-sur-Inclination and worshipped love as an insatiable Moloch.' He might have written Masoch. The comparison is preposterous. To imply any connection between the ' love-ravings ' of *Chastelard*, and the artificial conceptions current in the salon of that egregious prude, ' Sappho ' de Scudéry, is either to miss the point entirely or to be wilfully blind to the facts. Swinburne's contemporaries, while praising the artistic qualities of the play, denounced the book as a ' lamentable prostitution of the English Muse ' and proclaimed that there was ' reason to fear that Mr. Swinburne is wanting in the higher beauty of moral dignity and sweetness '. However, although deeply shocked at Chastelard's ' constant exhibitions of passion ' the contemporaries do not seem to have clearly discovered what lay behind the hero's passive but highly sensuous attitude to his cruel mistress :

> her sweet lips and life
> Will smell of my spilt blood

might pass unnoticed : but they were horrified at the

thought of Chastelard in hiding under the bed of his
queen while she undressed for the night !

An incident which occurred right at the close of
Swinburne's glorious year (1865) may be here mentioned as not devoid of significance. At the beginning of December Houghton arranged a meeting between Tennyson and Swinburne ; but the author of
Atalanta was no longer the modest undergraduate who
had visited Farringford with Nichol in 1857, nor even
the ' rimailleur inédit ' who in one of the intervals of
the composition of his tragedy had vainly called at the
same place in the winter of 1864. To Tennyson's
company, Swinburne preferred that of Palgrave and
Lewes, and it seems that he turned his back on the
Laureate. Houghton accused him of being under the
influence of drink, which he denied. It seems however that he spoke to Lewes and Palgrave of other
things than 'Blake and Flaxman'. Anyhow the echoes
of Swinburne's wild talk went as far north as Wallington ; Lady Trevelyan probably refers to the same incident when on 6 December 1865 she writes urging
Swinburne to ' deny the talks attributed to him ' and
to be ' more guarded about what you say when men
get together and take alcoholic stimuli . . . It is horrid
for your friends to have to deny some things '. Swinburne may on this occasion have been sober ; he may
not have insulted Tennyson ; he may have confined
his talk to remarks on Blake and Flaxman. All this
does not alter the fact that the faults with which he is
here reproached are true psychologically and describe
accurately his state of mind at the time. All tends to
show that after the publication of *Atalanta*, for just
over a year, Swinburne bore the strain of high nervous

and intellectual tension and physical irregularities :
those culminated in the composition of *Dolores* which
illustrates the seething and somewhat chaotic condition
of the poet's inspiration in the summer of 1865.

It was perhaps at the beginning of 1866 that Swinburne's reputation stood highest. The notoriety of
Chastelard had just added a little spice to the triumph
of *Atalanta* : he had in the course of six months chal-
lenged literary opinion with two masterpieces. In
spite of an occasional censure, there was absent from
the chorus of criticism that note of contemptuous mistrust and resentment which was to be found in the
reception of most of his books after 1866. Payne on
behalf of Moxon had agreed to publish his poems and
his *William Blake* ; he was also requested, from the
same quarter, to write critical essays for several volumes
of anthology from Byron, Keats and Landor ; he was
even asked to accept the editorship of a literary magazine : in the course of March he was chosen to represent modern literature at the Royal Literary Fund
Annual Dinner.
    This must not however blind us to the fact that a
wave of hostility, arising partly from envy, partly from
misconstruction, partly from the conversations and doings of Swinburne himself, slowly surged towards the
poet. In March the *Spectator* ' slated ' the *Essay on
Byron* asserting that Swinburne was perhaps a poet but
no critic. More significant still are the difficulties of
Swinburne over his membership of the Arts Club,
Chelsea, to which he had been elected in 1864. Towards the end of March, owing to some wild behaviour
on his part, there was a talk of expelling him, but

W. M. Rossetti smoothed matters over.[1] Swinburne's irregular habits culminated in the spring in what he calls a ' bilious attack '. Those bilious attacks which occasionally assumed a semi-epileptic form recurred from now on at fairly regular intervals and placed an all too frequent bar on Swinburne's activities.

Meanwhile Payne[2] was a little apprehensive of a possible scandal. To pave the way for the publication of the forthcoming poems, he printed *Laus Veneris* separately in January as a test of public opinion : no one paid attention to so slight a volume. On the other hand Rossetti, Meredith, Ruskin and even Lady Trevelyan pleaded for a serious ' pruning ' of his book of poems. Letters of advice were sent from various quarters and regular consultations held, probably at the instigation of Rossetti or Ruskin. The excision of some pieces was advocated. Swinburne consented in ' one or two instances '. But he resented those hesitations ; he was full of self-confidence, and perhaps persuaded that his friends were too shy, and failed to anticipate the all-transmuting power of his genius which could turn vice into virtue and virtue into vice. One cannot but sympathize with him to a certain extent : after enduring for over four years the censure and admiring disapproval of Rossetti and Meredith, he had now found his real style and in his forthcoming *Poems and Ballads* he felt that he was going to express himself more fully and more deeply than he had yet been able to ; he was going to show in those lyrical

---

[1] The reconciliation was only temporary. In the spring of 1870 the Committee of the Art's Club asked Swinburne to resign. (See *Life* : chapter vii.)

[2] Gosse states that through Lord Houghton the manuscript of *Poems and Ballads* was offered in March to the firm of Murray, who declined to publish it. (*Life*, page 131.)

pieces the full range and resonance of his varied inspirations ; and he believed that his finished art would
lull puritanical hearts to sleep. Anyhow he had found
his true voice, and he was going to use it.

He was now revising the proofs of his volume with
all speed : on 21 March fifty-six pages were ready.
But the printing went on very slowly and in April–
May we find him still busy over his proofs. He wrote
in an unpublished letter to Powell : ' I cannot see my
book fairly out and blunder follows blunder with these
unblessed printers, delaying me and all things. If they
could be *put in the bill* each time as their betters have
been it might do some good.' Doubtless Swinburne
had his share of responsibility in this delay : Mr. Wise
has shown that, some errors having escaped Swinburne's attention, they had to be corrected at the last
moment which cost much expense and trouble ; it
seems that some poems—like *Félise*—were included,
and perhaps composed, only a few weeks before the
date of issue.

However, the first copies were out on July 1st, on
which date Swinburne sent an accompanying letter to
Victor Hugo, and most papers had received theirs by
the end of the month. The first article (in the *Reader*)
appeared on the 28th. John Morley's attack in the
Saturday Review followed on August 4th. The story
of the withdrawal of the book by Payne is now well
known. [1] To quote Swinburne's own words, written
four days after the event, ' My hound of a publisher
has actually withdrawn from circulation my volume of

---

[1] Swinburne and his friends complained bitterly that Payne went on selling odd
copies of the original impression of *Poems and Ballads* in an underhand way. Hotten
at one time thought of taking action against him. (*Rossetti Papers*, 27 December
1866.)

poems—refuses to issue any more copies—"through fear of consequences to himself " . . . C'est embêtant.' It remains however for me to point out one fact which is apt to be overlooked. Behind Payne's decision there was more than the influence of Morley's strictures ; when D. G. Rossetti, accompanied by Sandys, consented to devote one afternoon of his valuable time to an interview with Payne, he found that ' the publisher was distracted with terror of the public prosecutor and desired nothing so much as to be rid of the poet and his friends '. What put the fear of prosecution into Payne's head ? Morley said nothing about it. It has been vaguely asserted that a rumour was current to the effect that a review demanding this course was going to appear in *The Times*. Most fortunately the *Hardman Papers*, published in 1930, supply here a few precise facts ; unreliable as they may be in some cases, we must not forget that they are a contemporary record and that Hardman was associated with many of the reviewers. He wrote under the date November 1866—' It seems that Dallas was the cause of Moxon's withdrawing of *Poems and Ballads*; he had written a crushing review for *The Times*, in which *both poet and publisher* [italics mine] were held up to the execration of all decent people. The article was in type when a private hint was given to Moxon, in order that he might, if so inclined, disconnect himself from the bawdry . . . So he wisely threw the whole thing up and it has since been purchased by J. C. Hotten, a publisher who is far from particular what he gives to the world.' If this Dallas review is ever found, it should be printed, as an additional proof. For (this has never been sufficiently emphasized) all the evidence tends to show that there was a distinct attempt at suppressing the book ; that for some of the reasons I have tried to set out most of the critics were after Swinburne, and cared little about morality and decency. The ' hint ' given to Payne is particularly significant. The attempt at making the publication of *Poems and Ballads* impossible was to a great extent a private *vendetta*, and I know of no more dishonourable episode in the history of literary journalism.

All the more so as the attempt seems now, whatever the ulterior motives may have been, unjustifiable. Whatever the secret springs of his inspiration, we must recognize that Swinburne managed (and this was a true artistic *tour de force*) to give us the crystal flow of the rushing stream and conceal its painful origins. We may re-read and study the text of *Laus Veneris*, *Les Noyades*, *Félise*, even *Dolores* and the

Ah that my lips were tuneless lips

in *Anactoria*—we shall find little which may strike the uninitiated as strange or suspicious ; we shall hear nothing but the simplified or disguised expression of some of the deeper forms of passion, bitterness and desire.

The proof is that the contemporaries failed to spot the passages to which the biographer may point to support some of his statements. Objection was taken not to the intensity of some ideas of pain and pleasure,[1] not to the key-note of death and murder which is here and there struck with unusual power ; but to the

[1] One or two exceptions only serve to prove the rule. See *Examiner*, October 6 (the pseudonymous letter is by Lord Houghton) and *Saturday Review*, November 17, 1866.

poet's 'lack of sincerity' (!) ; to the parallel between Venus and the Mother of God in *Laus Veneris* ;
to the pagan and mythological subject of *Hermaphroditus* ; to the names of Sappho and Faustine ; to the
'atheistic' verses of *Félise*. It was in vain that the
virtuous Morley denounced in Swinburne 'the feverish carnality of the schoolboy over the dirtiest passages
in Lemprière' ; we now have to turn to Lemprière
if we want to discover the feverish carnality. It was to
a great extent Morley who created the immorality
of *Poems and Ballads*[1] by pointing to relevant passages
in the lexicon. He confesses that the 'fevered folly'
of many pieces will be unintelligible to the readers,
and presently proceeds to enlighten them. *Poems and
Ballads* is quite different from *Les Fleurs du Mal*, in
which three at least out of the five condemned pieces
are of a very obvious character. Powell wrote to
Swinburne that two dear old ladies in Wales believed
Anactoria to be an Hymn to the Holy Virgin ; if
ever their pious illusion was destroyed, Morley is to
be blamed for it.

Nothing is further from my mind than to imply
that all was sham and hypocrisy in the outburst that
followed the publication of *Poems and Ballads* ;
much on the contrary was heart-felt and genuine ;
Swinburne received, as well as letters of wild enthusiasm, epistles which were certainly sincere in their
indignation. I merely wanted to distinguish between
the prejudiced opinion of some reviewers and the out-
cry which arose, partly from the scandal created by the
Press, partly in a spontaneous fashion. There can be

[1] ' The Saturday Review Temperament is ten thousand thousand times more damn-
able than the worst of Swinburne's Skits ' (letter from J. A. Froude to Skelton,
19 August, 1866).

no doubt that Swinburne shocked a great many of his contemporaries and that, in a way, he revelled in that idea. But the indignation he aroused was but an inverted form of admiration. By his picture of sheer passion intense and cruel (*vide* the Marquis de Sade), careless of consequences and unmixed with sentimental reverberations (*vide* Gautier, Baudelaire and ' Art for Art's Sake ') Swinburne managed what had not been contrived perhaps since the days of Byron and Keats, probably since those of Shakespeare and Spenser : he struck the emotional bed-rock of pure passion which had been buried for years and was only allowed to emerge here and there in its less rugged form in the nuptial poems of Patmore, the cautious idylls of Tennyson, or the too dramatic pieces of Browning. In brief Swinburne's harmonious slogan (' we must do justice to that much misused and belied thing, the purely sensuous and outward side of love ') created echoes in the heart of his contemporaries, and those echoes had to be stifled, which created confusion, distress, and consequently indignation and scandal. Who knows how many complex reactions were caused by the lines

> Rise up, make answer for me, let thy kiss
> Seal my lips hard from speaking of my sin
> Lest one go mad to hear how sweet it is. . . .

not only in the breasts of undergraduates and budding poets, but even in the more austere sentimental stronghold of the older generation—in the hearts of puritans and country clergymen ?[1]   The result was

---

[1] In the years that followed *Poems and Ballads* and *Songs before Sunrise*, references to Swinburne as the archetype of the unbeliever become frequent in sermons, religious articles, etc. : ' While Renan, with his treacherous praise said, " Master, Master," and kissed our Lord, Swinburne insulted him as he hung on the bitter cross.' (Prebendary Thorold in the *Guardian*, October 18, 1871).

that Swinburne became not merely a writer to be criticized and despised, but an imminent danger which had to be crushed. Hence the scandal. Thomas Hardy has admirably expressed this in a self-analytical stanza of his elegy :

> It was as though a garland of red roses
> Had fallen about the hood of some smug nun,
> When irresponsibly dropped as from the sun
> In fulth of numbers freaked with musical closes,
> Upon Victoria's formal middle time,
> His leaves of rhythm and rhyme.

And the nun did not remain icy-cold and indifferent as to a meaningless accident ; even though she may not have discerned the exact nature of the flowers, she breathed in the fragrance, blushed, hung her head in shame, and strove in a violent though not perfectly dignified manner to get rid of the obnoxious garland.

What was Swinburne's attitude while the storm raged ? First the weight of his uncontrolled anger gathered on the head of the not altogether responsible Payne. Then all his energies were directed to one end : overcoming the obstacle which had been maliciously placed in his way, rescuing a work which had been censured but not read, securing at once the re-publication of his book. In this he was singularly fortunate : as early as August 6th he received from Lord Lytton, who, since he had read *Atalanta*, was a warm admirer of Swinburne, an invitation to come and consult with him and Forster about the transfer of his book to another firm. He stayed at Knebworth, Lord Lytton's country house, from the 11th to the 24th of August. During that week he received an offer

from J. C. Hotten to publish his book at once :
Howell (who, it should never be forgotten, had his
good points) seems to have been responsible for
bringing Swinburne and Hotten together. The
latter was not of course one of the most reputable
publishers in London. But his offer at such a
juncture was unhoped for ; it was all-important for
Swinburne that his book should come out at once. He
accepted straightaway (in a letter which was not perhaps very carefully worded and afforded to Hotten
later on a commercial hold on Swinburne) and could
write to a friend on the 24th : ' My book will be
reissued in a few days '. At the beginning of October
the volume was again ready and review copies sent so
that reports began to appear regularly in the Press.
But it was decided to delay publication until Swinburne's ironical and impassioned plea, *Notes on
Poems and Reviews*, came out towards the end of the
month[1]. Swinburne had won the day. The journalists
had merely succeeded in holding up the book for a
few short weeks. Not only was *Poems and Ballads*
published, but no alteration of any kind had been
made to the original text. The author on this point
had been adamant and had declined to comply with the
representations of nearly all his friends. ' Now ', he
explained to Lord Lytton, ' to alter my course or
mutilate my published work seems to me somewhat
like deserting one's colours.'

But now the struggle was at an end and the resistance

[1] Hotten did not make up his mind to bring out the book till he had obtained a
confidential letter from a police-magistrate to the effect that Swinburne's book was
neither ' seizable nor indictable '. See Rossetti Papers (October 13 and November 20,
1866). Swinburne believed that J. M. Ludlow, the social reformer, was trying to
get a prosecution (*Life*, page 143). W. M. Rossetti's *Defence* appeared on November 12.

battered down, a strange weariness came over Swinburne. A feeling of disgust convulsed him at reading the poem of Buchanan in the *Spectator*, the abuse and caricatures poured on him in *Punch* (in which he was called ' Swineborn '), the malicious insinuations of the reviewers. He could not help noticing how some of his acquaintances avoided meeting him ; in his closest friends he discerned various shades of reluctance and disapproval. He was not free from anonymous abuse of the worst kind : under the date November 1866 the *Hardman Papers* have the following amazing entry ' It has been [Shirley] Brook's great amusement lately to circulate epigrams full of wit and indecency about the poet [Swinburne] and to manage that they should be communicated to him by kind friends.'[1]

In this frame of mind Swinburne left London on the eve of the publication of the *Notes* and spent the last days of October at the residence of Powell, Nant-Eôs, near Aberystwyth. On November 2nd he proceeded to Holmwood where he remained a few days ; he then returned to his London lodgings in Dorset Street where he stayed during the last days of November and the first fortnight in December. But his health gave way : he was again the victim of ' one of those damned bilious attacks which prove the malevolence of the deity ' and by the end of the year he was back in Holmwood for a prolonged stay. During those periods of calm, while away from London, he meditated a great deal ; the days of illness were also favourable to introspection. After the fight, the dust of the battle began to abate ; from his bitter experience he drew

[1] See also *Hardman Paper* under January 1867.

some conclusions. He remembered the half-hearted defence of friends who had been his masters and his guides and were responsible for the growth of his inspiration. The time of the publication of his book and the months that had preceded seemed now to him a period of stress and noise, a revelry, a sort of prolonged Bacchanal ; he knew the beauty but also the emptiness of it. He longed for some spiritual reaction from his sensuous ecstasies, for some period of ascetic relief, after his severe and strict service of Fleshly Beauty

> Sous le fouet du Plaisir, ce bourreau sans merci . . .

as had said his brother Baudelaire, to whom he was more than ever looking up as a fellow-martyr. He bethought himself of his admiration for Italy, of his youthful *Ode* to Mazzini ; he believed that his early republican fervour, his boyish love of liberty were the truer and nobler form of his inspiration ; as an artist he felt that it would open to him new lyrical themes. As early as 9 October, 1866 he wrote to W. M. Rossetti :

> After all, in spite of jokes and perversities—malgré ce cher Marquis et ces foutus journaux—it is *nice* to have something to love and believe in as I do in Italy. It was only Gabriel and his followers in art (l'art pour l'art) who for a time, frightened me from speaking out ; for ever since I was fifteen I have been equally and unalterably mad—tête montée, as my mother says— about *this* article of faith ; you may ask any tutor or school-fellow.

He had already begun *A Song of Italy*. There is nothing more remarkable in the whole life of Swinburne than this sudden and spontaneous change of attitude.

It is fitting that this chapter should close with such a sharp, clear-cut division. If we look back on those seven years of the poet's life we are struck by two things : the mental and artistic activity they display, the many important experiences which Swinburne crowded into a comparatively short time, from the death of his grandfather to that of Lady Trevelyan, from the *Triumph of Time* to *Dolores*, from the failure of *Rosamond* to the notoriety of *Poems and Ballads*. But we are also struck by the chaotic character of this tireless activity : lyrical poetry, political satire, art and literary criticism, the drama, the novel, Swinburne, perhaps not uninfluenced by Hugo's example, has attempted everything. But there is no deep underlying unity in his inspiration or his style : the classical and the pre-Raphaelite manners, vice and the depth of passion, politics and art for art's sake, atheism and medieval pastiche form a strange medley which is best exhibited in *Poems and Ballads*. The intellectual influences which Swinburne has undergone are no less conflicting ; Houghton, Rossetti, Sade, Blake, etc., are not easily reconciled. This diversity is both wonderful and disconcerting. There was a time about 1866 when his friends may have thought that Swinburne was about to become one of the great literary leaders of the age ; that he would achieve equal success as poet, dramatist, critic and novelist. This was not to happen : but when giving up everything to concentrate on *Songs before Sunrise* the poet gained in depth and unity of thought what he lost in wealth and variety of inspiration.

At the stage we have just reached, Swinburne makes use with characteristic *naïveté* of metaphors

borrowed from school-slang : ' What awful rows I
have got into ' he remarks to Powell after the crisis
of *Poems and Ballads.* ' You may ask any tutor or
schoolfellow ' he protests to W. M. Rossetti about
the genuineness of his interest in Italy. We may then
be forgiven for the following allegory : after many
years spent in that strange school in which Rossetti,
Baudelaire, Hugo and others had been successively
or concurrently Principals, Swinburne, after a final
scandal, was now about to be transferred to a new
establishment of which Mazzini was Headmaster.

CHAPTER VI

SONGS AFTER SUNSET
(1866-1872)

BUT to this new school Swinburne went spontaneously and voluntarily. To be quite fair and if the metaphor may be strained a little further, he ought to be compared, not to a public-school boy, but rather to one of those middle-aged students of the Renaissance who, convinced of their own ignorance, started their studies all over again under some scholar of deeper learning. It has been asserted that the meeting between Swinburne and Mazzini was deliberately engineered : that a sort of *conseil de famille*, which Lord Carlisle and Jowett attended, considered what could be done ' with and for Algernon ' ; and that Swinburne never suspected the ' collusion '. We have seen how inaccurate the reminiscences of contemporaries are apt to be though given in perfect good faith. If such a meeting took place, and if Mazzini gave his consent, why should the services of Purnell and Karl Blind have been required to introduce the poet to the patriot ? Why should the latter have written probably in the course of March 1867 ' Quant à Swinburne, dont je sais tout, je ne comprends rien au désir d'être introduit etc. etc. Il a déjà une lettre de moi qui lui donne mon addresse et le droit de venir chez moi quand bon lui semble. Etes-vous sûr que le désir exprimé à Mr. Purnell soit d'une date récente ?' The attitude, only too common even among the friends of the poet, to treat him as a child of genius, yet as a child, to pat him on the back and call him ' Algernon ' in a mild hectoring fashion, cannot be too strongly deprecated. Swinburne's boyish manners may have encouraged such an attitude though it must have been at times irksome to him[1] ; but to us, who know only the poet and have not met the man, this style is entirely out of date.

We shall therefore refuse to believe that, but for Jowett and Lord Carlisle, *Songs before Sunrise* might never have been written ; in fact the *conseil de famille*, if it ever was held, must have slightly overestimated its own importance. We know from the letter quoted above that as early as October 1866, when *Poems and Ballads* had barely been published, Swinburne had *spontaneously* turned from ' Rossetti and his followers in art (l'art pour l'art) ' to Italy and Mazzini, and that he was haunted by the thought of writing a ' not inadequate expression of love and reverence towards him'. This poem (which was, after undergoing many modifications, to become the *Song of Italy*) once written, it was only to be expected that Mazzini would read it and seek to know the author, who, by the way, happened to be the friend of men like Nichol, the Rossettis and Madox Brown, who were all acquainted with the Italian patriot.[2] Indeed, indeed, if the authors of the ' unsuspected collusion ' ever deceived anyone, they must have deceived themselves.

---

[1] It is on the contrary quite probable that most of Swinburne's acquaintances in the seventies observed with him a marked attitude of admiration and respect. The late Sir Edmund Gosse told me that when he became intimate with Swinburne about 1871–75, he ' realized what a great privilege he was enjoying and used to follow him about like a dog '.

[2] Aurelio Saffi, as Mr. John Purves points out to me, claimed that he had been instrumental in introducing the two men. But this is doubtful. See page 79, note.

The great fact which from 1866 to 1871 gives unity to the life of Swinburne lies in his relations with Mazzini and the consequent composition of more or less ' political ' poems, which were later to form a whole and become *Songs before Sunrise*.   It is therefore indispensable to analyse briefly what those relations were and how far they affected Swinburne's mind as reflected in his poetry.   The other elements in his life during this period may be considered as distinct and secondary and treated separately.

Swinburne's enthusiasm, not only for Italian unity, but also for the personality of Mazzini, reaches back very far.   It is possible that, to quote his own words, ' ever since he was fifteen ' he had been ' tête montée ' about it.   It is however probable that blind admiration for the patriot developed chiefly at Oxford under the influence of Nichol and others : besides the *Ode to Mazzini*, the *Temple of Janus*, which in some lines as

The visioned Rome that nobler hours shall bring . . .

has a distinct Mazzinian ring, go far to prove it. This early worship suffered however an eclipse, at least as far as its literary manifestations were concerned, and from 1860 to 1866, even in the course of Swinburne's trips to Italy, if we hear much about Landor, Hugo and Baudelaire, Mazzini and the Italian cause are somewhat neglected.   But towards the end of 1866, from motives which seem chiefly internal, enthusiasm sprang to life again and embodied itself in the poet's work.   While *A Song of Italy* was expanding into a very considerable poem, Swinburne agreed at the express request of Ford Madox Brown and some Greek friends

(Strauss-Dilbenghi, Mrs. Spartali) to write an ode on the Cretan insurrection, for which, as Gosse observes, he must have cared very little ; his ulterior motive was perhaps not to displease Mazzini. His wish to meet ' the chief ' was indeed evident, although, as seen in the letter already quoted, he seems to have dreaded and postponed at the last minute, with typical shyness, the interview he longed for. I have suggested that this enthusiasm was not altogether disinterested ; that the artist as well as the man hoped to benefit by Mazzini's intercourse, that Swinburne felt obscurely how his lyric genius might derive fresh vigour from what had proved to many others a living source of strength and inspiration.

The depth and extent of the Mazzinian influence over Swinburne have never been precisely gauged. The reason may be that, despite Swinburne's repeated assertion that the *Songs* were ' infiltrated and permeated with Mazzini ', there is but little direct *external* evidence. Of the correspondence which one would expect to have passed between the two men there is practically nothing extant ; it was in vain that the late Sir Edmund Gosse searched for Swinburne's letters to Mazzini in Italy and elsewhere. It is even doubtful that there were many. The *Letters from Mazzini to an English family*, published in 1926 by Mrs. Richards, as well as several references in the still unpublished correspondence of Swinburne with W. M. Rossetti, reveal the fact that Mazzini rather unnecessarily adhered to those mysterious methods of conspiracy which had so long been his, and only communicated with Swinburne when abroad through a third party (generally Emilia Venturi) ; writing directly to him would in his eyes

have been more dangerous still ; Swinburne seems to
have had from him chiefly indirect or oral messages,
or, as he says somewhere, impersonal ' bulletins from
headquarters '. When in England, Mazzini, relying
on his magnetic personality, preferred to have personal
interviews with ' his ' poet.

There is at least one exception to what seems to have
been the rule. On March 10, 1867, Mazzini, possibly
at the instigation of the *conseil de famille* to which reference has been made, bethought himself that he had
not acknowledged the copy of *Atalanta* which two years
earlier had been duly sent to him, and wrote to Swinburne a fine and powerful letter which sounded like
a clarion-call in the ears of the poet ; after congratulating him on the Candiote Ode, he went on as follows :

> Whilst the immense heroic Titanic battle is fought, christ-
> ened on every spot by the tears of the loving ones and the blood
> of the brave, between Right and Wrong, Freedom and
> Tyranny, Truth and Lie, God and the Devil—with a new
> conception of Life, a new Religious Synthesis, a new European
> World struggling to emerge from the graves of Rome, Athens,
> Byzantium and Warsaw, kept back by a few crowned un-
> believers and a handful of hired soldiers—the poet ought to be
> the apostle of a crusade, his word the watchword of the fighting
> nations and the dirge of the oppressors. Don't lull us to sleep
> with songs of egotistical love and idolatry of physical beauty :
> shake us, reproach, encourage, insult, brand the cowards, hail
> the martyrs, tell us all that we have a great Duty to fulfil, and
> that, before it is fulfilled, Love is an undeserved blessing,
> Happiness a blasphemy, belief in God a Lie. Give us a series
> of 'Lyrics for the Crusade'. Have not our praise, but our
> blessing. You *can* if you choose.

On March 16th Mazzini learned through some friends
that Swinburne was ' already writing an Ode on Italy
in which he mentions me ! . . . If he goes on I shall

feel very proud.' The fateful and now inevitable meeting took place on March 30th at the house of the German exile Karl Blind, to whom Swinburne was introduced by Thomas Purnell. Towards Blind and Purnell Swinburne ever afterwards considered that he had contracted a bond of eternal gratitude.[1]

This memorable event was recorded the following day in two letters. In the one, addressed to his mother, the poet gives very full and significant details both about the meeting and his state of mind : ' The minute he came into the room, which was full of people, he walked straight up to me (who was standing in my place and feeling as if I trembled all over) and said : " I know *you* ", and I did as I always thought I should and really meant not to do if I could help—went down on my knees and kissed his hand. He held mine between his for some time while I was reading, and now and then, gave it a great pressure. He says he will take me to Rome when the revolution comes, and crown me with his own hands in the Capitol.' The other letter, addressed to George Powell whom Swinburne had disappointed on the previous evening so as to keep his engagement with Mazzini, is shorter but more impressive still : ' You will not wonder at the care I took to keep it when I tell you that it was an engagement to meet Mazzini. I did ; I unworthy spent much of last night sitting at my beloved Chief's feet. He was angelically good to me. I read him my Italian poem all through and he accepted it in words I can't trust myself to try and write down. I will be with you to-morrow at six at the St. James's Hall if

[1] ' Believe me for ever, most truly and gratefully yours, A. C. Swinburne ', from a letter of thanks to Karl Blind, c. 31 March, 1867.

well enough—but to-day I am rather exhausted and
out of sorts. Il y a bien de quoi. There's a tradition
in the Talmud that when Moses came down from Sinai
" he was drunken with the kisses of the lips of God " '.
To say that ' Mazzini also was conceivably rather
exhausted ' is a poor joke, and may give a wrong impression : A Song of Italy (for there can be no doubt
that this was the poem which Swinburne read) had not
probably reached its final length by then ; moreover
Mazzini was enough of a student of men, as well as
of an artist and lover of poetry,¹ to have enjoyed the
performance.

Nor was this one spectacular interview all, as had
been the case with Landor ; in the course of April
Swinburne, to whom Mazzini had given permission
to ' come and see him whenever he liked ' paid him
two private visits. ' I have had two long interviews
lately with the Chief ' he wrote on April 29, 1867 in
an unpublished letter to W. M. Rossetti. ' He is
more divine the more one sees of him. We are quite
on familiar terms now, and what a delight this is to
me I need not tell you. . . . He said things to me and
told me stories I can't write about.' On May 5th
Swinburne called on him once more, but it is doubtful
whether he saw him again before Mazzini left for
Zurich and Lugano in the course of the Summer.
However, Mazzini was back in London early in
January 1868 and Swinburne saw him in the first days
of February and had probably ample opportunities of
meeting him until he went back to Switzerland, from
which he was soon exiled (1869) ; in August 1870 came

---

¹ ' Mazzini takes great interest in poetry ' (Rossetti papers, May 7, 1867).

the news of Mazzini's arrest and his imprisonment at Gaëta. Messages were scarce until his release at the close of 1870. In the course of 1871 Mazzini continued to follow Swinburne from afar in the midst of his many activities in Switzerland and at Pisa. The news of his death overwhelmed Swinburne in March 1872. ' You will see by to-day's papers that I have lost the man whom I most loved and honoured of all men on earth.'[1]

What is to be emphasized is that, even when away from England, Mazzini was always careful to give Swinburne the impression that he watched him attentively. When he wrote to common friends in England there was always a message for ' the Poet '. ' Do write yourself to Swinburne that I am ill, *cannot* write, but read, mark each step of his, feel grateful and admiring and touched ' (December 3, 1867). ' You ought to write one note of thanks and encouragement to Swinburne. I shall, most likely ' (May 13, 1868). Mazzini insisted on having reports of the poet's health sent to him by his medical attendant, Dr. Bird. In March 1869 he acknowledged the manuscript dedication of *Songs before Sunrise* by the following sentence : ' The last beautiful lines[2] will strengthen, if there be need, the firmness of my actual purpose ; they must be prophetic or a branding reproach.' How well calculated those words were to fill Swinburne with pride and inspiration will be seen from his own comments : ' If there be need—par exemple ! Anyhow you see my poetry is " art

---

[1] To his mother, 12 March, 1872.
[2] ' Yea, even she as at first ... Shall cast down, shall build up, shall bring home. ...
First name of the world's names, Rome.'

and part " in the immediate action of the republic,
having given this feeling at so practical a minute to
the leader.'

For it seems that, in spite of obvious difficulties,
Mazzini read Swinburne's riddle aright and discerned the mainsprings of his personality. This in-
curable romantic and idealist may have been unable to
create and rule a nation ; we know that in the field
of politics he was strangely mistaken. But we also
know that he possessed the gift of galvanizing individual energies ; unable as he seems to have been to
organize a great collectivity, he had no difficulty in
persuading one man to go to his death. Swinburne
was probably wrong when he wrote : ' He is born
king and chief and leader of men, he is clearly the man
to create a nation—to bid the dead bones live and
rise.' But he expressed a reality when he added:
' I know, now I have seen him, what I guessed before : whenever he has said to anyone " Go and be
killed because I tell you " they have gone and been
killed because he told them. Who wouldn't I should
like to know ? ' It was not long before Swinburne
fell under the magnetic spell[1] : ' You know they say
that when Mirabeau was dying a young fellow with
healthy blood came and asked if it could not be trans-
fused into *his* veins out of his own—so as to restore
life *there* by degrees as it was exhausted *here*. I wish
it were true and I might (if necessary—I don't want to
die or live superfluously) do that office for a greater
and better than Mirabeau. But he wants no alien

---

[1] ' Swinburne speaks of Mazzini's ' immense magnetic power' which he feels oper-
ating upon him' (Rossetti Papers, 7 May, 1867). As a token of friendship Mazzini
gave Swinburne a ' beautiful white angora with a tabby tail' (Rossetti Papers,
19 September, 1869). Swinburne was fond of all animals, especially cats and snakes.

blood—his spirit supports him and will ' (December 24, 1867).

Yet in spite of, or perhaps owing to, this immense worship and admiration, which went so far as to express themselves in strictly theological terms (the parallel between Mazzini and Christ is often to be found, implied or expressed, in the poems and correspondence) it was extremely difficult for the Chief to assume a spiritual leadership over Swinburne. First it was essential that the poet should not be disappointed in his expectations, and those were high indeed. Mazzini's personality was however equal to the task. But it was also essential to realize that whatever influence Mazzini might gain had to be limited to a certain field—that of political poetry and propaganda. Had Mazzini attempted to reform Swinburne's morals and private life, the latent powers of revolt would have been reawakened in the poet, and everything put in jeopardy. This Mazzini, although he thoroughly disapproved of some of the sources of Swinburne's inspiration (' I wish very much that he would write something . . . giving up the absurd immoral French art for art's sake's system '), fully understood and did not infringe the limits it would have been dangerous to cross. When the photographs of Swinburne and the Menken were on sale in the shop windows and the rumour circulated that ' Swinburne was going to act on the stage ', Mazzini refused to interfere : ' No, I did not ask Swinburne about the stage or the double photograph ; I really cannot play the part of spiritual father to him except when he himself offers means and opportunity.' Another difficulty arose precisely from the fact that Swinburne's long cherished dogma of Art for Art's sake, which he had publicly defended, was in open conflict with the composition of a book of ' Lyrics of the Crusade ' (' Tout ce qui est utile est laid '—Th. Gautier). From this perhaps more than from anything else Swinburne the artist shrank : ' All Mazzini wants is that I should dedicate and consecrate my writing power to do good and serve others exclusively ; which I can't. If I tried I should lose my faculty of verse even. When I can I do ; witness my last book ' (to his Mother, May 7, 1867). All those obstacles Mazzini, through his tact and personality, overcame : during the years 1867–70 Swinburne devoted the best of his time and powers to the composition of political poems ; he gave up his 'aesthetic ' novel *Lesbia Brandon*, then in course of composition, and interrupted or slackened considerably the writing of erotic verse. There is in the history of poetry no more striking or successful instance of a complete and clear-cut transformation in the inspiration of an artist.

It seems therefore that Mme. Galimberti's conclusion in her interesting review of the letters of Mazzini (' il grande occhio bruno che leggera in fondo alle anime, con tanta sicurezza, s'era ingannato '—*Giornale di Genova*, 10 March 1927) cannot be accepted. On one point, perhaps, was Mazzini mistaken : he believed that Swinburne was to die soon (' he will not last more than one or two years '—June 1870. ' My faith in his improvement is very weak '—February 1871). Hence an occasional harshness in some of his comments : ' I wish very much that he would, before vanishing, write something . . .' (January 1869). He would probably have been surprised had he been told that Swinburne would survive him by nearly forty years. But there can be no doubt that ' the Poet ' was then drinking himself to death, and the way in which for about twenty years Swinburne sustained the strain of his many activities and vices is a puzzle to modern doctors.[1] On the contrary, the depth and insight of Mazzini's remarks are exceptional for one who had but a recent knowledge of the ' subject ' and had so many other preoccupations on his mind. He wrote to Mrs. Taylor in April 1867 : ' Between blind worshippers and blind revilers he will remain what he is ', a pregnant analysis of the lack of equilibrium then obvious in Swinburne's state of mind. He also had the intuition that the best way of effecting a lasting change in Swinburne was to get a woman to take moral and perhaps physical charge of him : ' He might be transformed but only by some man or woman—better a woman of course—who would like him very much and assert at the same time a moral superiority on him ' (April 1867). It seems that Mazzini went as far as to encourage an intimate friendship between Swinburne and Emilia Venturi, to whom he was bound by bonds of such a mysteriously close friendship : ' I should like a certain degree of intercourse between you and him : it might do good, in your sense, to him ' (June 1867). ' Swinburne wants to see you as soon as you are in London and speaks of you often as of a chosen sister and as an exceptional woman ' (April 1868). About the same time other friends of Swinburne were endeavouring to entangle him in a liaison with the notorious Adah Menken. The

[1] See Dr. H. Baruk's review of my *Jeunesse de Swinburne* in *L'Hygiène Mentale*, December 1, 1930.

two attempts were widely different, but they sprang
from the same pious motives and both met, it seems,
with moderate success.

It remains to point out that the benefit and influence
of the intercourse between Swinburne and Mazzini
was not entirely one-sided. True, many things re-
pelled the Italian doctrinaire in the poet's personality :
his aggressive atheism, the sensuous tendencies of his
poetry, etc. True, he was sometimes bewildered by
Swinburne's wild enthusiasm, the unintelligible way
in which he read out his poems (' He talked about art
and poets, recited—almost unintelligibly for me—
Siena and *La Pia* '—April 1868). But we feel that
Mazzini's instinctive mistrust soon yielded to a feeling
of genuine affection. For at times he must have felt not
a little proud, if not of the praise bestowed on him
(' Who am I whom he praises ? '), at least of the work
he had suggested. In his bitter days of old age, ill
health and disillusion he had been able to inspire a
poet, his Poet, and what a lyrist that was, he cannot but
have realized. Sometimes Mazzini must have felt
obscurely that his own province was spiritual propaganda in Italy and chiefly abroad, rather than action in
the field : to have won Swinburne to his side was for
the tireless journalist and lecturer no mean achievement. Perhaps, in hours of pain and defeat, when the
long-deferred hopes seemed further away than ever,
the old idealist and conspirator, who was also at heart
a poet, felt that his ' visioned Rome of the People '
might never come true ; but that it had and would
preserve an ideal existence, being now safely en-
shrined in the purest verse of *Songs before Sunrise*.

What passed between the two men during those

long frequent interviews they had together ? We suspect that they did not speak of Italy and politics only : Mazzini was a critic of Dante as well as a patriot, an artist as well as an apostle, which only served to increase his hold over Swinburne. But we shall never know exactly, as Swinburne, acting on the Chief's instruction, was extremely reticent ; Mazzini was fond of wrapping the simplest things in an atmosphere of mystery. It is indeed safest to turn to the poems of Swinburne themselves, if we want to form an idea of what he learnt from Mazzini and to what extent he accepted or rejected his doctrine.

It is a common attitude to treat the political basis on which Swinburne's Songs of Liberty rest apologetically ; to admit freely that he was entirely mistaken, as was proved by the course of later events ; to confess that ' this liberty was largely a chimera, a vain fancy of the poet's own unselfish imagination '. Even Mr. Welby is reduced to plead that although Swinburne's realization of Freedom was wrong in individual cases, yet his praise of Freedom in the abstract remains admirable. However, if the reader is to understand these poems he should be aware that Swinburne's views on European affairs between 1867 and 1870 (*not* before or after those dates) form a coherent whole ; that they do not represent the disconnected ravings of a fevered brain, but that they were shared, rightly or wrongly, by a group of thinkers and patriots. What he added to those opinions was a superstructure of ideas and sentiments which did not materially affect them.

When in October 1866 Swinburne turned from the worship of Sappho and Dolores to the cause of Italian Unity, it was high time for him to draw on a source of inspiration which he had since 1860 sorely neglected. ' Gabriel and his followers in art ' (and perhaps also his own personal inclination) had so far succeeded in ' frightening him from speaking out ', that he had left such splendid lyric opportunities as Garibaldi's conquest of Sicily and Naples and the battle of Aspromonte slip without writing even an ode or a song. The few political allusions in the *Poems and Ballads* of 1866 (*A Song in Time of Order, of Revolution, To V. Hugo*) are highly disappointing. Now it was rather late in the day : Italian Unity was almost achieved though through means and men that Swinburne and Mazzini equally hated. In true Mazzinian fashion Swinburne despised ' the Savoyard ' (Victor Emmanuel) and asserted that ' If that satellite of a dead dog Victor Emmanuel goes to Rome, I shall be furious, and would kiss the toes of a priest who would poison him in a wafer.' It is no use saying that in the Italian cause Swinburne was chiefly attracted by the principle of nationalities ; to him, as to Mazzini, Italy and Democracy were inseparable ; the new nation must be a republic, free from kings or priests, or must not be at all. Yet although practically the whole of Italy had now (October 1866) passed under the rule of the Piedmont Monarchy, there was one exception, one issue which had not been solved and which made Swinburne's poems possible : thanks partly to Napoleon's intervention, Rome was still in the hands of the Pope. The attention of all patriots was of course focussed on the town which could not but become the capital of the new state. But to Mazzini and his friends the question was whether the king would sooner or later transfer his residence from Florence to

Rome, or whether the ' Universal Republican Alliance ' founded by the Italian Patriot in 1866 would succeed in fomenting a revolution, which would establish on the banks of the Tiber a democratic Republic whose example would spread like fire through a unified Italy. To all monarchists, catholics and republicans, Rome had become an *idée fixe*. Its name recurs ever and again in Swinburne's *Songs*, which are not at all an epic of the Risorgimento but a series of manifestoes and appeals to the republican Soul of the Eternal City. This is also why when, in December 1869, Swinburne bethought himself of a title for his collected poems he chose the rather disconcerting one of *Songs before Sunrise*. The obvious objection is that they should more accurately have been called *Songs after Sunset* ; all the more so as when the book appeared in 1871 everything was practically settled. But this objection entirely overlooks the fact that all true Mazzinians were still hoping against hope that Republican Rome would shake the domination of King and Pope. In their eyes what had been achieved towards Italian Unity was as nothing ; the true sunrise had not yet begun ; but when it did, the burning sun of Freedom would light up first the Roman hills, then the whole of Italy, then the limitless ' Republic of a world made white'. It was only when in August 1870, after months of fruitless agitation in Switzerland and Italy to over-throw the king, Mazzini was arrested and imprisoned at Gaëta, that all hope of ever seeing the gorgeous sunrise began to fade away. By that date most of Swinburne's *Songs* were written and even printed, and, but for unforeseen circumstances, would have been published.

It does not follow that Swinburne's volume suffers from having been begun so late. What it may have lost in breadth and variety, it gains in unity and concentration : in the Italian poems a few rare facts, connected by a constant preoccupation, make for clarity of outline and strength of purpose. Historically, there is no doubt that the book came out too late ; from an artistic point of view the thing is not perhaps to be regretted.

When, at the end of 1866, Swinburne took up the pen with an irrepressible urge to write on Italy and Mazzini, the circumstances were not however encouraging. Venetia had indeed been freed, but Italy was forced to accept it from the hands of Napoleon III, and what was worse the patriots had been shamefully defeated at Custozza and Lissa. However, Swinburne undertook with commendable courage to write ' a little gratulatory song on Venice '. He felt the difficulty, and with poetic diplomacy proceeded to explain that the Prussians would not have conquered at Sadowa had it not been for the unhappy efforts of the Italian army. Thus, he proceeds, Austria was defeated if not exactly ' by ' the Italians, at least ' through ' their hands. The distinction is subtle and the passage worth quoting :

> Their swords at least that stemmed half Austria's tide
>   Bade all its bulk divide ;
> Else, though fate bade them for a breath's space fall,
>   She had not fallen at all.
> Not by their hands they made time's promise true,
>   Not by their hands, but through.
> Nor on Custozza ran their blood to waste . . .

This is all very well, but, since Austria's strength was

equally divided, how is it that it was not the Germans
who fell and the true patriots who conquered ? Swinburne leaves the point unanswered, but he must have
realized how difficult it was to write a song of triumph
in that half apologetic strain. From the original
design of a ' gratulatory song ' on Venice ' free of
things dead and done ' the poem was enlarged so as
to cover a Shelleyan allegory (in which Swinburne was
beset by reminiscences from his poem of 1857, *The
Temple of Janus*), an apology of tyrannicide and the
Martyrs of the Cause (including Pisacane, Agesilao
Milano, and Felice Orsini), a fiery praise of Garibaldi
whose ' sacred blood is fragrant still Upon the bitter
Hill ' (Aspromonte), and of Mazzini, an invective
against fallen Austria, a hymn to the tri-coloured flag
and a final invocation to Republican Rome. The poem
begun in October 1866, was started afresh in November and concluded in the course of February 1867.
But it is probable that, after it was read to the Chief
on March 30, it underwent additions and modifications
which delayed for a few days its being sent to press
(April 30th). At least the stress laid on the ' limitless
Republic ' and the ' Capitolian Rome ', and the sharp
rebuke given not only to France, but also to the
English flag :

> Let England's, if it float not for men free,
>   Fall, and forget the sea . . .

point to a direct Mazzinian influence, which could not
have exerted itself before the beginning of April.

The *Song*, published at the time when Lord Derby
and Disraeli, who were rather averse to Italian Unity,
had just taken office, was not a success ; the reviews

proved few and brief ; Mazzini complained of what
he called ' la conspiration du silence ' ; after *Poems
and Ballads* it frankly disappointed Swinburne's
admirers . . . and enemies. The larger part of the
edition was still unsold in 1876, and the book was not
yet out of print at the end of the century. Nor have
modern critics relented. Edmund Gosse considered
the *Song* as a ' verbose manifesto, vociferous and yet
vague '. While allowing that the opening lines are a
failure and recognizing that the metre has a not
unintentional (indeed sometimes very effective) monotony, it is time to point out that Swinburne's poem
contains one sublime passage : the comparison of
Mazzini nursing the newborn Italian nation which
suddenly grows and becomes his mother, with St.
Christopher carrying Christ across the flood :

>   . . . for he
> Father of Italy
> Upbore in holy hands the babe new-born
> Through loss and sorrow and scorn,
> Of no man led, of many men reviled ;
> Till lo, the new-born child
> Gone from between his hands, and in its place,
> Lo, the fair mother's face . . .
> As in faith's hoariest histories men read
> The strong man bore at need
> Through roaring rapids, when all heaven was wild,
> The likeness of a child
> That still waxed greater and heavier as he trod,
> And altered, and was God.

When one considers that this grand passage is
immediately followed by a solid verse-paragraph of
some 230 lines and that Swinburne succeeds in keeping
that interminable period afloat through sheer magic

of irresistible rhythm and power of lyric breath (a feat unequalled and unapproached even by Milton and Shelley) one does not see very well how historians of English poetry can in future afford to ignore *A Song of Italy.*

It seems that after this great lyrical effort Swinburne expected some rest : but Mazzini would not hear of it. He had demanded ' a series of Lyrics for the Crusade ' ; the poet could not be let off so lightly, and he was soon to find out that Italy could be a deity as cruel and insatiable as Dolores. In fact it was this necessity of constant service, heedless of actual results and hopeless of any ulterior reward or period of rest, which, being repeatedly preached by Mazzini, became one of the finest themes of the *Songs.* Swinburne realized that he must give up, or at least postpone, most of the work he had in hand, and, more particularly, his long cherished scheme of a poem on Tristram and a sequel to his *Chastelard.* It is interesting to note how he tried to adapt his previous work to new circumstances : in the course of 1867 he introduced in his unfinished novel, *Lesbia Brandon,* two new characters who were not of course part of the original plot : the one, an Italian patriot, Attilo Mariani, who preaches that it is ' an inconceivable honour to die for Italy ', who is ' ready to forge, murder, betray for the Cause ' and ' wants all to give all they have ', but is called in the papers ' assassin and conspirator ' and refrains from going back to Italy because ' there is hardly room for a general in Caprera '—(a typical trait illustrative of the bickerings between Garibaldi and the Chief)—is but a slightly modified portrait of Mazzini. The other character, a French exile somewhat preposterously called Pierre Sadier, though ' sincere, clean and brave ' and possessed of ' a hatred of treason, lie, and perjury ', lacks the warm national patriotism of Mazzini, as he belongs to a nation whose unity was achieved ages ago ; he may stand for a picture of Louis Blanc, Armand Barbès or some other French exile whom Swinburne met at Blind's. Sadier's conceptions are more abstract and universal, less ' municipal ' than those of Mariani, but he is no less disinterested. Mariani, just before his death, said that ' Italy could do without him '. Pierre Sadier, as sincere a man, could not have said ' La France se passera bien de moi maintenant '. This marks the main difference between two perfect patriots. Mariani had ' broken his soul at the feet of Italy ' as ' Magdalen the alabaster box at the feet of Christ '.

But Swinburne soon found that it was no use, that he could not reconcile Mazzini and ' l'art pour l'art ', and he gave up *Lesbia Brandon*. The Spring and Summer of 1867 were not however likely to stimulate the republican Muse. Nothing did happen. The Conference of London seemed to establish the status quo for a long time. Pius IX announced that he would soon summon an Oecumenical Council. Mazzini's plots in the Pontifical States were doomed to failure. Was Swinburne really too late ? Was the new Pindar to remain mute for lack of any Olympic games ? In disgust he turned to a poem of a general, uncompromising character : ' I am writing—I add it to fill up —a poem on Siena of a discursive sort ' (17 September 1867). *Siena* (which was not completed and published till April 1868) is an extremely beautiful and serene piece of work in which Swinburne has perhaps achieved his loveliest cadences. An unwonted calm and restraint give it a sort of classical beauty. The poet reveals himself a consummate artist by blending in a strange symphony the favourite themes of his conflicting inspirations : religious and anti-religious (Saint Catherine, Christ, the Church), Greek (the three Graces) and political. The Mazzinian influence is obvious, as in the verse in which it is asserted that ' God and the People should be one '. But it is all extremely vague, it is about the past, not the present ; it is hardly calculated to stir men's hearts, but rather to lull them to sleep. However one verse is interesting from the biographical point of view—for in it we see Swinburne becoming fully conscious of his new function as poet of liberty and asserting that long service has qualified him for the job :

> Me consecrated, if I might,
>   To praise thee, or to love at least,
> O mother of all men's dear delight,
>   Thou madest a choral-souled boy-priest,
> Before my lips had leave to sing,
> Or my hands hardly strength to cling
> About the intolerable tree
> Whereto they had nailed my heart and thee
> And said, ' Let be '.

However, just about this time, things were beginning to hum. It was rumoured that Garibaldi was on the point of resuming his everlasting march on Rome. At the beginning of September he went over to Geneva as president of the Peace Congress, which Hugo later attended ; he was acclaimed as an international hero ; while in the chair he pronounced words which sent a thrill through the world : ' It is our duty to go to

Rome and we shall soon go.'   On his return to Italy
he was received everywhere with fiery enthusiasm, and
marched towards the Roman frontier.   Everybody
expected something decisive to happen, when Rattazzi had Garibaldi arrested and shipped off to Caprera (24 September, 1867).   But Swinburne would not
be defrauded of his chance of a poem ; out of those
great hopes suddenly disappointed he made up the
Halt before Rome, which was dashed off in a few days
and sent to the *Fortnightly Review* (to which Swinburne,
through Joseph Knight, had been introduced) [1] :

> Is it so, that the sword is broken,
>   Our sword, that was half-way drawn ?

bitterly asked Swinburne, with something like Mazzinian impatience, of the ' netted lion ' Garibaldi.
Alas ! lo and behold ! those few insignificant facts
were but the prelude of greater events : On October 21
the brothers Cairoli with seventy-five patriots were
defeated and killed a short distance from Rome ; on
the 22nd Rattazzi resigned ; on the 23rd Garibaldi,
who had escaped from Caprera, crossed the frontier at
Passo Covese and on the 29th seized Monterotondo.
But a French corps was hurried from Toulon under
de Failly, landed at Civita Vecchia and on November 3rd, at Mentana, met Garibaldi who was defeated
and captured : the *chassepots* ' had worked wonders '.
What could Swinburne do ? All that was to be said
was already embodied in the *Halt before Rome* which
the *Fortnightly* had just published (November 1st).
Here was a great opportunity wasted.   After being so

---

[1] ' I have written a poem on this check of Garibaldi's expedition which (the poem,
not the check) pleases me more than most things I have done '. (To Powell, October,
1867.)

late, Swinburne had been too early ; he had shot his
bolt too soon. And this is how the poet, who was
later to celebrate the first, second, and third anniver-
saries of Mentana, failed to commemorate the event
proper. [1]

However, this Garibaldian poem, although it had
been something of a false start, had given Swinburne
the impulse he needed to launch on a sustained enterprise ; for, in spite of Mazzini's pressing requests, he
was still hesitating on the border-line between aesthe-
ticism and political poetry. Since *A Song of Italy*, he
had written practically nothing. But now he had, with
Garibaldi, crossed the Rubicon. His mind was made
up ; he was going to write the book Mazzini wanted.
On October 6th, 1867 he wrote to W. M. Rossetti :

I may tell you between ourselves that I have now done
enough to enable me to speak with some hope of a design which
must come either to nothing or to much—much (that is) for
me, if I may so speak of my own aims and achievements. I
think I may some time accomplish a book of political and
national poems as complete and coherent in its way as the
Châtiments or Drum Taps. This, as you know, Mazzini
asked me to attempt—' for us ', as he said. Phantoms and
skeletons of national songs I have for some time seen floating in
the future before me in plenty, but now I have also done one or
two into words and so embodied them that I think they will
turn out in good marching order—*des soldats viables !* This
week I have worked off one on the news of Garibaldi's arrest
which I am tempted to think my best lyric ever written ;
although as a rule I always feel discouraged at first with any
work I have strongly desired and laboured to do well for any
outer reason such as moves one in these matters. But this time
I am thus far satisfied ; and I am hopeful that it will seriously
please Mazzini—rather confident that it must. I thought of

[1] One should also mention that Swinburne was now in poor health, and in the
midst of his *liaison* with Adah Menken (see below). He seems for a short time to
have neglected the development of Italian affairs.

sending you a sample, but will wait till we meet. It is all up with our monarchico-constitutional Savoyard friends this time I suspect. There is I think room for a book of songs of the European revolution, and, if sung as thoroughly as Hugo or as Whitman would sing them, they ought to ring for some time to some distance of echo. The only fear is that one may be disabled by one's desire—made impotent by excess of strain.

During the three years that followed he worked steadily at his book of poems, but always leisurely ; he was aware that work of the kind he had undertaken, arising as it did from purely local events and happenings, must needs be of the very highest quality if it is to survive and prove of general interest to all ; to the remonstances of his friends who urged him to publish his book as soon as possible, he replied that ' work of this sort cannot be finished off to order ' (January 1869). He was right, but his friends were not quite wrong.

During the last months of 1867 and in the course of 1868 he composed several *Songs* (*A Watch in the Night*, *The Litany of Nations*, *The Song of the Standard*, *Blessed Among Women*—on the death of the brothers Cairoli, etc.) but none of the highest order. It was also then that he wrote *Mentana : first anniversary*, in which he tried, in a rather ineffective manner, to make amends for the lost opportunity of the preceding year.

In 1869 he began to compose some of the best of his Italian songs. The *Dedication* of the unfinished volume was sent to Mazzini as early as March and gladdened the heart of the sick patriot. It asserted, in no doubtful terms, the share Mazzini had had in the poet's inspiration :

> Take, since you bade it should bear,
>   These of the seed of your sowing . . .
> That the dew of your word kept growing . . .

Super Flumina Babylonis, Christmas Antiphones, A New Year's Message and several others also date from the same year, but Swinburne refrained from printing most of them at once in order to keep them fresh against the publication of a complete volume. It was not until the end of 1869 (December 2) that he made up his mind about the title of his future collection :

I must settle on a name for my progressing book ; ' Songs of the Republic ' is generally liked, and seems to myself presumpt-uous for any man but Hugo to take by way of title ; ' Songs of the Crusade ', Mazzini's proposed name, is ambiguous and suggests by derivation the Galilean gallows. I think of calling them ' Songs before Sunrise ' ; will you tell me how you like that or ' before Dawn ' or ' Morning ' ? (Unpublished letter to W. M. Rossetti.)

1870 was Swinburne's *Annus Mirabilis* ; it saw the completion of the greatest poems of the book ; the sun of his inspiration had risen at last and was now flooding like an unexpected meteor the darkened sky of European politics : *Tiresias, The Hymn of Man, Hertha* were all finished in that year, though the subject of *Tiresias* had been conceived long ago— as early as April 17, 1868 he wrote to G. Powell :

I have such a subject before me, untouched—Tiresias at the grave of Antigone—i.e. (understand) Dante at the grave of Italia. I do not say the living heir and successor of Dante as a patriot, for *he* sees her slowly but hopefully rising, tho' with pain and shame and labour. My beloved chief is still with us, very ill and indomitable, and sad and kind as ever. I have worked much at *his* book since we met.

But it was not until August 1870 that he made up his mind to ' touch ' the subject. By that time the con-ception had been slightly modified, and the symbolism had become more complicated, so that *Tiresias* stands not only for Dante, but also for Mazzini and Michael-Angelo. On the 28th Swinburne wrote to W. M. Rossetti :

I am writing a poem on Tiresias at the grave of Antigone—the living buried woman representing liberty in the abstract (or more especially as incarnate in Italy—but I always identify the two, as it were, in this book) during the years while ' the Earth cried, where art thou ? '. And the prophet, any patriot or free-thinker you will from Dante to Mazzini ; but it is difficult clearly and comprehensibly to combine without confusing the type and the antitype, especially as the Theban story with its infinite suggestions and significances fairly carries me away like a wave, forgetful for the time of symbol and modern application. I, like Arnold's Callicles, ' ever loved the Theban story well '. But I think to make something of it.

Once again Swinburne had here combined with great cunning the Greek or classical motif with the modern or political one. In spite of the truly admirable diction of the first part it is the second which must retain our attention. For towards the close Swinburne introduces Mazzini himself as an actor, and renders in convincing terms the magnetic power allied with an appearance of supreme benignity which seems to have made up the unique charm of the patriot :

> The living spirit, the good gift of grace,
>   The faith which takes of its own blood to give
>   That the dead veins of buried hope may live,
> Came on her sleeping, face to naked face,
>   And from a soul more sweet than all the south
>   Breathed love upon her sealed and breathless mouth.

It is to be noted that this poem, one of the latest of the collection, ends in a cry not of triumph, but of despairing doubt : ' Art thou dead, Italy ? ' A few days before, Mazzini had been arrested and imprisoned in Gaëta.

The Hymn of Man is one of the few poems in Songs before Sunrise which is closely connected with one precise historical fact ; the circumstances, which have never been fully stated and are essential to the understanding of the piece, deserve to be summarized:

In December 1869 the Oecumenical Council, which Pius IX had been preparing ever since 1867, met. Everybody knew that it would be asked to adopt, together with the dogma of infallibility, the famous syllabus which condemned in the most intolerant terms the liberal doctrines of the age ; and these two measures were duly passed a few months later. For the Pope Swinburne entertained a fierce hatred only comparable to that he felt for Napoleon III ; he saw in him not only an adversary, but a renegade who had drawn back from his liberal manifestations of 1846–48, when even Mazzini had been deceived into congratulating him. In the Halt before Rome he had already denounced the monster

> who hath claws as a vulture,
> Plumage and beak as a dove.

And he depicted him in the midst of his Council as one whose hands

> with sharp edge tools oecumenical
> The leprous carcases of creeds dissect.

Now in October 1869 the Italian Radical Ricciardi decided to hold at Naples an anti-Catholic Council which would sit at the same time as the Roman one,

and would among other transactions read and publish
letters and manifestoes from all sympathizers who
were unable to attend ; Vacquerie's paper *Le Rappel*
gave wide publicity to the scheme. Michelet's and
Quinet's replies were made public and Swinburne and
W. M. Rossetti decided to send a letter of sympathy
to Ricciardi. This epistle was duly drafted by W. M.
Rossetti, modified and enlarged by Swinburne, then
turned into Italian by his friend and dispatched
(November 1869). Here is the central passage of this
manifesto which has never been published. The first
paragraph was written by Rossetti, but the second is
entirely Swinburne's and throws light on his religious
and political conceptions at the time :

' A poor old Italian Man ' (as our illustrious Carlyle phrases
it) is congregating at Rome the powers of darkness. Another
Italian—one long known and proved worthy of that great name
—is doing his best to flash upon Rome some ray of light out of
Naples, and to turn these powers into visible impotences. May
the endeavour be successful in proportion as it is admirable.
The Liberty we believe in is one and indivisible : without
free thought there can be no free life. That democracy of the
spirit without which the body, personal or social, can enjoy but a
false freedom, must, by the very law of its being, confront a
man-made theocracy to destroy it. Ideal or actual, the Church
or priests, and the Republic, are natural and internecine enemies.
Freedom, which comes by the law of the life of man—flame of
his spirit, root and heart and blood and muscle of his manhood—
can take no truce with the creeds or miscreeds which inflict, not
(as some kings of our past) upon the flesh, but upon the souls of
men, the hideous and twofold penalty of blindness and eviration.
She expects no non-natural message from above or from
without ; but only that which comes from within—faith,
born of man, in man, which passes in contagious revelation
from spirit again to spirit without authority and without sign.
Truth, Right, Freedom are self-sufficing, and claim service
from the soul that suffices to itself.

The Anti-Council duly met in December, but it seems that the Italian and French members soon began to quarrel. The authorities, under the pretext that the French Republic had been acclaimed, suppressed and dispersed this Congress which savoured not a little of parody. 'Heaven preserve us from "regalantuomini"!' exclaimed Swinburne indignantly when he heard the news. He vainly tried to get his manifesto printed in England, in February 1870 ; but, since prose was of no avail, he hastened the composition of a *Hymn* which he had begun a few weeks earlier and which in his mind was to have been read before the Anti-Catholic Council ; this was the *Hymn of Man* :

> I have in my head a sort of Hymn for this Congress—as it were a ' Te Hominem Laudamus' to sing the human triumph over ' things '—the opposing forces of life and nature—and over the God of his own creation, till he attains truth, self-sufficience and freedom. It might end somehow thus with a cry of triumph over the decadence of a receding Deity :
> ' And the love-song of earth as thou diest sounds over the graves of her kings
> Glory to Man in the highest ! for man is the master of things '.

The poem took its final shape[1] in August 1870 when the councils of both Ricciardi and Pius were things of the past. But one should keep in mind when reading the *Hymn of Man*, with its fierce antitheism and its glorification of humanity, in what circumstances it was first conceived : it is not, as is too often supposed, a tide of vague and purposeless rhetoric. It was composed for a precise occasion ; it was written

[1] In its first form it was finished by February 5, 1870 : ' I have written a modern companion in arms and metre to my *Hymn to Proserpine* called *Hymn of Man* (during the Session in Rome of the Oecumenical Council), by the side of which *Queen Mab* is as it were an archdeacon's charge and my own previous blasphemies are models of catholic devotion '. (Letter to Powell.)

for Ricciardi's Congress ; it is, in its twofold aspect, destructive and constructive, a protest and a declaration of faith.

With the *Hymn of Man*, however, the cause of Italian Unity recedes into the background, and we are only concerned with general problems of a metaphysical character. *Hertha* is the most outstanding instance of poems of this type, which Swinburne introduced in his book so as to give a wider appeal and value to what might have been considered as the work of a partisan. Here, the only allusion to Italy is to be found in the line

> Green leaves of thy labour, white flowers of thy thought, and
> red fruit of thy death . . .

a harmless reference to the national flag. *Hertha* was begun towards the end of 1869 and finished before the middle of January 1870. We know that Swinburne set great store by this poem and even claimed that there was ' a good deal of clarified thought ' condensed in it. If we read it in the hope of discovering an original system we shall be disappointed. Swinburne starts from an essentially Mazzinian doctrine : ' Humanity is not an aggregation of individuals but a Collective Being . . . Humanity is a man who lives and works for men . . . The best Interpreter between individual man and God is Humanity ' (Mazzini's *Credo*, 1867). But to this conception, already introduced in the *Hymn of Man*, and so common in the nineteenth century that it can easily be traced back to Auguste Comte and even further, he has added various inspirations derived from his wide reading : Cleanthes' Hymn to God, Blake, Emily Bronte, Tennyson's

Higher Pantheism, Whitman, Schopenhauer.[1] Indeed, to strengthen the essential tendency which is at the root of the poem Swinburne went further—even to the pantheistic poetry of the East which he mentions in his essay on Blake : ' Swinburne is excessively enthusiastic about the Mahabharata which he has been looking at in a French translation under the auspices of Bendyshe' (*Rossetti Papers*, 12 January, 1869). And of course we must recognize in the background the great Darwinian ideas of evolution which were agitating the age. Swinburne's great merit is to have combined and vulgarized (or as he says ' clarified ') those scientific and sentimental conceptions, by a direct appeal to feeling and imagination. He cleverly speaks in the name of Hertha (a Germanic deity to whom his friend Powell, who had an interest in Northern religions, may have introduced him) by which he means, the earth considered as an active, living and growing force, or, as he himself puts it, ' the vital principle of matter '. It is this spiritual principle and no longer, as in the *Hymn of Man*, the poet himself, who demands the destruction of the ' false gods '. This makes the tremendous antitheism of such lines as

God trembles in heaven and his angels are white with the terror of God. . . .

more acceptable ; but this antitheism, worthy of the Marquis de Sade, is there all the same, witness the

---

[1] ' I am very much struck by finding in Wagner a disciple in matter of thought of A. Schopenhauer. I read some extracts from his works and a condensed summary of his life and views given in a review of Fouché de Careil's book on the subject (cited he.e [in Gasperini's *Wagner*] by Gasperini) now years ago which impressed me unforgettably with their beautiful force, clearness and fearless depth of truth. I quite understand their power upon the kindred spirit of a great artist, as clear-sighted, straight minded and heroic in his own line of spiritual work ' (To Powell, October 21, 1869).

supplementary stanza which Mr. Wise has printed on page 87 of his *Swinburne Library Catalogue*.

According to Swinburne himself (letter to W. M. Rossetti, 8 January 1870) the essential thought of the poem is that Hertha, the principle of growth, ' prefers liberty to bondage, Mazzini to Buonaparte ' and is a ' good republican ' because in liberty only can man's soul reach its full stature and growth :

> I bid you but be,
>   I have need not of prayer ;
> I have need of you free
>   As your mouths of mine air
> That my heart may grow greater within me, beholding the
>   fruits of me fair.

' This much ', adds Swinburne, ' I think may be reasonably supposed and said, without incurring the (to me) most hateful charge of optimism—a Creed which I despise as much as ever did Voltaire.'

It seems to me that Swinburne's triumph lies rather in having made of the scientific law of evolution a spiritual necessity ; the natural compulsion to grow, live and change, apart from any idea of perfection or progress of the species, has never been rendered in a finer or more powerful way than in this stanza :

> Though sore be my burden,
>   And more than ye know,
> And my growth have no guerdon
>   But only to grow,
> Yet I fail not of growing for lightnings above me or deathworms
>   below.

In that sense, *Hertha* is a great philosophic poem. The *Songs* also include several pieces in which the

Mazzinian influence, although never quite absent, is far less noticeable. Such are the *Songs* dealing with countries other than Italy, more particularly France[1]. Swinburne's views are here violently coloured by his fierce hatred of Napoleon III, which is to a great extent to be accounted for by his early admiration for the *Châtiments*. I should however like to point out that, although in *A Song in Time of Order* and his anonymous article of 1858 (*Church Imperialism*) he had referred to the Emperor in abusive terms, it was not until 1869 that he chose to take ' Buonaparte ' personally to task in his *Songs*. Mentana passed and its first anniversary as well without Swinburne making more than a casual reference to

> the wrongdoer grown grey with his wrong.

But in the summer of 1869 Swinburne made a prolonged stay in France, and from what he heard or saw in the course of his visits at Vichy and Paris his hate and scorn rose fiercer than ever. From September 1869 to January 1870 he wrote no less than eight sonnets of tremendous vituperation on the now sick Emperor :

> O Death, a little more, and then the worm . . .

More than two years after Mentana he began to discover how great and unforgivable Napoleon's guilt was : ' Looking this morning at my poem just before Mentana [*The Halt before Rome*] I was reminded of the upshot of our hopes then . . . and the rage of the thought exuded into a sonnet.'

---

[1] For the references to England and other countries and in particular the *Appeal* for the condemned Fenians (1867) see below, pp. 230–232, 288.

This was *Mentana : Second Anniversary.*

France was bound to share in most of the insults lavished on her Emperor, as we see in fact in *Quia Multum Amavit* (October-November 1869). But Swinburne never quite lost faith in her ; and it was from this quarter that came the single confirmation of the vain prophecies which Swinburne's Muse poured upon an unheeding world. The Empire fell on September 4, 1870 ; on the 7th Swinburne wrote to W. M. Rossetti : ' I feel inclined to go out and kiss everybody I meet—to roll on the ground and come naked in contact with the earth as Whitman says somewhere . . . I have been in a state of lyric discharge with brief intermission ever since the news came on Monday afternoon. An Ode literally burst out of me . . . Think what this is to me . . . now to see France for the first time.'

When in January 1873 Napoleon died at Chislehurst, Swinburne thought fit to write *The Descent into Hell*, a sequence of sonnets which are in the worst of taste. Less than a year before Mazzini had gone to his grave. Those two men, between whom his verse had accumulated unbridgeable gulfs of hate and unscalable peaks of admiration, stood in a nearer relation than he thought. Both had been dreamers and conspirators ; both, though in a different degree, had loved Italy, and helped in the making of its unity. When reading the *Songs*, though the poet in us may sympathize, the sober historian remembers Racine's line and is forced to the conclusion that neither Napoleon nor Mazzini had deserved

Ni cet excès d'honneur ni cette indignité.

Songs before Sunrise, which had been begun so late and at first composed rather slowly, were nearing completion at the beginning of 1870 ; in May Swinburne was hard at work so as to get his volume published in the Summer, his friends urging him to make haste. As Swinburne had reasons to be dissatisfied with Hotten, his publisher since 1866, he made arrangements for the firm of Ellis to bring out the volume as soon as ready. This was the source of endless difficulties and delays. The quarrel came to a head in June, when Hotten heard that he would not have the *Songs*. He argued that, in August 1866, Swinburne had entered into an agreement with him under which he had a right to publish all Swinburne's works for ever ; he even asserted he possessed a document, written from Lord Lytton's house, to that effect, but was unable to produce it. He threatened legal proceedings, in the hope, it seems, of gaining time and money. Hotten's case, which appears doubtful, was stated by him as follows in a letter to Powell (July 9, 1870) : ' The poet announced thro' me sometime since " Songs of the Republic " to include all his recent political ballads. I duly advertised the work and sold copies in advance, but somebody made him a better offer than mine and now he is preparing to issue the book under the new title " Songs before Sunrise " '. Swinburne flatly denied all this in very energetic terms, but was genuinely afraid of legal complications. The proofs of the *Songs* had been corrected by September, but Ellis, who was nervous too, put off publication first till the autumn, then till the end of the year. However, through the intervention of Howell (who had been a party to the 1866 agreement) and of the Rossettis, some sort of truce was reached. On December 28th Swinburne could write to Lord Morley[1] that although he had been 'rent in twain between two midwives or publishers, . . . all was now settled'. But Ellis would wait till the next publishing season : early in March the book had not appeared ; it came out about April, 1871.

By that date Italian Unity was an accomplished fact ; in May France was to sign the Treaty of Frankfort ; Mazzini, Guarini, Napoleon III, Rattazzi had only a few months to live. The King of Italy might well say in opening the first Roman Parliament ' Our work is done '. *Songs before Sunrise* was a total misnomer ; the amended title, *Songs after Sunset*, is scarcely an epigram. The book in spite of its unique poetic quality was briefly reviewed and attracted little attention. Swinburne far from being, as he would have us believe, the lark whose morning song was the harbinger of ' birds voiced and feathered fairer ' who were to be the true bards of liberty, had proved a love-sick full-throated nightingale whose evening lays were ample consolation for the troubled visions of a summer day.

It has been found necessary to enter into a detailed account of *Songs before Sunrise*, its publication and the purport of its chief poems, because such an analysis alone could give us a key to Swinburne's relations with Mazzini. Moreover this book, standing as it does at a crucial period of its author's career, is part and

---

[1] According to Gosse, Swinburne had been introduced to Morley, then editing the *Fortnightly Review*, by Joseph Knight, and the same authority asserted that Morley believed that Swinburne never knew the authorship of the *Saturday Review* article of August, 1866 ; that Swinburne did is however certain (see my letter to *The Times Literary Supplement*, July 1st, 1926). As early as October 6th, 1866, Hotten knew that Morley had written the article. (*Rossetti Papers.*)

parcel of his intellectual and sentimental life. When he wrote on July 22, 1875 ' my other books are books, that one is myself ' he was not so much asserting in a rhetorical manner the sincerity of his purpose, as merely stating a fact which his biographer has had to recognize.

Far be it from me, however, to assert that from the day he met Mazzini Swinburne turned over a new page and pronounced, in the lay orders of Italian Unity, vows of ascetic abstinence. The transformation he underwent merely affected his inspiration—and that only temporarily. Besides, it would not be impossible to discover, even in *Songs before Sunrise*, some of the features of the sadic sensuality which is so characteristic of *Poems and Ballads*[1], although this is rather exceptional. Be this as it may, it would be a mistake to believe that when on November 2, 1866 he returned from Aberystwyth, where he had daily bathed in stormy seas much to the alarm of the shore keepers, to the ' domestic joys ' of Holmwood, the author of *Poems and Ballads* was at heart a changed man. He had, as we must now consider, preserved in fact the same mental and bodily habits. It was, it seems, in the summer of 1866 that Swinburne, who through the influence of Burton and other friends had long been addicted to *occasional* excesses, began to have recourse to alcoholic stimuli in a more constant way and with serious consequences to his health. He wrote on September 28, 1866 to W. M. Rossetti : ' As to

[1] This sensuality is turned to good purpose in the attitude of complete self-surrender and sacrifice to the cause of Liberty : ' Touch you and taste of you sweet . . . Trodden by chance of your feet ' (*The Oblation*). As already noted above in connection with *The Unhappy Revenge*, Swinburne would have made an excellent martyr. Cf. *A Year's Burden* (' Smite, we will shrink not, strike, we will not bleed ', etc.) Now is the time to quote from Dilke's reminiscences of Swinburne : ' He assured me that he was a great man only because he had been properly flogged at Eton '. (*Life of Sir Charles Dilke*, I, 230).

your screed of friendly counsel concerning Bacchus
. . . I own the soft impeachment—now and then—
notamment when we met last. It's the fault of good
conversation—never so good as tête-à-tête of a night—
and that means Bacchus. " L'ivresse, mes amis, est
un vice vraiment délicieux et dont le véritable phil-
osophe ne saurait se passer " . . .' His mother's
illness in September, then his visit to Wales at the end
of October, and a fresh stay at Holmwood until the
middle of November, tore him away from what
Mazzini called ' the perilous stuff '. But he was back
in town from November 21st to December 12th and
he was promptly laid up with one of those ' bilious
attacks ' (to quote his own words) which will now
become more and more frequent and in which it is easy
to detect, without medical knowledge, the outcome
of habitual drunkenness, though Swinburne would
not admit it and was prone to blame somebody else !
' I have been bedridden or helpless upwards of a week
with another of those damned bilious attacks which
prove the malevolence of the Deity ' (To Powell, 12
December 1866).

He was back in Holmwood to recover by December
25th, and invited his friend W. M. Rossetti to
come down and visit him. Rossetti has left us a
very pleasant record of his visit (January 12th–15th,
1867) : ' Visited Swinburne's father at Holmwood.
Old gentleman kindly, conversible—has seen and
observed. Lady Jane has an attaching air and manner
and seems very agreeable in home life—simple,
dignified and clever. There are three daughters at
home, all sensible and agreeable ; the second with a
handsome sprightly face, and the youngest evidently

talented. The younger son was unwell and has not shown. Swinburne shows well at home, being affectionate in his manner with all the family, and ready in conversing.'

Swinburne returned to London with Rossetti on the 15th in order to work on the Blake designs and manuscripts at the British Museum for his forthcoming essay. But he was soon back in Holmwood where early in February G. E. J. Powell paid him a return visit. The friendship between the two men was fast ripening. Apart from a common taste for a certain kind of literature there existed other ties between them which made intimacy possible and durable. Powell was an old Etonian. He was wealthy, tactful and obliging. Frequent gifts and sundry services made him all the more appreciated. His great fondness for music was not distasteful to the poet. It has been written that Swinburne was ' totally devoid of ear ' and that music ' drove him wild with impatience '. This is an exaggeration. There is a strangely Wagnerian atmosphere about *Laus Veneris* and Baudelaire's criticism may have contributed to open Swinburne's eyes to a new world of beauty ; *Atalanta* owes something of its inspiration, he asserted, to the choruses of Handel ; references to music are not absent from Swinburne's poetry. It seems that Powell initiated him to a certain extent ; on the evening he met Mazzini, he was to have attended with Powell a concert of Mme. Schumann's. He read with interest Edouard Schuré's musical articles in the *Revue des Deux Mondes*. He was enthusiastic about *Lohengrin*[1]

[1] ' I think of going to Munich in the autumn with an old schoolfellow and friend to see the opening of Wagner's theatre and the performance of his as yet unknown opera which is to take four nights to represent and embodies the whole Nibelungen—conceive—if you know the Lohengrin—what a divine delight it would be ' (To

and had for Wagner a genuine admiration. In this respect it is perhaps not uninteresting to quote what Ferdinand Wagner wrote to Powell : ' I always feel happier and better when I have dived into the turbulent waves of Swinburne's gigantic mind. The masterly hand with which he holds the threads that seem to float unconnectedly—as if driven by the wind—and which he always succeeds in tying together when least expected seems to me exactly like Richard Wagner '. There would indeed be, for a more competent critic, an interesting parallel to attempt between the two masters who, about the same period, renovated music and poetry.

Swinburne was of course back in London in the month of March : he seems to have stayed in town till well on in the Summer. On April 10th he received the visit of P. B. Marston, the blind poet, introduced by his father Dr. Westland Marston, the journalist, who had written reviews of Swinburne's works in the *Athenaeum*. In such circumstances the satanic atheist and admirer of the Marquis de Sade could act with almost angelical kindness. He recited some of his poems, encouraged the young man, and later was instrumental in getting Marston's poems accepted by several magazines. Many years later, the recollection of that evening still haunted Marston : ' I remember so well the first evening I came to see you in Dorset Street. It was the 10th April 1867. I testified of it in a sonnet called *To a Day* . . . I had no sleep the night before, and I recited in my room choruses from *Atalanta*.

Nichol, July, 1867). In August, 1872, Swinburne wrote a poem on the overture of Wagner's *Tristram*. (See below.) A large number of poems in *A Century of Roundels* are devoted to Wagner or Music in general. See also *Music : an Ode* (1892), in *Astrophel and other Poems*.

The servants thought I was in prayers.' Swinburne
was in poor health towards the end of April, and
again in May. He sat to Watts who was painting the
now famous portrait, but found the strain almost intolerable. On July 12th while on a visit at Lord
Houghton's house he was seized with a bad fainting
fit ' of a really dangerous kind ' which prevented him
from meeting Louis Blanc at Blind's house ; the
Admiral was telegraphed for and removed his son to
Holmwood on the 15th. This little scene was to be
repeated several times in the years that followed, until
the Admiral's death. Then, there was no one to take
Swinburne home in a cab, and he went from bad to
worse, till, in precisely the same circumstances, Theodore Watts took him in hand.

It required over two months for him to recover completely. Steeped in ' domestic virtues ' Swinburne,
who had been prescribed ' a torpor of mind and body
for months ' found that ' things were awfully slow '.
He was however able to work a little : since January
he had been contributing fairly regularly to the *Fortnightly Review*. His reviews of Morris' *Jason* and of
Arnold's *Poems* written about this time show that, as
a critic at least, he was still believing in ' l'art pour
l'art '. The latter article contains a terrific denunciation of philistinism, so severe indeed that the editor
of the *Fortnightly* cut out part of the quotation from
the alleged French critic (i.e. Swinburne himself) dealing (as in the as yet unpublished *William Blake*) with
the true nature of poetry.[1] But it also had some very

---

[1] ' In the next *Fortnightly* there will be an article of mine on Arnold—curtailed
of much I had written . . . (which is a bore, for the part I have to resorb contained
an eloquent exposition of the real nature of Urizen and his crucified son—mais ils ne
perdront rien pour attendre)'. (To W. M. Rossetti, September 17, 1867.)

uncharitable, if eminently deserved sentences on Arnold's inability to judge of French poetry (' The English poet is here hopelessly at sea without oar or rudder, haven or guiding star '). But Arnold's answer was enough to disarm the most carping critic : ' You will own that I at least have a conscience when I tell you that I have twice refused to lecture at Edinburgh on the literature of the grand siècle or any other period of French literature alleging that my knowledge was too imperfect ' (10 October 1868).

After several months' enforced rest Swinburne, whose strength had returned, obtained permission from his doctor to leave Holmwood for a short week-end on condition that he would be ' regular as here '. He seems to have met his friend Powell at Slough and gone with him to Étretat [1] where he stayed for three days from 25 to 28 September. By the beginning of October he was safely back in Holmwood and met there Henry Kingsley : ' Kingsley has just been here : I never met him before and like him—especially as in a minute's talk on Italy I found him of one mind with me ' (To W. M. Rossetti, October 11, 1867). A week or so later he was back at his old lodgings of Dorset Street after an absence of nearly four months ; ' bilious influenza ' was not long in overtaking him and by the end of November he was again laid up. But in spite of this and of a slight accident (he was at the beginning of December ' spilt ' out of a hansom and disfigured) he made up his mind to stay in London where he was to remain during most of the year 1868.

---

[1] This is asserted by Gosse. It is not impossible, as Mr. Myers told Gosse, that Swinburne had then with him the proofs of Menken's *Infelicia*. There is, however, no direct evidence of Swinburne's connection with the actress till some weeks later.

It is in December 1867 that we find for the first
time direct evidence, in a letter to Th. Purnell on the
4th of that month, of Swinburne's acquaintance with
Adah Menken, and there is no reason to believe that
their intimacy began more than a few weeks before.
This *liaison* attracted at one time much attention. The
contrast between Swinburne and the Menken was indeed of great violence, and without indulging in the
cheap witticisms which were then circulated we must
recognize that the thought of those two being lovers
must have appealed to many as a joke. Dolores Adios
McCord, was born at New Orleans in 1835. After
showing great proficiency at school (it is even claimed
that she knew Latin, Greek and French perfectly) she
went on the stage as a dancer. In 1856 she married
a Jewish music master, Alexander Isaac Menken,
whom she soon deserted to follow a chequered career,
now as an actress, now as a sculptor's model, all the
while contributing many poems and articles to newspapers. In 1859 she married a prize-fighter from
whom she was not divorced until 1862. The year
before she had scored her first real theatrical success
by appearing as Mazeppa, riding bareback a white
horse on the stage, in a melodrama adapted from Byron
by H. M. Milner. So great was her triumph that she
took *Mazeppa* over to Europe in 1864 ; she appeared
in London from July to December, then returned to
the States via Paris. From October to December 1865
she was again in London. After a short stay in the
States she revisited Europe at the end of 1866 and
stayed chiefly in Paris, where her *liaison* with Dumas
the elder was notorious ; she had by then been married
no less than five times. In the course of October 1867

she went to London and appeared at Astley's and on various other stages until the end of May 1868, when she transferred her activities to the Châtelet in Paris. She died in the French capital on August 10, and was buried at the Père Lachaise, her remains being in 1869 transported to the Cimetière Montparnasse.

How and when were Swinburne and the athletic circus rider brought together ? The idea of such a *rapprochement* was worthy of Houghton or Victor Hugo. It had the picturesqueness of the meeting with Burton with something in addition. When Swinburne first saw Menken, we can only conjecture ; it is not impossible that it was in the course of her first or second visit to England, which might explain the title *Dolores* given to one of the most remarkable pieces of *Poems and Ballads* ; but in that case she supplied only a name. It was in October 1867, on Menken's return from Paris, that the relation must have become of a closer nature. Why ? We are here again confronted with the story of a *conseil de famille* of which people like D. G. Rossetti and Purnell are supposed to have been members. Where Mazzini had only half-succeeded, why should not Menken succeed ? If Swinburne, flattered by the advances of a fair actress of literary proclivities and not displeased by the notoriety, began to think a little less of whisky and other perversities, where would the harm be ? As for Menken it might not be over difficult to incite her to play that game ; would it not be for her excellent publicity ? Was she not on the other hand genuinely fond of the society of men of letters, and did she not preside in London over a sort of literary salon where Dickens and others had been seen ? Was she not also anxious to get her volume of poems, *Infelicia*, published in England ? Could not Swinburne's publisher, Hotten, be persuaded to accept it at the poet's request, supported by that of Swinburne's secretary, John Thomson, the dramatic critic of the *Weekly Dispatch*, and a warm admirer, who had copied out for her the manuscript of her poems ? Is it so impossible to believe that this strong, passionate woman, with an inclination towards literature, could feel a genuine interest and affection in the author of the finest love-lyrics in English poetry ? And might not Swinburne also like the company of one who was obviously no fool, whose personality was full of picturesqueness, and whose sculptural body showed no violation of the canons of ' Art for Art's Sake ' ?[1]

Menken assumed the active part. As Mr. Wise puts it, Swinburne was the sought, not the seeker. On December 9th he wrote to Purnell explaining that he was shy of appearing before Dolores ' sick and disfigured ' after his hansom accident. This impression is strengthened by the set of cartoons entitled ' Ye Treue and Pitifulle historie of ye Poet and ye Ancient Dame ' sent by Burne-Jones to Swinburne on April 24, 1868 in which we are shown in turns the poet ' inviting the Ancient Dame to his abode, the Ancient Dame ringing the Poet's bell, the Poet bidding an accomplice say that he is grievous sick,

---

[1] Just about the time of this affair Swinburne was translating in one of the finest stanzas of *Ave Atque Vale* Baudelaire's sonnet, *La Géante*, where lines sound here very appropriate :

> J'eusse aimé vivre auprès d'une jeune géante,
> Comme aux pieds d'une reine un chat voluptueux . . .
> Parcourir à loisir ses magnifiques formes,
> Ramper sur le versant de ses genoux énormes . . .
> Dormir nonchalamment à l'ombre de ses seins,
> Comme un hameau paisible au pied d'une montagne ?

the Ancient Dame returning homewards, weeping, and writing anxious notes of inquiry with which the poet lights his cigar, while the Ancient Dame raveth by the side of the Ocean at St. Leonards on Sea '. For Dolores indeed was showing the greatest concern, as Purnell took great care to inform Swinburne (December 4th, 1867) : ' she fears you are ill ; she is unable to think of anything but you . . . She has become a soft-throated serpent, strangling prayer in her white lips to kiss the poet. . . . She concludes " Tell him all—say out my despairing nature to him. Write at once ; believe in me and my holy love for him. Let him write one word in your letter. He will, for he is so good ".' Would a mere £10 bet be worth all that trouble, and was not Menken giving Rossetti more than his money's worth ?[1]

Meanwhile Swinburne was giving publicity to his affair and, having had photographs of Menken and himself taken together, distributed them among his friends. On January 26, 1868 he wrote to Powell : ' I must send you in a day or two a photograph of my present possessor—known to Britannia as Miss Menken, to me as Dolores (her real Christian name)—and myself taken together. We both come out very well. Of course it's private.' By February the facts were widely known, and the *liaison* taken quite seriously by people who were in a good position to judge. Shirley Brooks wrote to Hardman : ' I am Ada's. . . . She lives at No. 26 Norfolk Street, S.W. . . . Swinburne is the only rival I dread—he knew her first. But I shall sit upon his corpse. He boasts—but he

---

[1] It is said that Rossetti had invited Menken to conquer Swinburne's affections (see Adah Isaac Menken. A Fragment of an autobiography, 1917).

lies.' Brooks does not seem quite so easy as he would have us believe about his rival's boasting.

Swinburne's well-intentioned friends, in order to secure publicity and perhaps money, circulated the photographs so widely that in March they were publicly exhibited for sale in the windows of several shops.[1]

Soon the whole town was talking about it. The wildest rumours circulated, such as, in Swinburne's own words, that ' Menken was going to play Psyche to my Cupid in a new ballet or opera buffa— . . . complimentary to my appearance of youth at the time, if not to the discretion of my age '. The report even reached the ears of Mazzini who exclaimed in a letter : ' Swinburne is going to act on the stage ! ' (April 10, 1868).

Matters had gone a little too far and Swinburne's friends had succeeded only too well in advertising the poet's amours. The Chief, possibly also Lady Jane and the Admiral, knew of his extravagance. In a private letter to Powell (April 17, 1868) Swinburne expressed his annoyance in a childish and engaging style :

> There has been a *damned* row about the photographs ; paper after paper has flung pellets of dirt at me, reissuing or asserting the falsehood that its publication and sale all over London were things authorized or permitted or even foreseen by the sitters ; whereas, of course, it was a private affair to be known (or shewn) to friends only. The circulation has, of course, been stopped as far as possible, but not without much irritating worry. The one signed I think good—the other not—except for the pose of her shoulder and bosom.

Menken's departure from London at the end of

[1] See *Pall Mall Gazette* for March 17, 1868.

May further contributed to pour oil on the troubled waters of scandal. But in spite of these unpleasant circumstances Swinburne's affection for Menken remained strong and genuine. On August 26th, eighteen days after her death, he wrote to Powell :

I am sure you were sorry on my account to hear of the death of my poor dear Menken ; it was a great shock to me and a real grief. I was ill for some days. She was most lovable as a friend as well as a mistress.

We may well leave it at that. Of course he had no difficulty in forgetting Menken, and she, on the other hand, was not when she met him in a state of maidenly innocence. But those two strange beings had met and felt for each other genuine interest and perhaps affection. Suffice it to say before we pass on that their *liaison*, on whatever basis it rested (and it seems to have been more than purely platonic), was not ignoble.[1]

At the beginning of 1868 Swinburne published two works whose importance should not be overlooked : *William Blake*, begun in 1862, finished and printed in the course of 1866, but delayed owing to a change of publishers and modified till the last minute, appeared in the month of January ; it contained together with a brilliant and intuitive, if sometimes inaccurate, study of the mystic, a logical and definite exposition (the best which has appeared in English) of that doctrine of Art for Art's Sake from which Swinburne's bark, borne by Mazzinian breezes, was gradually

---

[1] Menken's volume of verse, *Infelicia*, was published in the summer of 1868 by Hotten, with a dedication to Dickens, and an epigraph from Swinburne's *Dolores*. As most of the poems had appeared before in American magazines, the rumour that Swinburne wrote *Infelicia* has no foundation. He may have corrected the proofs and touched up some lines, being tempted to try his hand at short *pastiches* in the Whitmanesque style of the original.

drifting away. *Ave Atque Vale*, the elegy on the death of Baudelaire which was printed in the *Fortnightly* of the same month, has a somewhat different story : on April 19, 1866 Swinburne had read in the papers a false report of the death of Baudelaire, who a few days before had been struck with paralysis. He wrote to Powell : ' I hope to write a little notice of his death as I did before of his work and I want to lay hold of any facts I can'. On hearing that Baudelaire had survived, Swinburne perforce held back his notice which was later incorporated in a footnote of the *William Blake*. About May 22, 1867 a fresh report reached Swinburne who wrote again to Powell : ' I am writing a sort of lyric dirge for my poor Baudelaire which I think is good as far as it has gone. But London and business or (worse) society are awful clogs on poetry'. Soon after the rumour was again denied and Swinburne put his elegy away in disgust. When however he learned that on August 31, 1867 Baudelaire had at last passed away after a painful struggle of over two years, he revised and completed his poem and, after waiting a little to make sure that the dead poet would not come to life again, sent it off to the *Fortnightly*. Among many other things, we are struck in this very beautiful poem, by the insistence laid on the ' farewell theme ' and the irrevocability of Baudelaire's fate. Written in the first period of Mazzinian fervour, *Ave Atque Vale* displays on the part of Swinburne a consciousness that one stage of his career is now closing and that he must turn to new inspirations.[1] The publication of *William Blake* and *Ave Atque Vale* marks the end of the

---

[1] I may perhaps refer the reader to my study on ' Swinburne et Baudelaire ', published by the *Revue Anglo-Americaine* in February, 1924.

Pre-Raphaelite and Baudelairian phase in Swinburne's development.

Although his name was thus well before the world, little work was done by Swinburne in 1868 : apart from the *Notes on the Royal Academy* published in June and undertaken at the request of Hotten in conjunction with W. M. Rossetti who did most of the task, he simply revised and touched up for the *Fortnightly* (July) his Notes on the *Old Masters at Florence* written in 1864, and worked rather casually at some of the *Songs*. Moreover, being in disagreement with the editor of the *Fortnightly* who had not paid him for the *Halt before Rome*, he decided not to send any contribution for the time being. He had, in November 1867, planned a sequel to his *Chastelard* (the two dramas which were to become *Bothwell* and *Mary Stuart*) and a narrative poem on *Tristram and Iseult* [1], which had haunted him since his false start at Oxford. He had already done some work on them, but in June 1868 he managed to lose both manuscripts in a cab, which was a severe check. The truth was that ' London, business and society were awful clogs on poetry '. He might well write to Powell : ' I have been so worried of late with influenza, love-making and other unwholesome things—such as business, money etc. that I have left undone what I should have done ' (January 26, 1868). On March 18th he attended the meeting of the Anthropological Society and spoke on American Literature. On April 28th he fell at his lodgings while

---

[1] It was recorded in the Weekly Gossip of the *Athenaeum* for March 14, 1868, that ' Swinburne was composing a poem on Tristram and Yseult, and writing an Essay on the women of Arthurian Romances for the Early English Texts Society, in which Tennyson's views will not be adopted '. Unfortunately the latter scheme, if it ever existed, does not seem to have materialized.

carrying a lamp in the dark and injured his head and foot ; the reason was no doubt a fainting fit brought about by intemperance, but on May 15th Dr. Bird was able to advise Mazzini that ' for five days past Mr. Swinburne has avoided " the perilous stuff " and is consequently very much improved in body and mind '. A more serious attack overcame him on July 10 while working at the British Museum. Edmund Gosse has given his version of the incident. Here is Swinburne's as retailed by the Admiral to Powell : ' His account was that he had gone to the British Museum to make some references directly after breakfast, that working for a couple of hours he found the atmosphere of the reading-room so close and oppressive that he got up to go away, when he fainted, and in fainting, hurt his forehead. They kindly plastered him up and took him home in a cab. . . . He was going out as usual the day he wrote'. But the papers published pessimistic reports of his health. Mazzini, Nichol, Jowett were alarmed. The latter wrote ' a really kindly and friendly letter on the hypothesis that I have been injuring my natural health by intemperate and irregular ways and offering even pecuniary help if needed to set me straight ' (to Nichol, July 22nd, 1868). But Swinburne would not be ' set straight '. He delayed his visit to Holmwood, and on July 28th wrote from London in the following terms : ' My life has been enlivened of late by a fair friend who keeps a maison de supplices[1] à la Rodin—There is occasional balm in Gilead'. This was not going to improve

---

[1] This ' maison de supplices ' was in the Euston Road. In an undated letter Swinburne mentions a ' Mrs. A.' who was perhaps connected with it. See also the reference to ' Florence ' in Nichol's letter to Swinburne (January 22, 1877, *Swinburne Library*, p. 208).

his health. After a very short stay at Holmwood, he
was back in London by the end of August on his way
to his friend Powell who had rented a house at Étretat
for several months. He had however to postpone his
departure till the 12th owing to ill health. On the
14th he was settled at Étretat and wrote to his mother
describing Powell's habitation as ' the sweetest little
old farmhouse fitted up inside with music, books,
drawings etc. There is a wild garden all uphill, and
avenues of trees '. What he did not say was that the
' sweetest little old farmhouse ' was called ' Chaumière
Dolmancé ' and the avenue in the garden ' Avenue de
Sade ',—' in remembrance of our walk there '.

The chief event which connects Étretat with
Swinburne in the minds of lovers of poetry is the
episode of his rescue from drowning by the local
sailors. In a haunting stanza the poet has embodied
his experience :

> When thy salt lips well-nigh
> Sucked in my mouth's last sigh
> Grudged I so much to die
> This death as others ?

and Gosse, in his *Portraits and Sketches*, has given us a
delightful cameo of the incident, adorned with all the
graces of rhetoric. He drew his biographical material
from a cutting of the *Journal de Fécamp* which he
found in the collection of George Powell, at Aberystwyth[1] ; upon this rough bit of journalese Gosse
poured the lacquer of his style and completely transformed it, to such an extent that it is highly entertaining to compare with the original his polished, though
slightly inaccurate, narrative. George Powell's own

[1] For this information, as for many other courtesies, I am indebted to Professor
A. Barbier, of Aberystwyth University.

plain description of the facts may seem rather insipid
in comparison but is well worth printing :

During one of Mr. Swinburne's visits to me at Étretat [early
in October 1868], he was, whilst bathing carried out to sea
through a rocky archway, and entirely out of my sight, by one
of the treacherous undercurrents so prevalent and so dreaded
on that dangerous coast. After I had lost sight of him for about
ten minutes, I heard shouts on the cliffs above me, to the effect
that 'a man was drowning'. Guessing what had occurred, I
gathered up Mr. Swinburne's clothes by which I had been
sitting, and running with them through the ankle-deep shingle
to where some boats lay, sent them off to the rescue. In but a
few minutes, however, a boat coming *from* the point at which
I feared a catastrophe had taken place, brought us the welcome
news that my friend had been picked up by a fishing smack
bound for Yport, but a few miles distant. I, therefore, took a
carriage and galloped off at fullest speed, with the clothes of the
rescued man to the village of Yport, whence we returned
together to Étretat in the smack which had picked up Mr.
Swinburne—he declining to use the carriage.

On two points Gosse's narrative is slightly misleading : first it seems impossible that Swinburne, as
he was borne away by the current may have reflected
with satisfaction that ' his republican poems were
nearly ready for the press ', as we have seen that, by
October 1868, only a few, probably no more than ten,
and those among the less important, had been composed.   Lastly, it seems that the Sieur Coquerel
' guetteur au sémaphore ' who first raised the alarm
and attracted the attention of the Marie-Marthe is
entitled to share with ' le patron Théodule Vallin '
the honour of having saved the poet, or, as the *Journal
de Fécamp* irreverently puts it, ' l'individu', ' qui se
serait infailliblement noyé sans la présence sur ce
point du guetteur et l'adresse du Patron Vallin '.

In fact there were more than two men who claimed

to have saved Swinburne ; we have seen that Powell
implies that he had some share in the rescue. Guy de
Maupassant, then a young man of eighteen, who
happened to be on the shore at the time of the accident, hearing Coquerel's and Powell's cries, gallantly
joined in the shouting. This was enough to incite him
after the rescue to introduce himself, and he was on
several occasions invited by Powell to the ' Chaumière
Dolmancé '. Of his visit, or visits, he gave in a preface
to Mourey's translation of *Poems and Ballads* a highly
coloured and somewhat exaggerated description. In
fact, after a few years, his fertile imagination had completely transformed the facts, so that this great master
of realism would say freely that he had saved Swinburne's life and that the sailors at Étretat admitted
that ' it was lucky for Swinburne that that morning
M. Guy had been in the water too '. There is no
doubt that the furniture and decoration of the ' Chaumière Dolmancé' must have been rather special. Swinburne's taste for the *macabre* was at one time genuine :
Baudelaire, Poe, Rossetti, Balzac had confirmed him in
it. He had read with admiration Meinhold's *Sidonia
Von Bork*, Petrus Borel's *Contes Immoraux*, and shared
Powell's delight in Le Fanu's *Uncle Silas*.

By the end of October Swinburne was back in
Dorset Street. He passed most of the month of No-
vember at Holmwood where he received an ' admiring
and sympathetic letter ' from Emmanuel des Essarts
(Swinburne's reputation in France was growing apace).
He came back to London in December and spent
Christmas at Cambridge as the guest of his friend
Bendyshe to whom reference has already been made :
' I spent Christmas at Cambridge very agreeably with

an Etonian friend of mine of a remote date (to us) now
Senior Fellow of King's—a great ally of mine—a
raging and devoted atheist at whose talk God trembles
on his tottering throne—and a perfect host. . . . We
attended divine service (to universal amazement of the
whole college) and for once I sat in the seat of a
bishop—" the seat of the scorner "—and walked out
actually preceded by a man with a silver poker ! '

During the first months of 1869 Swinburne remained at Holmwood. He was working industriously
over a textual study of the poems of Shelley, which he
had started when, in April 1868, Payne (of Moxon and
Co.) had entrusted with the task of editing the works of
Shelley W. M. Rossetti, who frequently applied to the
poet for help and advice. Swinburne decided to publish some of his remarks in the *Fortnightly* (May) ;
he embodied in his article fragments of a verse translation of the *Cyclops* which completed Shelley's own
unfinished version. It is probable that Swinburne, who
was then at work on the *Songs*, found this study of
Shelley very useful, for Mazzini supplied the inspiration, but not the style , and the works of the great
lyrist were particularly to the point. Hence the
numerous reminiscences or resemblances which occur
in many of the *Songs*. Swinburne recognized this in a
noble fashion when he introduced in his volume the
sonnet *Cor Cordium*, in which he addressed Shelley's
heart in a parody of the terms of ritual theology, this
being a common and sometimes effective trick of
Swinburne's style :

> O wonderful and perfect heart for whom
> The lyrist liberty made life a lyre—
> Love of Loves, holy of holies, light of lights . .

At the end of April Swinburne paid a short visit to
Jowett at Balliol College ; then went to Dorset Street,
where he remained until June, writing for the *Fortnightly* (July) a review of *l'Homme qui rit*. Towards
the end of July he set out in the company of Richard
Burton, who was shortly to take up his new appointment at Damascus, on a trip through Auvergne with
the ultimate object of settling at Vichy for a few weeks.
This was necessitated by Burton's health which had
been affected by tropical climates among many other
things. But Swinburne, who had not been subjected
to such hardships, also benefited from the stay (' I am
better than I have been for five months ') and forgot
about bilious attacks. After visiting Clermont and
climbing to the top of the Puy de Dôme the travellers
reached Vichy on the 24th. They stayed until about
the 20th of August. Frederic Leighton and Mrs.
Sartoris hunted them up, and many years later (1896)
Swinburne remembered her delightful singing and
wrote with emotion of

> A woman's voice, divine as a bird's by dawn.

But at the time he simply told his mother : ' She plays
and sings to me by the hour, and her touch and her
voice are like a young woman's. *But*—they have sent
her here to get down her *fat*—and—— ! '

Above all, Swinburne was enjoying Burton's company [1] ; it was the first occasion on which he was alone
with him for such a long time. ' I feel now as if I knew
for the first time what it was to have an elder brother'.
Shortly after August 10th Mrs. Burton arrived, and

---

[1] He then introduced Burton to the works of Petrus Borel and read out to him
Madame Putiphar in a copy borrowed from the local library which, despite Swinburne's endeavours, would not part with it at any price.

the party, after having visited Le Puy and the castle
of the Polignacs, from whom Swinburne, in the face
of all evidence, insisted that he was descended,[1] broke
up.   Burton and his wife went South, while Swinburne
made for Paris where he stayed a few days at the beginning of November.   Shortly before he had written to
Powell (29 July) : ' I shall stay in Paris not more than
a week, but I hope to meet Paul de St. Victor, Th.
Gautier and perhaps Flaubert.   Tu conviendras que
cela vaut bien la peine de s'y arrêter.   If you were
with me I could bring you acquainted with the friend
at whose house I expect to meet them'.   It is to be
regretted that we have no details about Swinburne's
stay at Paris, and also about the hospitable friend.
But it is possible that all his hopes came to nought as
also did his intended visit to Hugo at Guernsey.
After a short stay at Étretat he was back in London
about September 15th ; he soon proceeded to Holmwood where he stayed until March 1870.

He was now engaged again on his *Tristram*, having
been stung into inspiration by Tennyson's publication
of *The Grail*.   ' Having read a few pages . . . I fell at
once tooth and nail upon *Tristram and Iseult* and wrote
at an overture of the poem projected all yesterday ' he
wrote to D. G. Rossetti on December 22nd.   This was
indeed a period of regular correspondence between the
two friends : Rossetti had decided to have the manuscript of his poems recovered from his wife's coffin,
and, after much revision was submitting them to Swinburne both for criticism and also because his friend
had undertaken to write a review of them which appeared in the *Fortnightly* for May 1870.   Swinburne

---

[1] See *Summer in Auvergne*, etc.

was now very active : although he was writing his finest *Songs*, he displayed in his *Tristram* and his article on Rossetti that his interest in Pre-Raphaelite poetry remained as keen as ever.

Most of what concerns the year 1870 has already been said. The completion of *Songs before Sunrise* and the quarrel with Hotten absorbed most of Swinburne's activities. He came to Dorset Street in the course of April and remained until June, when he was taken seriously ill while at D. G. Rossetti's house in Cheyne Row : Rossetti and Fanny Schott nursed him back to health. He then went back to Holmwood where he remained till the end of the year except for a short visit to town in October.[1]

At the beginning of 1871 Swinburne was in London to supervise the much-delayed publication of *Songs before Sunrise*. His volume being now completed he indulged, as a natural reaction from the works of the months which preceded, in a reckless mode of living which his much shaken health could not by any means stand. It is characteristic that his relations with Simeon Solomon, to which allusion has already been made, seem then to have grown more intimate than ever. At Solomon's request Swinburne was now writing for the *Dark Blue Magazine* an estimate of the works of his friend. In a very beautiful style, which reminds one at once of Ruskin and Pater, Swinburne did not hesitate, with extraordinary frankness if with much psychological insight, to analyse sympathetically the most abnormal tendencies of Solomon's inspiration.

---

[1] There seems to be no authority for asserting that he went to Étretat in the summer of 1870, and was driven back to England by the war. At any rate it is certain that the *Ode on the French Republic* was composed at Holmwood on September 7, *not* in France.

'There is a mixture of utmost delicacy with a fine cruelty in some of these faces of fair feminine youth which recalls the explanation of a philosopher of the material school whose doctrine is at least not without historic example and evidence to support it : " Une infinité de sots, dupes de cette incroyable sensibilité qu'ils voient dans les femmes, ne se doutent pas que les extrémités se rapprochent, et que c'est précisément au foyer de ce sentiment que la cruauté prend sa source. Parce que la *cruauté n'est elle-même qu'une des branches de la sensibilité*, et que c'est toujours en raison du degré dont nos âmes en sont pénétrées que les grandes horreurs se commettent ".' We may well understand poor Solomon's feelings when he complained to Swinburne that this article had done his reputation more harm than good.

On February 11th the Swinburnes were greatly alarmed about their son, who was staying in London at an unknown address. Lady Jane wrote with much insight : ' He must not take lodgings in town. He should stay here to overcome his fearful propensity : his health is better, he is happy. But books are not sufficient, he should have intellectual society '. From May to July[1] he stayed at Holmwood and his health consequently improved : he worked happily at *Bothwell* and his essay on Ford. But in July, in the course of a short stay in London, he fell so seriously ill that the Admiral had to come and take him home according to the usual method. In a letter to Frederick Locker Swinburne recognized with engaging frankness his

---

[1] In June he visited Jowett at Oxford. It was on the 3rd that he met at the Master's House Hippolyte Taine, who was not very favourably impressed, as appears from a letter to his wife. Taine must have sensed that his famous ' method ' would have been powerless to account for a phenomenon like Swinburne.

own folly in having ' made himself ill ' and that he was ' ashamed to think of my friends knowing it was my own fault '.

About August 12th he went on a long holiday to Scotland under the supervision of Jowett. He remained at Tummel Bridge till well on in September enjoying numerous excursions (in the company of Edwin Harrison, Jowett's student) and a moderate amount of society (Browning and Millais visited him). He then went on to his uncle Sir Henry Gordon's residence at Aberdeen ; he had only been back to London a short time when he suddenly became so ill that the Admiral was again informed by some ' fool or rascal ' to quote Swinburne's own words. The old sailor realized that emergency measures were imperative. He carried his son 'literally out of bed' and, to make sure against a repetition of the same farce-tragedy, gave the landlord notice that his son was leaving. Here is Swinburne's own account of the incident : ' My father came up to town again and was most kind—got my things packed up for the warehouse and carried away, and brought me finally out of that damned hole where I was dying for want of air and light. There were most unpleasant and irritating circumstances connected with it which I may tell you when we meet. For the present I am here to rest and recruit and do perhaps a stroke of work'.

In December, Jowett invited him to Oxford and then accompanied him to London. He was staying there at a new address in North Crescent when on March 12th, 1872 the news of Mazzini's death reached him.

In the great mental and physical distress through

which he had recently passed, Swinburne felt this as a fresh blow. Although he had not seen Mazzini for many months, he realized that he was now deprived of a great moral support. Indeed throughout those chequered years of many activities, intense creative work, moral chaos and gradual physical decay, it is the influence of Mazzini which gives strength and unity to the life of Swinburne ; the trend of a great purpose, however hopeless or mistaken it may at times appear, is visible in his writings during that period. He was now left with nothing to comfort him but the fragments of his (and other men's) dreams and the beauty of the work he had accomplished.

CHAPTER VII

THE COMING OF WATTS
(1872–1879)

WITHIN the dates which limit this chapter the life and works of Swinburne have in common certain marked features : the strong lyrical and emotional impulse which had since 1860 been so conspicuous is for a while at least distinctly checked. One would expect that this continuous flow of inspiration, at first versatile and disorderly, then, under Mazzini's influence, more powerful and concentrated, should in the long run exhaust itself ; this, to a certain extent was the case, ill-health, money, and other worries concurring to the same effect. But it seems chiefly that Swinburne the poet was utterly puzzled and disconcerted for want of any practical *goal* to which he might direct his inspiration. He could not, as had been the case in 1867, find a new outlet for his lyrical faculties ; Italian unity and the Universal Republic had been an *impasse*. He could not now return to Art for Art's Sake. Swinburne did not repudiate these phases of his career, but he had *outgrown* them. It was all very well for Mazzini to die in 1872 when his work was done, but what was *his* poet to do ? For this, the Chief had not provided. As a consequence we shall see Swinburne endeavouring to shift for himself in the fields of art and politics, but without much confidence. After following up some lines of inspiration, which were soon exhausted, we

shall see him gradually turn from purely lyrical poetry
to dramatic and critical activities ; satire and parody
prevail over Pindaric odes ; prose almost outweighs
poetry. In proportion as the lyrical faculties decrease,
the intellectual ones grow stronger ; the discrepancies
between facts and principles appear more obvious to
the poet : self-analysis and introspection, which had
never been absent but could not have much scope
during the great lyrical period, become more and more
pronounced. As Baudelaire noted, a poet often grows
into a critic. Swinburne is now chiefly a critic, not so
much because he writes at this time most of his best
criticism as because his chief effort is to understand
everything, himself included. This phase, despite all
the interest it offers, is bound to be an anti-climax
after the hectic days of inspiration that preceded.
The poet himself feels it, and his mood is often tinged
with bitterness and melancholy. It looks like the
final stage of a great career. And, in fact, it very nearly
was.

At first, after the grave physical breakdown which
marked the year 1871, it seemed that things were
improving all round ; thanks to the Admiral's energetic action Swinburne had now no chambers in town,
and when he paid a short visit to London in March,
he had to engage furnished rooms at a new address,
12 North Crescent, supplied by Powell, where the
owners, the Von Horns, seem to have looked after him
with devotion. In the summer he was again one of a
party which Jowett took to Tummel Bridge, Pit-
lochry ; he stayed there from early in July till the
middle of August, his chief occupation being to bathe
in the neighbouring cataracts ; Jowett duly encouraged

those amusements, and by the end of his stay Swinburne was well and strong again. Another illness
however soon became acute and proved more difficult
to cure—that particular form of disease which Rabelais
described as 'faulte d'argent'. There is no doubt
that in the preceding years Swinburne had been living
far beyond his yearly allowance of £200. He now
(September 1872) decided to rent new lodgings at
3 Great James Street from a Mr. Bateman, and the
expenses accruing from his moving in further upset
his finances. To make matters worse, he was involved
in endless quarrels and bickerings with his former
landlady, a Mrs. Thompson, who, taking advantage
of the irregularities and ill-health of her lodger, insisted on a parting gift as a well-merited reward. This
claim infuriated the poet who denied it in a high-
flown style worthy of a nobler occasion : ' I therefore
wholly repudiate and flatly deny the existence of any
claim on her part, especially when backed up by two
deliberate and impudent lies of which she seems by
your account to have been guilty in her communication
to you etc., etc. . . .'

And this was not all : there was also the latch-key
which was lost, the carpenter's bill which had remained
unpaid, the movable filter and the Turkey carpet which
Mrs. Thompson had spirited away, and all this coupled
with the usual worries of the poet's life, was enough to
drive him into fits of exasperation. But most important of all was the money question. Vainly did Swinburne stay at Holmwood during the three autumn
months ; bills found their way to Holmwood. He
wrote to Morley on November 21st : ' I am at present
in a fair way to be pressed to death by unpaid bills,

which really worry me out of power to work at all regularly or comfortably, and to earn wherewith to discharge them'. By December 22nd matters were still worse, or perhaps he was franker with his correspondent, George Powell : 'I must look to pounds just now as I am pressed by duns and am still worth about £200 less than nothing, which I have to make up somehow'. He dared not go to his new rooms in London, and had to seek some diversion during the month of November in a visit to Jowett at Oxford, in the course of which he met Lionel Tennyson.

For reasons of economy he continued at Holmwood during most of the year 1873, and it may even be asserted that in the years 1872–79 Swinburne's health, and perhaps life, were miraculously preserved on several occasions by lack of money more than by anything else. The problem remained more pressing than ever, and he had to settle bills with cheques drawn by his father : 'I am harrassed by utter want of money and various unpaid bills' (January 31). 'To return to town, I must have *some* money at my banker's to go on with—whereas having been informed in November that I had overdrawn my account by upwards of £100, I shall have none in the ordinary way till Midsummer' (March). Towards the end of May he slipped off on another 'week-end' to Oxford and met at Balliol, to his intense gratification, the Bishop and the Dean. For this atmosphere of respectability, in which Jowett unobtrusively steeped him, Swinburne felt truly grateful. It was in the course of that visit that the poet had a long conversation with Walter Pater at Brasenose on the subject of their common friend Solomon. From the first days of July to the beginning of August, Jowett had no difficulty in inducing Swinburne to go to Grantown with him. The two friends stayed at a Mr. McGillivray's whose hall-table was covered with books entitled ' " Tell Jesus ", " The Gospel in Ezekiel " and other Evangelical effusions ' which the poet approached in a ' devout and humble spirit of piety '.[1]

Midsummer had by now been reached and Swinburne's exchequer had, through paternal generosity, been partly replenished. In August, and again in October, Swinburne was able to stay in London and use the chambers he had engaged nearly a year ago. His new friend and legal adviser, Theodore Watts, about whom more will be said later, was then living in the same street, a few doors from him. But Swinburne was again unwell and compelled ' to leave town suddenly and everything in my rooms at sixes and sevens '. Until the end of the year, to quote Frederick Locker's phrase, ' the frail vessel was in port again ', safely moored in the calm waters of Holmwood.

The year 1874 was divided between Holmwood, the Isle of Wight and London. On the 10th of January Swinburne took Jowett, who had so often managed his holidays for him, on a ten days' trip to Cornwall, the beauty of whose rocky coast had lingered in his mind since the autumn of 1864 : ' I have just returned from a prosperous ten days' tour to the Land's End with the Master of Balliol which has left me in love for

[1] Moreover, Swinburne was helping Jowett in the compilation of his *School and Children's Bible* (see *Recollections of Professor Jowett* in *Studies in Prose and Poetry*). . . . This sounded incredible even to Watts who wrote in 1874 : ' Sandys believes Knowles' hoax about you : that you are engaged in translating the Bible with Jowett ! ' But translating the Bible or reading sacred books would not be calculated to have a religious influence over Swinburne. What would have been needed on the contrary to ' improve ' his theological outlook would have been to abstain strictly from any reference to Scriptures or use of biblical metaphors.

life with Kynance Cove where (to use an original expression) I could live and die ' (To Powell, January 21). He took the Master up the crag of Tintagel ; in those cliffs and rocky bays, which he had learned to climb, it was Swinburne's turn to assume a controlling attitude towards Jowett : ' I knew and had reason to know what it was to feel nervous . . . for he would stand without any touch of support at the edge of a magnificent precipice as though he had been a younger man bred up from boyhood to the scaling of cliffs and the breasting of breakers'.

From January to the middle of March Swinburne spent two long months at Holmwood, well in health but longing for that intellectual company which, Lady Jane Swinburne felt, was sadly lacking. He was reading with interest Mérimée's *Lettres à une Inconnue,* which had just come out, and beside his own poems and critical work, was much engrossed in (and highly incensed by) Emerson's and Carlyle's sayings as reported by the Press. At the beginning of March came the news of William Michael Rossetti's impending marriage and Swinburne sent him ' the expression of such feelings and such wishes which will not seem less trustworthy or the less cordial that it comes from lips which must refrain from invoking the benediction of Urizen on the head of a friend whom they would rather commend to the favourable communion of Hertha '.

March and May were spent in London ; Swinburne paid a brief visit to Holmwood in April and stayed for a few days in London in June ; it was then that he made the acquaintance of a ' very famous veteran of the sea ', ' the one Englishman living I was really ambitious to know ', John Trelawny. His admiration for this somewhat dubious but undoubtedly picturesque character steadily grew until in 1880 the *Songs of the Springtides*, that wonderful collection of sea-poems, was rather aptly dedicated to him. In July, Swinburne accompanied by part of his family went on a prolonged visit to the Isle of Wight, at The Orchard, Niton, the home of his uncle, Sir Henry Gordon. He stayed there reading Homer and studying Chapman as late as the middle of September. He wrote to Morley in August : ' I am like you enjoying sea and sun (though the latter has been capricious of late, and allowed such gusts and swells of bad weather, that last week bathing off an unsafe shore I could hardly regain it, and even had I been drowned, as I reflected on regaining land in rather a spent condition, could not have enjoyed the diversion of reading the notices of my death in the papers, which is an unreasonable dispensation of an ungracious Providence). As for the sun's heat I bask in it, swimming or sitting ; it is never too hot for me in summer and seldom too cold in winter ; what I hate is the autumnal halfway house, *brumeux et suicidal* [*sic*]'.

Professor Tyndall's address to the British Association in Belfast he read in the Press towards the end of August with great admiration, and wrote to Watts about it as follows, thus showing that his mind, though untrained to science and probably unfit for such a training, was perhaps more closely akin to the scientific spirit of the age than either Browning's or Tennyson's :

Science so enlarged and harmonized gives me a sense as much of rest as of light. No mythology can make its believers less afraid or loth to be reabsorbed into the immeasurable harmony with but the change of a single individual note in a single bar of the tune, than does the faintest perception of the lowest chord touched in the whole system of things.   Even my technical ignorance does not impair, I think, my power to see accurately and seize firmly the first thread of the great clue, because my habit of mind is not (I hope) unscientific, tho' my work lies in the field of art instead of science, and when seen and seized even that first perception gives me an indescribable sense as of music and repose.   It is Theism which to me seems to introduce an element—happily a fictitious element—of doubt, discord and disorder.

From the Isle of Wight Swinburne went to London where he stayed until the end of December.   Christmas, New Year's day and the season of ' Galilean orgies ' were as usual spent at Holmwood.

At the beginning of 1875 Swinburne went on his customary January visit to Jowett, and spent a week with him at Ashfield House, West Malvern, but he was back on the 14th at Holmwood where his aged father was in poor health.   He stayed in the country till the middle of February when he came to town to attend an anniversary dinner of the birth of Charles Lamb, ' a somewhat Pagan passover, but *enfin* !'   Gosse has given us in one of the best pages of his biography a delightful vignette of the dismal ceremony and its still more dismal conclusion.   Swinburne now stayed in town till the end of May.   In February he had sent to E. C. Stedman that long autobiographical letter which cannot be accepted literally as to facts, but which is none the less typical of the tendency to self-analysis which has been duly noted in the poet.   Swinburne's finances with the help of his father and the sound advice of Theodore Watts were being gradually restored, but he still had to be extremely careful during

his visits to London. ' Of my own or my friends'
finances I never professed to be a judge (God—or something better—help my friends if I did!)' he comically
exclaimed to Gosse in a letter of March 13th,
and when in the course of April Jowett applied to him
for a subscription to some fund or other he had to
implore the Admiral's assistance. This was not refused : ' I enclose a cheque for £10 to enable you to
answer Jowett's application by sending him such part
of it as you may judge suitable ; I should say not more
than a half at any rate. Your income for a man about
town is a small one'.[1] After a short stay at Oxford
he was back in Holmwood about June 15th. His
stay in the country was fortunately protracted owing
to a slight accident : ' I have been in bed ', he wrote
on July 4th, ' a week to-day, laid up with a badly
sprained foot . . . I sprained it in trying to climb and
jump from a garden-fence—rather schoolboyish at
my grave and reverend time of life—and the consequence has been worse than twenty swishings'.
He beguiled his enforced inaction till the beginning of
August by working and exchanging with some friends
the most unedifying correspondence (' one always
writes " des horreurs " when one is " en famille " ').
On August 3rd came the news of Gosse's marriage.
He answered wishing him ' all the joy and good fortune
that can be wished, without admixture of envy of that
particular form of happiness which I am now never
likely to share. I suppose it must be the best thing

---

[1] Swinburne's total income was at that time well under £400, as appears from
this sentence occurring in a letter of January 22, 1876 : ' . . . no great sum to a rich
man, but not unimportant to me whose allowance is just £200 a year and who
certainly cannot count on making as much annually by the entire profit of his
writings'.

that can befall a man, to win and keep the woman
that he loves while yet young ; at any rate I can congratulate my friend on his good hap, without any too
jealous afterthought of the reverse experience which
left my own young manhood " a barren stock "—if
I may cite that phrase without seeming to liken myself
to a male Queen Elizabeth '. Swinburne henceforward
maintained towards marriage the slightly sceptical
and somewhat embittered attitude of a hardened
bachelor.

The month of August and the beginning of September were spent with Jowett at West Malvern
where the two friends went into raptures at the news
of Captain Webb's swim across the Channel. Swinburne entertained the Master by reading to him fragments from the parodies of Browning which were to
appear later in the *Heptalogia* ; but work of a far more
serious sort was also done, and when Swinburne left
West Malvern for Holmwood about September 7th
he had planned and written a large part of *Erechtheus*.
He continued the tragedy at Southwold, Wangford,
where he remained with Watts until the end of October. The end of the year was spent at Holmwood
except for a short stay in London about the middle of
December.

During practically the whole of 1876 Swinburne
stayed at Holmwood, immersed in work and engrossed
in the various controversies, literary or political, in
which he was now taking an active part. One of his
chief reasons for coming to town would have been the
possibility of working at the British Museum ; but he
had for some time been in difficulties with the authorities, and after vainly applying to Gosse, he now

(January 2nd) urged Watts to be 'the means of reopening to me the now closed doors of the British Museum without sacrifice of self-respect or dignity on my part ... I cannot expose myself to be addressed like a schoolboy suspected of pilfering or convicted of carelessness'. In the course of March he slipped off to London to view the Old Masters Exhibition at Burlington House, but was back at Holmwood after spending only a few hours in town. He had plenty of time for reflection and meditation about his own work and the nature of his inspiration. This is illustrated by the letter written to Nichol on April 2nd, 1876, in which he analyses his early poems and endeavours to show with great critical acumen that the word 'Pre-Raphaelite' does not apply to them : 'The always (I think) rather foolish and now long since obsolete word Pre-Raphaelite was never applicable to any but the work of my earliest youth written at college, and has so long ceased to be applicable (at least in its original sense) to the poetic work of my two elders that I think for the sake of accuracy it should now be disused'. During those months, not of inaction, but of (comparative) intellectual solitude, he read with varying degrees of admiration the works of Leconte de Lisle and James Thomson.

In May he went with Nichol on a holiday to Sark and Guernsey, it being the first time since 1857 that the two friends found themselves together on a pleasure-trip. ' Moi, nourri sur les bords de la mer, je n'ai jamais rien vu de si charmant ', he wrote soon after to Mallarmé. This simple sentence he amplified and developed to saturation in the *Garden of Cymodoce* which became the third sea-poem of *Songs of the*

Springtides. Only one thing was lacking to make his enjoyment complete : the presence of Victor Hugo.

He went back to Holmwood in June, as Watts, in view of the Buchanan-Taylor case,[1] which was now being heard, had advised him to ' make himself scarce for three weeks ' in order not to have to appear as a witness. However, ' wishing to meet some friends ', he came to town in the middle of June, but hastily retreated to Holmwood when he had received a subpoena on the 27th. Then after this unfortunate experience he does not seem to have stirred from the family shelter until the end of the year. The only other incident worth noting is that, in October, under somewhat obscure circumstances, Swinburne suffered from having slept in a room with a ' large Indian lily in full flower near the bed ' ; he was for some time, he asserted, ' at the doors of delirium, if not of death ' and felt like ' a rag of manhood '. During the months that followed, Swinburne was fond of referring to and describing this incident which, had it been fatal, would have been a fitting close to the career of the author of the long-forgotten novel *Lesbia Brandon*[2], which he was now again thinking of publishing. During the first months of 1877 Swinburne remained at Holmwood, and it seemed that he would now settle almost permanently there, paying a few brief though all too long visits to London. On January 10th in answer to some invitation of Mrs. Gosse's he could write : ' I am not likely to be in town for months and have not been since the middle of September ' ; but an unexpected event changed everything : on March 5th

[1] See pp. 247–248.

[2] In the last chapter, *Leucadia*, the heroine poisons herself slowly with flowers and Eau de Cologne.

Admiral Swinburne, whose health had long been unsettled, died. On the following day Swinburne announced the news to his two closest friends; Nichol and Watts. The letter to Nichol is the more remarkable : ' I write just a line to let my oldest and best friend know that on the day before yesterday my father died. Among many points of feeling and character that I like to think we have in common, I doubt if there is any stronger on either side than our *northerly* disinclination for many or effusive words on matters of this kind. So I add nothing beyond a word to say how confidently, and in no conventional sense, I may reckon on the sincerity of your sympathy and that to know this is some genuine relief and satisfaction'. Under the Admiral's Will Swinburne was left two thousand pounds on the sale of his father's valuable collection of books and manuscripts, and five thousand pounds at his mother's death. But Lady Jane preferred to make the latter sum over to her son at once, so that the poet became comparatively independent and this (coupled with Swinburne's resentment at his brother Edward being appointed executor instead of himself) may have contributed, as Gosse suggested, to make further residence at Holmwood distasteful. At the beginning of May Swinburne was contemplating an early departure, and we find him at Great James Street early in June. A prolonged stay in London did not fail to produce its usual effects, and by the end of September we learn from a letter to Karl Blind that he had been seriously ill and could ' hardly hold his pen '. But there was now no Admiral to come and take him home *manu militari*. On October 8th he wrote to Howell that he had been ' prostrate for weeks beneath the double scourge of sore-throat and indigestion . . .' ; which however did not prevent him from parodying Patmore in a very effective manner. In his rooms at Great James Street, where he would lie prostrate on his bed for weeks attended by the ever faithful Mrs. MacGill, the most fearful disorder prevailed : poems, essays, novels were mislaid or lost ; important letters remained unanswered. ' Que voulez-vous c'est la bohème des célibataires ', as the poet frankly acknowledged in a letter to Mrs. Lynn Linton.

By the beginning of 1878 the conditions at 3 Great James Street had become appalling ; it seems that Swinburne fell into long spells of mental and physical torpor, from which he emerged only to indulge in fresh excesses. A letter of January 15th to his American friend P. H. Hayne gives a fairly vivid picture of the chaos, mental and otherwise, in which he struggled :

After an intermittent illness of some months' duration, I find on turning over a fearful mass of unsorted papers, proofs, correspondence, etc., etc., a note from you dated as far back as last October 12th, asking if I had received two likenesses of Generals Lee and Wade Hampton. . . . During my illness . . . my books, papers and parcels have got into such confusion that for two days I thought I had lost the most important manuscript I have of unpublished prose and verse combined [*Lesbia Brandon*]. That has turned up—but many other things are yet missing. Among these I fear must be the biographies you mention of Edgar Poe and (if they were ever delivered) the photographs aforesaid— alas ! . . . Generally I am as yet, being still somewhat of an invalid, quite unable to say what has or has not come to hand here during the last few months.

To make matters worse it was decided to pull down at an early date the building in which ' a poor poet of unpopular opinions has been able to live peacefully in five old chambers which he[1] would have delighted to describe '. This meant hunting for new quarters— no easy task as we know. To escape from this chaos and uncertainty, Swinburne unwisely decided to accept John Nichol's long-standing invitation to come and spend a month at Glasgow. Early in February he was the guest of the Professor at 14 Montgomerie Crescent, Kelvinside. Among other diversions, he was shown some 'erotic correspondence and Priapic poetry of Burns which are simply sublime. Oh ! how frail are *our* attempts on the Chastity of the Muses to that " large utterance of the early Gods " '. Nichol ' took him round ', and persuaded him to contribute to the University Magazine the four sonnets on the Russian question which Chatto had declined to print. To put it mildly, it was for the poet a month of intense mental and physical strain.   The usual symptoms, forerunners of an impending crisis, reappeared. ' I am £40 out of pocket ', he wrote to Watts. ' I want money. What terms do I stand on with Chatto ? ' He had however enough energy to prepare his second series of *Poems and Ballads*, and to put together the scattered fragments of *Lesbia Brandon*. At last on February 21st he came back from Glasgow by a night train accompanied by Nichol. In the course of March, his health broke down completely : ' I am hardly yet recovering ', he wrote on April 11th, ' from a very tedious and painful attack of sickness . . . which re- sulted in depriving me for weeks of all natural sleep and appetite—nay, well-nigh of all power to swallow or digest anything . . . I literally *can* write no more this morning'. And again a month later : ' I have

[1] Edgar Poe.

been a bedridden invalid for many days'. . . . So weak was he that he had to decline Victor Hugo's invitation to attend the Centenary Commemoration of the death of Voltaire as representative of English poetry. The fact that there is no extant letter from Swinburne between May 1878 and June 1879 is in itself significant. It is obvious that the poet who on April 11, 1878 could only write with ' much difficulty, fatigue, and even physical suffering ' was for a few months practically unable to correspond with anyone. But documents are not entirely lacking to confirm this. In July, Lady Swinburne received at Holmwood an alarming letter from Lord Houghton and wrote in great distress to Watts who was able to answer reassuringly. ' Anxious as I must always be about Algernon ', wrote Lady Swinburne, ' Lord Houghton's letter alarmed me terribly'. Towards the end of July Swinburne went on one of his usual visits to Jowett's. But by the end of August things had not much improved. Swinburne ignored friends and family, and remained weeks without communicating with anyone. On August 29th, Powell inquired from a friend : ' I feel great anxiety about the Bard. I have had no answer to several cards and gifts. Has the old tempter seized him ? What is the matter ? ' On November 16th, Lady Swinburne wrote to Watts : ' I was greatly distressed at hearing from Mrs. Mac-Gill yesterday that he had been ill ten days. If I had known I would have gone to him and perhaps have induced him to do something that might do him permanent good'. And the anxious mother announced that she would herself come to London and fetch him. It seems however that her attempt, if it materialized, had no effect. Swinburne lay in his chambers in London in a state of increasing exhaustion until the beginning of June 1879, when Theodore Watts, assuming after much hesitation a kind of paternal authority, made up his mind to intervene.

We must now break up the narrative just before what bode fair to be the last scene of the tragedy : the purpose of this chapter has been to show the change which came over Swinburne's mind in those years, how he became less given to enthusiasm and the lyrical expression of his emotions, more prone to analysis and introspection. He was thus led by circumstances and a kind of inner necessity to develop those critical faculties which education had done nothing to awaken. It has been possible to detect the causes and some of the effects of this new tendency in his life ; but when we turn to his work during that period, the change becomes self-evident. It is not so much that Swinburne wrote more prose and less poetry as that in the considerable body of verse he then composed there is, in contrast with the works which preceded, extremely little that is properly speaking lyrical. His two major enterprises, *Bothwell* and *Erechtheus*, are not only nominally, but also intrinsically dramatic ; and it is highly characteristic that, while the biographer could not ignore *Chastelard* and *Atalanta*, he will have little to say about them. *Bothwell*, an enormous drama of almost epic proportions, begun about 1868, but chiefly composed from 1871 (when the first act was privately printed) to March 1874 when the last line was written, bears witness to Swinburne's erudition (he had read chiefly Froude, Hill Burton and Knox, apart from contemporary letters and documents), to his tireless energy as an artist, and in a few instances to a fine dramatic instinct ; but it lies entirely outside Swinburne's life. With the death of Chastelard, all personal interest disappeared from the tragedy of Mary Stuart ; even the Queen's character changed, became more subtle, more complex, and far less effective. Swinburne himself unconsciously recognized this when he wrote to Nichol emphasizing the historical value of his play : ' One link dropt in the whole chain of public or private circumstances would throw the rest into chaotic confusion. Strike out these passages and the poem would sink from an epic in dramatic form to a simple drama of personal intrigues and passion on a somewhat larger scale and stage than Chastelard'. The only lyrical bit in the play is the French sonnet to Victor Hugo, which originally was very fine in spite of some awkward constructions and pauses :

> Comme un fleuve qui donne à l'océan son âme
> Je verse entre vos mains d'où le vers tonne et luit
> Tout ce que mon livre a de musique et de flamme,
> Tout ce qu'il peut tenir de lumière et de nuit .. etc.

But the sonnet was beaten and hammered out of shape by José Maria de Heredia who had unwisely been consulted : as though Rossetti would have been the right man to touch up Milton's sonnets ! From July 1874 to the beginning of 1876 there were protracted negotiations between Swinburne and John Oxenford and others with a view to producing *Bothwell* : the scheme was wisely abandoned. If any of Swinburne's

plays has any chance of succeeding on the stage, it
would be *Chastelard*, with all its imperfections. It
was very nearly produced by Lugné-Poe in 1904, in a
French version by Maeterlinck, at the Théâtre de
l'Œuvre. Since then, no producer has been brave
enough to attempt the task.

What has been said of *Bothwell* may, with few modifications, be repeated of *Erechtheus*. The play was composed from August to December 1875, under the
supervision of Jowett. Swinburne was obsessed by the
dread that there might be any ' non-Greek touch or
allusion in it ' ; the result is that the tragedy is neither
Greek nor Swinburnian. It is dedicated to his mother ;
a perfect birthday offering, cold, pure, and harmless.
Lady Jane, who had taught her son Italian, deserved a
warmer tribute.[1]

Of the three (comparatively) slender volumes of
verse, which include most of the pieces Swinburne
wrote during those years, a large number of poems
must be discounted from the lyrical total either because they were composed before (*Ave Atque Vale*, *At
A Month's End*) or after (*Off Shore*, *Odes* to Hugo and
Landor, etc.) or chiefly because they are not lyrical at
all : such in particular are the translations (from Villon
and Aristophanes) and the ' necrological ' poems or
occasional pieces (on Gautier, Barry Cornwall, *A Birth-
Song*, etc.). When such deductions have been made,
the reader is confronted with a small body of lyrical
poems which are distinguished by very special features.

---

[1] For instance *Atalanta* ; witness the lines :

> For there is nothing terribler to men
> Than the sweet face of mothers. . . .

Swinburne may have felt the inadequacy of his former gift when, much later, he
dedicated to Lady Jane that subtle and powerful poem, *A Tale of Balen* (see below).

Nearly all of them exhibit a perfection of form, or more exactly a subtlety of music unmatched in the poems that preceded them : Swinburne's calmer inspiration gives him a mastery of rhythm, an understanding of the technique of harmony, which make some of his work of this period comparable to that of Spenser or Keats. He delights more particularly in two highly elaborate forms : the sestina and the ballade. But he occasionally creates for his purpose intricate stanzas of pure original beauty as for instance in the *Year of the Rose, A Forsaken Garden, A Vision of Spring in Winter.* As regards matter, the poet has exchanged the lyrical outbursts of *Poems and Ballads* and *Songs before Sunrise* for the vaguest themes of undefined melancholy and sorrow. Never was perhaps the art of Swinburne so closely akin to music, so elusive of translation, and yet, in a way, so perfect. It was then that several of his shorter songs began to be set to music at the request of publishers and composers. Swinburne's elaborate rhythms are generally meant to create in the mind of the reader a neutral state which is neither joy nor sorrow, waking nor sleeping, yet is tinged with dreamy melancholy. However, in spite of the tenuity of the theme it is not impossible to find even in these poems a tendency to retrospection, and a sort of dramatic detachment from self. The note is struck in the *Sestina* :

> I saw my soul at rest upon a day
>   As a bird sleeping in the nest of night . . .

and again in the *Ballad of Dreamland* ('the most finished example of workmanship I ever " sculped " '. To Watts, April 4th 1876) :

I hid my heart in a nest of roses . . .
Lie still, I said, for the wind's wing closes . . .

and chiefly in the *Vision of Spring in Winter* :

I send my love back to the lovely time . . .

   In some other poems however (very few, but essential) the matter as well as the form assumes importance,
and the poet delights in conjuring up in a way that is
semi-dramatic, rather than lyrical, the various moods
which made up his personality in the past.   I do not
mean to say much about *Thalassius*, that ' symbolical
quasi-autobiographical poem after the fashion of
Shelley or Hugo ', because it was written at the Pines
in 1879–80.   But it had been conceived long before,
and Swinburne had with typical self-diffidence (a feeling new to him and uncommon in his days of lyrical
fervour) postponed it through fear of a possible accusa-
tion of ' arrogance and self-conceit '.   But *On the Cliffs*
was composed at Holmwood in July–August 1879
just before the country-house was sold and Swinburne
moved into the Pines.   The scene is made up of various
recollections and memories, as the poet is supposed to
stand by the seaside and listen to the song of a nightingale.   Full justice has not been done to this piece
which constitutes in my opinion the high-water-mark
of Swinburne's mature poetry.   Critics have com-
mented, in favourable or unfavourable terms, on the
form, its laxity of syntax and fluidity of rhythm which
come as near free verse as was possible for Swinburne's
poetry.   But the autobiographical accent, the incisive
and almost inhuman subtlety of analysis with which
the poet cuts through the gordian knot of his own soul
have not been sufficiently recognized :

From no loved lips and on no loving breast
Have I sought ever for such gifts as bring
Comfort, to stay the secret soul with sleep.
The joys, the loves, the labours, whence men reap
Rathe fruits of hopes and fears
I have made not mine ; the best of all my days
Have been as those fair fruitless summer strays,
Those water waifs that but the sea wind steers,
Flakes of glad foam or flowers on footless ways
That take the wind in season and the sun,
And when the wind wills is their season done.

Of course it is an echo from *Anactoria*. But the reference is here much more direct and clear, the parallel more minute and adequate. In comparison with this, *Thalassius* sounds coarse and artificial. Moreover those lines from *On the Cliffs* should be read in the light of the stanzas of *Poeta Loquitur*, that ferocious parody of himself written by Swinburne only a few months later :

Some singers indulging in curses,
    Though sinful, have splendidly sinned ;
But my would-be maleficent verses
    Are nothing but wind. [1]

Watts was horrified, and vetoed the appearance of this amazing and destructive piece in the volume *Heptalogia*. Nevertheless the passage I quoted from *On the Cliffs* is almost a poetical transposition of the parody.

In proportion as he became more critical, Swinburne found it extremely difficult to remain lyrical. This appears no less in the field of political inspiration. In fact it is nowhere so easy to perceive how truly disconcerted he was. In the days of Mazzini Swinburne

---

[1] ' Your letter gave me great pleasure and a sense of something in the rather dull monotonous puppet-show of my life which often strikes me as too barren of action or enjoyment to be much worth holding to, better than nothingness, or at least seeming better for a minute '. (To Churton Collins, March 27, 1876.)

was guided by the Chief's articles, letters and conversation, knew what to praise, blame or keep silent
about ; hence a real consistency in his views.   But
now Swinburne had to shift for himself.   In Italy he
had no great interest, for

> Rome [was] rent in twain of king and priest.

Germany he had at one time considered with some
favour, as, at Sadowa, she had broken the Austrian
might and helped Italian unity :

> Germany, what of the night ?
>   Long has it lulled me with dreams ;
>   Now at midwatch as it seems,
> Light is brought back to mine eyes,
> And the mastery of old and the might
>   Lives in the joints of mine hands,
> Steadies my limbs as they rise,
>   Strengthens my foot as it stands.

But after the French defeats, the fall of Napoleon III
and the constitution of the German Empire, the tables
were turned ; he wrote in 1872 : ' I hate them otherwise, but I must say the one good thing the Germans
can do—music—they do so much better than any other
people that no one even comes second.'

France might have taken in Swinburne's heart the
place vacated by Italy ; his feelings of love and admiration for her were never warmer than in 1872–79.
In a letter to Watts of December 8, 1876 in which he
explains why he did not dedicate the *Note on the Muscovite Crusade* to Karl Blind, he even went as far as proclaiming himself a Frenchman :

I had determined *against* my proposed dedication on the
single ground that, whatever feeling of personal loyalty and

gratitude towards Blind I might (as I do and always must and ought to) entertain, it would hardly seem consonant with my loyalty as a Frenchman (partly by blood and wholly in heart and sympathy and inherited duty) to inscribe my declaration of political faith in this matter to a man who, greatly to my regret, had publicly approved the violation, by Bismarck and his master, of Alsace and Lorraine.

But he was puzzled by the reactionary politics of the new French Republic, roused by the liberal opposition of *Le Rappel* which he read regularly, and indignant at a government which had exiled Victor Hugo. Had Hugo chosen to take charge of his political soul, as Mazzini had done, Swinburne would have felt relieved. Now, Hugo was a poet and a prophet, but above all a man of letters, not a leader. He was content with sending at regular intervals the most flattering messages : ' Bravo, O mon poète ', ' Vous êtes un grand esprit et un noble cœur ', ' Je suis fier de vous ', etc.—which was not of much help.

And this is why Swinburne, seeing how far off yet was the sunrise of the universal republic, began to leave off gazing on the horizon, and looked round him ; his interest in English politics grew in proportion as that in international affairs decreased. He began to discard that attitude of cold contempt for a nation of shopkeepers, too rich to care for Italy or a republican ideal, which Mazzini had dictated in the lines addressed to

> England, that bore up the weight
> Once of men's freedom, a freight
> Holy, but heavy to carry
> For hands overflowing with gold . . .

But, as he studied English affairs, he realized that his sympathies were not at all on the side they should have

been : Italian and French Radicals were all very well
—meeting Karl Blind, Mazzini, Louis Blanc, ' Attilo
Mariani ' and ' Pierre Sadier ' was all right.   But
against the English Radicals, Gladstone and Bright
and the Anglican business-men, all the aristocratic
instincts in Swinburne cried out.   Already in 1867 he
had made bold to ' tell the Chief that it was in our sort
of people that he must look for real faith and self-
devotion to a cause which could do us personally no
good and no harm—*not* in the Bright (Anglican-
Radical) set '.   But in spite of his ideology, Mazzini
was too much of a leader to listen to this sentimental
paradox.

As the years went on, Swinburne's confusion
increased.   He was for a little while supported in his
former attitude by a vague Jacobite hostility which
extended to all the Hanoverians (including Queen
Victoria, whom, despite what has been said, he treated
at that time with scant respect) and by a Mazzinian
distrust of all politicians, more particularly ' the author
of Codlingsby and such-like cattle ', as he graciously
described Disraeli.   But on January 8th, 1877 he had
reached the conclusion that ' Beaconsfield has the
merit (1) that he is not Gladstone (2) that he keeps
Gladstone out '.   On March 20th of the same year
in a letter to P. H. Hayne, he described in a final manner what were the horns of the dilemma on which he
was inevitably impaled : ' I find myself (an Englishman of the same class by birth and of the same opinions
by instinct as Shelley and Byron) utterly opposed to
the current of English Radicalism—and yet unable to
deny, or to disguise from myself, that the mass of
Englishmen on my side had adopted the same views

for reasons opposite to mine and on principles which I detested and despised.' In brief, Swinburne was unable to disentangle his principles from the personalities of those among his countrymen who upheld them, to separate the love inspired by the former from the hate aroused by the latter. What was he to do ?

For a long while, he kept silent. *Songs of Two Nations* (1875) is made up of poems practically all of which were composed before 1872, the one exception being the sonnets *The Descent into Hell*. But they only prove the rule : Swinburne was merely following up, with questionable taste, the old slogan that Napoleon III was a bastard and a coward. That, he could do very well ; to decide upon *new* issues was more delicate. Yet he was not allowed to hold his peace. *Songs before Sunrise* and his friendship for Mazzini had definitely committed him to the Liberal side. He had in November 1867 written a poem in defence of the sentenced Fenians, urging a reprieve. He had in 1868 been offered a seat in Parliament by the Reform League. Herbert Spencer now wrote to him asking the support of his name against English ' atrocities ' in Zululand and Afghanistan. At the end of 1876, Swinburne was solicited, probably by a Liberal body or paper, to ' say something on the Eastern Question '. The answer turned out to be different from what had been expected.

The circumstances were briefly these : in July 1875 the two Christian provinces of Bosnia and Herzegovina, secretly encouraged by Russian agents and relying on immediate help from Serbia and Montenegro, rebelled against Turkish authority. An arbitration between the Sultan and the insurgents was

offered by Russia, Germany and Austria, and at
Disraeli's instigation the Sultan accepted in January
1876 and even promised far-reaching internal reforms.
Russia and the insurgents however doubted Turkey's
sincerity. But Disraeli, whose foreign policy was
distinctly anti-Russian, declined to sign the Berlin
Memorandum which demanded immediate conces-
sions from the Turks. Russia's suspicions proved
well-founded when in May the French and German
consuls were murdered in Salonica, and in April the
Christian province of Bulgaria, in which the Tcherkess
or Turkish refugees from the Caucasian provinces,
now ruled by Russia, held the upper hand, was laid
waste by an army of 10,000 Bashi-Bazouks ; in a
few days 79 villages were burnt and 15,000 people
slaughtered. When this became known a wave of
indignation swept over England. Bright and Gladstone led the campaign in the Liberal Press and attacked Disraeli for his Turkish sympathies. *The
Daily News* wrote : ' If the question is whether
Bulgaria must be left at the mercy of the Turks or
conquered by Russia, let Russia conquer it and God
be with her.' The Press pandered to the sentimental
curiosity of their readers with detailed accounts of the
' Bulgarian atrocities '.[1] Famous men were enrolled
in the new ' crusade '. Morris and Carlyle wrote in
favour of Bulgaria. Disraeli had to yield and remon-
strated mildly with Turkey. But Russia at the end of
October sent an ultimatum to the Sultan, which
Disraeli criticized in a hostile speech on November 11.
At the end of December a European conference
opened at Constantinople to settle the situation ; the

---

[1] Gladstone wrote a pamphlet on the subject.

Russian ambassador wanted definite engagements, the English representative had instructions to spare the Turks.

It was then that Swinburne wrote his pamphlet, *Note on the Muscovite Crusade*. For reasons already mentioned, his sympathies were with Disraeli. Moreover he had been disgusted by the cheap methods used by the sensational Press in their effort to advertise and exploit the ' Bulgarian atrocities '. Russia he had never liked.

> I am she whose hands are strong and her eyes blinded
>   And lips athirst . . .
> By the stains and by the chains on me thy daughter
>   Hear us, O mother

exclaims Russia in the *Litany of Nations*. That attitude was partly a legacy of Mazzini's mistrust of Russian absolutism, partly, mostly I should say, a recollection of the boyish enthusiasm of the Crimean war, when to die at Balaklava was felt to be the highest bliss conceivable. Hate of Napoleon III and Russia were inextirpable feelings in Swinburne's heart. But Carlyle's intervention was the last straw ; the fascination which Nichol had, as early as 1857, taught Swinburne to feel for Carlyle, was gradually disappearing. Swinburne had deeply resented Carlyle's letter to *The Times* on the war of 1870. The circulation in 1874 of some unflattering comments on Swinburne (and in particular ' one beastly phrase ') by the ' philosophic nightman of Chelsea ' incensed him still further. The sonnets *Two Leaders* at the beginning of 1876 illustrate this evolution. With Carlyle's letter in favour of the Bulgarians, came for

Swinburne a great opportunity ; he realized his advantage, seized it and drove it home with tremendous strength. The *Note* is not so much a manifesto *against* the Bulgarians as a reply to Carlyle. But Swinburne at the beginning of 1876 had steeped himself in the *Areopagitica*, and with true Miltonic force, with metaphors and figures of speech not unlike Carlyle's own, he attacked the ' most foul-mouthed man of genius since the death of Swift ' in a style whose violence has never been matched, even by Carlyle himself. Swinburne very cleverly lays down that his quarrel is not ' with the Russian people as with an educated and adult nation ' but with the Czar and Carlyle, with the ' crusade which has Alexander of Russia for its Godfrey de Bouillon, and Thomas Carlyle for its Peter the Hermit '. He proceeds to show how Carlyle has no right to speak in the name of mercy, chivalry or Christianity ; now, although he sees ' nothing holier in a Sultan than in a Czar ', he prefers a ' waning evil ' to ' a waxing evil ' and, reversing the slogan of the Liberal Press, asserts that the Turkish scourge is preferable to that of the Russians. In the course of his argument, Swinburne hits upon some remarkable formulas and phrases, some purple passages of gorgeous oratory. The *Note* is one of the great vituperative pamphlets of English literature.

But Bright and the free-traders were let off lightly in the *Note* and Gladstone indeed received a handsome compliment. Swinburne proceeded to compose, as a supplement to his protest, a *Ballad of Bulgarie*, which however no magazine dared publish. Here contempt and anger are exchanged for parody and satire. The poet tells to ' robustious ballad tunes ' how ' the gentle

knight Sir John de Bright (of Brummagemme was he) '
would go and break a lance for Bulgaria :

> The mother maid Our Lady of Trade
> His spurs on heel she bound ;

He dons his ' basnet broad, no broader was to see ',
and exclaims before the fight in true epic fashion :

> Though Sir Thomas look black and Sir William go back
> What tongue is mine to wag
> By the help of our lady, tho' matters look shady
> It shall fight for the Red-Cross flag !

The ballad is a highly successful piece of burlesque.

But Swinburne felt that in his lust for personal
attacks, in his denunciation of the ' blazon on the shield
of the leader, the watchword on the preacher's lips '
he had lost sight of the ulterior purpose of the ' crusade ', and somewhat betrayed his principles. This
is why he solicited the approval of Karl Blind, the old
German Liberal and friend of Mazzini, and was glad
to receive his blessing : ' Thanks again and most
cordially for your most kind letter. It is a very great
honour to be accepted as a fellow soldier (tho' but a
humble private and good only as a trumpet or flag
bearer to some small regiment) in the great and noble
army of which you are one of the generals ' (December
31st, 1876). Swinburne was thus persuading himself
that he was still fighting in the same troops and for
the same colours.[1]

---

[1] The epilogue of Swinburne's anti-crusade was most unsatisfactory. Russia,
spurred to war by Turkey's impudence, crushed the Sultan in the war of 1877–78.
All that Disraeli could do was to deprive the Czar of some of the fruits of his victory.
But the *Bulgarian Crusade* was successful and a semi-autonomous Bulgaria consti-
tuted. Swinburne vented his rage in his sonnets, *The White Czar*, which the London
Press again declined to print. They found their way into the *Glasgow University
Magazine,*

It appears that Swinburne's chief activities in the years 1877–1879 were in the field of criticism. This is not literally quite correct : practically all the papers in *Essays and Studies* were written before 1872 ; *Joseph and his Brethren* was simply rewritten and re-cast from an early manuscript of 1860. Some seem-ingly critical works like *Under the Microscope* and the *Note on Charlotte Brontë* contain only digressive and indirect criticism. Swinburne found it impossible to continue the 'criticism of beauties' as he had practised it in *William Blake* and the *Poems of D. G. Rossetti* ; he passed on to the 'criticism of defects' ; he experienced difficulties in being enthusiastic or lyrical even in prose. This holds good in spite of fine eloquent passages which can be gathered here and there—on Byron and Whitman, in *Under the Micro-scope*—on Browning in *George Chapman*. The chief exception is the *Essay on Shakespeare* composed from 1875 to 1880 and published in book-form in the latter year. But here again, the book, despite Swinburne's boundless enthusiasm for his subject, is not, except for a few paragraphs, a work of blind admiration and lyrical raptures. It forms as clear a contrast as could be wished to Hugo's *William Shakespeare*. One could almost say that it is a work of cold logic and sound common sense. Swinburne, with poise and intelligence, though not without fine aesthetic sense, endeavours to steer clear of the rocks, to strike a middle course between the wild exaggerations of critics and scholars. The theory he submits (that of the 'three stages of Shakespeare') has, he knows, been 'forestalled by the common insight of some hundred or more students in time past'. He merely aims at

setting down ' what the writer believes to be certain
demonstrable truths as to the progress and development of style, the outer and the inner changes of manner as of matter '.   In brief he strives to eliminate from
his Shakespearean criticism (as he had from his
political and physical conception of the world) all
the ' metaphysics ' of German commentators and their
disciples, ' hypotheses of a floating or nebulous kind ',
all accounts and statistics which will ' help us exactly
as much as a naked catalogue of the colours employed
in one particular picture '—all the romantic excesses
of the pseudo-scientific school.   This he manages
admirably, and in fact, in spite of his subtle artistic
criticism here and there, his powerful refutation of
Hugo's parallel between Panurge, Panza and Falstaff,
his bold but always plausible conjectures concerning
Arden of Feversham, *Henry VIII*, *The Two Noble Kins-
men*—the *Essay* seems often too sensible, too sober and
matter of fact : from a poet, from such a poet, something more startling was expected.   What saves the
Essay however, what gives it point and a symbolical
value, is the attack on Furnivall and his school, the
ruthless condemnation of the ' critics by rule of
thumb ', ' who hear only through their fingers and
have not even fingers to hear with '.   As such, the
Essay is useful, and even epoch-making.   But this is
destructive, and has to do with controversy and satire,
rather than criticism.

It is in another direction, and in an unexpected
one, that we must look for criticism of positive value in
the work of Swinburne at that time.   I must here beg
leave to open what is only a seeming digression.   It is
rather late in the day to reveal new facts about

Swinburne's works, but I feel tempted, though with some hesitation, to claim that I may do so, even after Gosse's *Life* and Mr. T. J. Wise's *Bibliography*.

In December 1875, Stéphane Mallarmé on the suggestion of O'Shaughnessy wrote to Swinburne, who had given Augusta Holmes permission to publish a translation of his poem *The Pilgrims*, thanking him on behalf of his new-born review, *La République des Lettres*, and begging him to contribute *in French* ' une page ou des strophes '. Swinburne—who had in 1872 received a similar request from *La Renaissance*—was immensely flattered. He revelled in the thought, slightly exaggerated though not unjustified, that he had in France a large circle of admirers and disciples. It is well known that on February 20th, 1876 he contributed *Nocturne* to the *République des Lettres*. But Mallarmé had asked for ' une page ' as well as ' des strophes ', and on February 5, 1876 Swinburne informed the delighted editor that he had ' commencé un petit travail que je me propose d'offrir à la République des Lettres sur le grand peintre-poète William Blake ' : and Mallarmé answered : ' Oh oui ! que nous serons heureux des fragments de Blake'(11 February). In letters to Watts (February 8) and W. M. Rossetti (March 12) Swinburne refers to his French Essay on Blake, and fragments of a French translation from Blake's poems appear on the verso of the manuscript of *The Last Oracle* in Mr. Wise's collection. In June 1876 Swinburne told Mallarmé he had finished his ' notes sur Blake ' and Mallarmé answered that there was no hurry as the Review was going to be taken over by a new publisher and continued in a more important form. Nothing more has ever been heard either about the ' Notes sur Blake ' or a long article on Swinburne's works which Mallarmé had announced to the poet as early as January 1876.

However the *République des Lettres* went on appearing regularly until June 3, 1877. To pore over its files is not a fruitless task. It must first be stated, as Mr. Payen-Payne has done, that Swinburne's name is not appended to any article, and that Mallarmé printed under his name no study on Swinburne. But our attention is soon attracted by a series of articles entitled ' Les artistes étranges ' which are due to the pen of one Herbert Harvey. Those *artistes étranges* are : William Blake, A. C. Swinburne and the German poet Heinrich von Kleist. Our attention is maintained when we discover that those articles are truly remarkable in matter as well as in form.

Who is this Herbert Harvey who in 1877 could write with such understanding of Blake and, chiefly, of Swinburne ? No information is forthcoming. He wrote these three short studies and then for ever kept silent. Dictionaries, encyclopedias, histories of literature (French and English) are of no avail. Herbert Harvey is totally unknown. Unknown ? perhaps not quite, at least to the students and lovers of Swinburne's works. Herbert is the Christian name of the hero of the autobiographical novel *Lesbia Brandon*. As for Hervey (or Harvey), where have we seen that name before ? Is he not that chivalrous figure, that high-souled constable, who, blugdon [*sic*] in hand, plays such a prominent part in *La Fille du Policeman* ?

May it be then that Harvey is a pseudonym ? that Swinburne wrote the articles ? Although a positive proof is lacking (the letters to and from Mallarmé stop after June 1876) one is almost forced to this conclusion. The internal evidence is tremendous. The style is that of Swinburne, corrected or improved by Mallarmé or somebody else. In preference to the *Blake*, made up largely of translations, and to the *Henri von Kleist* which illustrates the interest the poet experienced in some aspects of German literature (*vide* his admiration for Heine) we must quote the following truly remarkable passage from his study on himself (*République des Lettres*, 18 February, 1877) :

Ce n'est pas sans dessein que j'ai nommé l'auteur des Fleurs du Mal ; il est une des deux ou trois personnes auxquelles Swinburne ressemble. Ils ont traité fréquemment des sujets analogues, sinon identiques. Ceux qui voient en eux des malades disent qu'ils ont la même maladie. Mais la ressemblance s'atténue et bientôt disparait quand on pénètre plus intimement dans leurs œuvres. Ch. Beaudelaire [*sic*] était retenu, méticuleux, circonspect ; Swinburne c'est la passion sans bride, qui ne s'arrête pas aux détails imprudents. Beaudelaire [*sic*] avait des remords au milieu même de ses plus hardis écarts ; c'est là ce qui lui donne ces façons de penser et d'exprimer, pleines de réticences dévotieuses ; il semble que l'on écoute non loin d'un confessionnal les confidences d'un pécheur, et cette impression ajoute un mauvais charme au plaisir qu'on éprouve. Les remords, Swinburne ne les connait point ; sa mélancolie ne lui vient pas de la crainte d'un avenir vengeur, ses élans ne sont point entravés par le souci du châtiment ; s'il souffre, s'il s'épouvante, c'est parce que les plus excessives jouissances sont incapables d'éteindre le désir allumé en lui. Il se livre tout entier, éperdument, sans retour, à la poursuite de la Volupté, ' la seule chose, dit-il, qui soit aussi certaine que la mort '. Il la veut, il la possède avec un furieux amour et avec une suprême indifférence de tout ce qui n'est pas elle. Il y a je ne sais quelle magnanimité farouche dans ses appétits coupables. Il songe souvent aux Héliogabales et aux belles impératrices impures. C'est un dieu bestial. Beaudelaire [*sic*] était catholique, Swinburne est païen. Il se sent violemment attiré vers ces époques pompeuses et

perverses ou ' le bien disait : mon frère le mal ', ou ' Aphrodite
sortait, rouge de vin '.   C'est à elles qu'il emprunte le plus
communément ses sujets.   Mais ne lui demandez ni exactitude
de mœurs, ni ce que nous nommons couleur locale.   La Revue
anglaise, qui a dit de lui, en étudiant *Atalanta in Corydon* [*sic*]
que dans ses poèmes antiques il n'émet jamais une pensée
moderne, cette Revue l'a fort maladroitement loué et s'est
trompée ridiculement.   Ne cherchez pas dans Phaedra, dans
Hermaphroditus, et dans l'Hymne à Proserpine, cette profonde
intuition du passé que révèlent les nobles poèmes de Leconte de
Lisle.   Swinburne est païen, non pas comme un Grec du temps
d'Aeschyle, mais comme peut l'être un Anglais du 19ᵉ siècle.

Even if Swinburne never wrote these words, they
deserve to be quoted, and the problematic Herbert
Harvey is entitled to a niche in the History of criticism.
But one's first impulse after reading these lines (with
their seemingly intentional misprints—Beaudelaire,
Atalanta in *Corydon*—their unfrench phrases—' réticences dévotieuses '—and striking alliteration—'*é*poques
*p*ompeuses et *p*erverses ') is to exclaim—in true Swinburnian style—' Aut Carolus Swinburne aut Dia-
bolus '.   And if it can be proved that Swinburne wrote
that essay, it will stand as a fresh and most striking
illustration of the intensity and precision of critical
analysis which he had then reached with reference to
himself ; it will be proved that there was no lyrical
poet—perhaps no man of letters—more exactly aware
of the strength and limitations of his genius than Swinburne was.

One last obstacle remains to be disposed of :
Swinburne, once he had published the pseudonymous
article on Blake may well have been tempted to use
the name of Harvey to write one on himself (' I should
like to review myself ', he wrote to Hatch in 1858).
But why not sign the Blake paper with his own name

in the first instance ? What incited him, after signing *Nocturne*, to use an assumed name ? Is there any reason for this ? There is : the *République des Lettres* was then publishing as a serial *L'Assommoir*, of which Swinburne highly disapproved. He vowed that he would not allow his name to stand as that of a fellow contributor of Zola. But the novel was interminable, and the *Notes on Blake* were ready. So Swinburne changed his name to Herbert Harvey. Thus is explained for the first time the enigmatic sentence in the letter on Zola which Swinburne had printed a little later in the *Athenaeum* : ' During the appearance of [*L'Assommoir*] I purposely and resolvedly abstained from contributing anything to [*La République des Lettres*,] tho' my name might still appear on its cover in the same list of contributors with his '.

If Swinburne is the author of those essays [1] they count as the most striking pages of criticism he wrote during the period now under consideration. But they are an exception, and the fact remains that Swinburne's critical works are chiefly remarkable for a tendency to satire and controversy. While the tendency to praise enthusiastically is now qualified and subdued, violent and often very effective denunciations abound in his prose works.

The most striking instance is of course to be found in the controversy with Buchanan. Between Swinburne and the Scotchman some private enmity can be traced as far back as January 1866, when Payne

[1] I do not state definitely that he is, but merely that the evidence in the favour of this hypothesis is very strong. As there is no reference to the authorship of the articles (Watts was not *au courant*—see Swinburne's letter of March 6, 1877) in the correspondence, the only proof positive might come from the records of the *République des Lettres* or from the Mallarmé papers. Let us hope it will some day.

decided to cancel an essay on Keats which Buchanan had
written on commission and transfer the work to Swinburne. Buchanan's retort was *The Session of the Poets*
published in the *Spectator* for October 1866 over the
name of Caliban ; Swinburne resented bitterly this
' last word of blackguardism '. A passing (and extremely sensible) reference to Buchanan's friend, David
Gray, in *Matthew Arnold's New Poems* may or may not
have aroused Caliban's wrath. But nothing of an irreparable nature had so far passed between the two men,
and about that time Swinburne attended at the Han-
over Square rooms one of Buchanan's lectures to which
he had been invited. It is Buchanan who is fully responsible for opening (or re-opening) the hostilities.
In October 1871 he published in the *Contemporary
Review* what claimed to be a general denunciation of
amatory poetry from Aretino onwards, but was really
an attack on Swinburne and Rossetti. Buchanan may
have been actuated partly by moral scruples, partly by
personal spite as shown by a letter to Robert Browning printed by Mr. Wise. It seems indubitable however that his chief desire was to create a cheap sensation. Although his name did not appear, and the
editor was alleged to have added the pseudonym of
Thomas Maitland to what was primarily intended to
be an anonymous attack, [1] it is probable that Buchanan
would have come forward and claimed the authorship,
had the article been the success he expected. It is the
curse of national prudery and moral sensitiveness,

---

[1] This was Buchanan's own version : ' I wished to publish my article on the
Fleshly School anonymously, to let the article stand upon its own merits.' He disclaimed responsibility for the pseudonym of Thomas Maitland by stating that he was
then ' on a cruise in the Hebrides ' and that the editor added the name without
consulting him.

feelings which are respectable in themselves, that they should always be liable to be exploited by those who are least endowed with them.

Swinburne's answer was *Under the Microscope* in 1872, a memorable pamphlet, which is not as well known as it deserves owing to the fact that, through Watts's intervention, it was not included in *Essays and Studies* in 1875. This ' fragment of a prose Dunciad ' is eminently a piece of controversy ; but a clever one. The author pretends to study with due parade of scientific jargon those germs and animalcules of literature, the journalists and critics. He is careful not to begin with Buchanan. He first brushes aside the anonymous, then after an indirect attack on Browning (whose cordial relations with Buchanan must have incensed Swinburne) he proceeds to examine ' under the microscope ' a ' germ ' of tolerable size and importance, Austin of the *Spectator* ; this allows him to indulge in a tremendous denunciation of the morality of Tennyson's *Idylls of the King*, in which Arthur appears as a ' wittol ', Guinevere as a ' woman of intrigue ', Lancelot as ' a co-respondent '. Next comes a panegyric of Walt Whitman, and it is only then that he descends to Buchanan, the ' germ ' of countless names and many addresses :

Now yachting among the Scottish (not English) Hebrides ; now wrestling with fleshly sin (like his countryman Holy Willie) in ' a great city of civilization ' ; now absorbed in studious emulation of the Persae of Aeschylus or the ' enormously fine ' work of ' the tremendous creature ' Dante ; now descending from the familiar heights of men whose praise he knows so well how to sing, for the not less noble purpose of crushing a school of poetic sensualists whose works are ' wearing to the brain ' ; now ' walking down the streets ' and watching 'harlots stare from the shopwindows', while 'in the broad day a dozen hands offer him indecent prints' ; now 'beguiling many an hour, when snug at anchor in some lovely Highland loch, with the inimitable, yet questionable, pictures of Parisian life left by Paul de Kock' ; landsman and seaman, Londoner and Scotchman, Delian and Patarene Buchanan. How should one address him ?

The 'scientific' hierarchy has been carefully observed throughout : first (introduced by way of digression but essential to the whole scheme) Byron and Tennyson, then Whitman and Lowell, then Austin, then Buchanan, 'as much beneath Mr. Austin as Mr. Austin is beneath the main objects of his attack'. Now the pamphlet is drawing to a fitting close, with the poet's comment on Buchanan's remark that 'inevitably a training in Grecian literature must tend to emasculate the student so trained' :

And well may we congratulate ourselves that no such progress as robbed of all strength and manhood the intelligence of Milton, has had power to impair the virility of Mr. Buchanan's virile and masculine genius. To that strong and severe figure we turn from the sexless and nerveless company of shrill-voiced singers who share with Milton the curse of enforced effeminacy ; from the pitiful soprano notes [1] of such dubious creatures as Marlowe, Jonson, Chapman, Gray, Coleridge, Shelley, Landor, 'cum semiviro comitatu', we avert our ears to catch the higher and manlier harmonies of a poet with all his natural parts and powers complete. For truly if love or knowledge of ancient art and wisdom be the sure mark of 'emasculation', and the absence of any taint of such love and any tincture of such knowledge (as then in consistency it must be) the supreme sign of perfect manhood, Mr. Robert Buchanan should be amply competent to renew the thirteenth labour of Hercules.

Swinburne let Buchanan's tedious piece of doggerel, *The Monkey and the Microscope*, pass unnoticed. But

[1] In the *Fleshly School*, Buchanan had alluded to Swinburne's 'falsetto'.

the anonymous poem entitled *Jonas Fisher*, published
in 1875, aroused his wrath. Jonas Fisher, a city mis-
sionary in Edinburgh, was supposed to make free comments on the various vices of the age. The same
criticism which Buchanan had levelled at the *Fleshly
School* was repeated ; this was not surprising, for the
author, Lord Southesk, knew Buchanan well. So
obvious was the resemblance that the critics of the
Examiner were deceived and wrote, in a sarcastic review of the poem, that the author was ' either Buchanan
or the devil '. Thereupon Swinburne sent to Minto,
the editor, a letter entitled the *Devil's Due* and signed
in jest ' Thomas Maitland ' which duly appeared on
December 11. Swinburne affected ironically to doubt
that Buchanan was the author, and proffered mock-
reasons to prove that the ' poet of many aliases ' was
not responsible for *Jonas Fisher*. Unfortunately he
added in an appendix that Buchanan could not have
written the poem because he was on a cruise ' in the
Philippine islands in the steam-yacht Skulk, Captain
Shuffleton '.[1] These expressions, coupled with others
used in the *Examiner's* review, might pass as libellous.
Buchanan, through Messrs. Russell and McClymont
took action. The attitude of Taylor (the proprietor
of the paper) and of Minto seems to have been very
unfair to Swinburne ; they completely lost their nerve,
gave up his name at once and suggested that action
should be taken against him alone. Fortunately one
of Buchanan's counsel, McClymont, was a former
student of Jowett, and had even been introduced
to Swinburne. He seems to have behaved very

---

[1] An allusion to Buchanan's letter, acknowledging the authorship of the *Fleshly
School*, dated from St. Kilda, March 1872.

handsomely and prevented Buchanan from prosecuting Swinburne and letting off Taylor. The case was tried in June–July 1876. Taylor's counsel, Hawkins, with unaccountable timidity pleaded ' that the question was about the conduct of Taylor, not that of Rossetti or Swinburne ; that Taylor had no animosity against Buchanan ; that Buchanan had been told who was the author of the article and offered the manuscript, but that he refused to take action against Swinburne '. After hearing Justice Archibald's summing up, which was in many ways far more dishonourable for the plaintiff than for Swinburne, the jury allowed Buchanan £150 damages instead of the £5,000 he claimed. Swinburne, despite Watts' ill-advised intervention, refused to make ' a graceful gesture ' and to bear part of the expenses of the trial. Documents which only came to light later show that in so doing he acted with great common sense and dignity.

It has been necessary to deal in detail with this controversy seeing that it plays such an important part in the life of Swinburne ; it is also typical of many others. Partly perhaps because he became ill-tempered and irritable, but partly also because his critical faculties were more alert than ever, Swinburne was led to engage in numberless quarrels and literary jousts. I can only mention here his public letter to that ' foul-mouthed and gap-toothed old dog ' Emerson, from whom some remarks, insulting to Swinburne, had been quoted in a newspaper interview ;—his brush with the sweet-named Collette, president of the Society for the Suppression of Vice, about ' the book called Rabelais ';—his letter on Zola's *Assommoir*;—his attacks on George Eliot in the *Note on Charlotte Brontë* ;—his parodies of

Lytton and Browning, published in 1880 but composed about this time ; his controversy with Furnivall and 'the Newest Shakespeare society' [1] which did not come to an end till well after 1879.

In such an atmosphere, which he was not alone responsible in creating, it is natural that the character of Swinburne should have become sour and defiant. He was intensely aware of the campaign of anonymous abuse which ever since 1866 had been intermittently raging about his name ; and though he would not let himself be influenced by it unduly, as Rossetti did, he could not but feel a sort of weariness at times. In a fine letter of April 1876 he wrote to Watts : ' If any insult is levelled at me in print of which, were it your own case, you would feel it due to yourself to take some kind of public notice . . . then and then only I trust you as my friend . . . to send me the printed attack on the spot. But in any less serious case than this it seems to me by no means worth while for any-one to trouble himself or his friend about the matter.'

His attitude to life was naturally altered. Many of his former friendships appeared to him in a different light. This, as I have already suggested, happened in the case of Rossetti. But here the painter-poet probably bears the entire responsibility of the estrangement. It seems that in the summer of 1872 Rossetti resented some criticism which Swinburne had passed (from the point of view of fitness for publication) on some of his poems—a criticism which was

[1] The controversy, which I have no room to describe in detail, is most entertaining to study. In the course of those heated polemics Furnivall came to call Swinburne ' Pigsbrook ' ; Swinburne retaliated with ' Brothelsdyke ', and henceforth always described as ' Furnivallscap ' the large blue sheets on which he used to compose his poems.

fully warranted by the frankness which had hitherto
prevailed between the two men.   From that date
Rossetti avoided Swinburne without giving any
reason : ' To this day I am utterly ignorant and unable
to conjecture why, after the last parting in the early
summer of 1872, he should have chosen suddenly to
regard me as a stranger. . . .'   And Swinburne, now
enlightened, knew that he had given more than he had
received.   But he learned from experience, and soon
after his intimacy with Lord Houghton and Howell
cooled off : ' Thank something ', he wrote in January
1877, ' there are spirits of another sort—and I have
met with my share of them as well as of Houghtons
and Rossettis (D. G.)'.   With Simeon Solomon the
case was different.   When in the summer of 1873
alarming rumours began to circulate about the young
painter, Swinburne reflected that he had done enough
to endanger his own reputation in many directions
and that he could not afford to let accusations of a
certain nature, however unjustified, be levelled at him
on the score that he was Solomon's friend.   In a certain way, in his own eyes, and within a certain circle
of people, the Burtons, the Mazzinis, the Rossettis,
he had preserved his respectability ; and that he was
not going to sacrifice.   On June 6th he wrote to
Powell : ' I saw and spoke with a great friend of poor
Simeon, Pater of Brasenose. . . . I suppose there is no
doubt the poor unhappy little fellow has really been
out of his mind and *done* things amenable to law such
as done by a sane man would make it impossible for
anyone to keep up his acquaintance and not be cut by
the rest of the world as an accomplice ? I have been
seriously unhappy about it for I had a real affection

and regard for him—and beside his genius he had such genuinely amiable qualities. It is the simple truth that the distress of it has haunted and broken my sleep. It is hideous to lose a friend by madness of any kind, let alone this. Do you—I do not—know of any detail of the matter at first hand ? Pater I imagine did.'

But there were ' spirits of another sort ', old and trusted friends like Nichol, Madox Brown, W. M. Rossetti, Knight, Purnell, Jowett,¹ whose interest in Swinburne was slowly ripening into affection and through whom he came to know many young Oxford men (Harrison, Julian Field, Bywater, etc.);—and also acquaintances of a more recent date, men for the most part younger than Swinburne ; these did not assume the controlling attitude or paternal authority of Houghton or Rossetti ; they did not treat him like Meredith as a wonderfully bright child to be petted and put to bed at the proper time. They had been stirred by his work to the depth of their souls ; they came to him with respect and loyalty ; they looked up to him as a Master. This was new to Swinburne and intensely gratifying. There was Edmund Gosse (far different from the Edmund Gosse we knew in later years) ' torn between the claims of a dying puritanism and those of a vaguely invading paganism ', who had written to the poet as early as 1867, and received an admirable letter, cold, dignified and manly, full of the most salutary advice ; but at the close of 1870 he was introduced at Madox Brown's house, and Swinburne was attracted by his pleasant conversation and tact, his

¹ One is tempted to add Barry Cornwall (Bryan Waller Procter), who died in 1874. (See Swinburne's poem in *Poems and Ballads, Second Series*) ; the two men had been on friendly terms since 1866, in spite of the fact that Procter had published very clever parodies of Swinburne. The poet was also Mrs. Procter's friend.

wide, or rather widening interests and reading ; as for Gosse, he was dazzled by Swinburne, and, as he told me, ' would follow him about like a dog '. There was the blind poet Philip Bourke Marston, who had a real hero-worship for him. There were O'Shaughnessy and others. It was at this time that Swinburne began to give private readings of his poems to those new friends (the first references to such ceremonies appear in letters dated 1873–1874). A real ' school ' began to spring around him. ' I have had so many readings ', he wrote to his mother on April 12, 1874, ' It is very fascinating and I don't wonder it killed Dickens. The intoxicating effect of a circle of faces hanging on your words and keeping up your own excitement by theirs which is catching even when your own words on mere paper are stale to you is such that I wonder how actors stand it nightly. . . . I have been gathering about me the circle of younger poets who are called *my* disciples " à moi " and bestowing the unpublished *Bothwell* upon their weak minds. They are very nice fellows and very loyal to me as their leader. There are five or six aged from 23 to 31 or so who have been presented to me at different times '.

Among those ' disciples ' there must have been, at the time, no more pathetic figure than Theodore Watts. I may, for many reasons, be mistaken, but it seems to me that during the first months of his mixing with literary society in London Theodore Watts was a touching and pathetic figure. This new friend at least was not Swinburne's junior. Born in 1832 at St. Ives, Huntingdonshire, the son of a country solicitor, Theodore Watts set out to study law so as to be

able to carry on his father's profession. A slow medi-
tative mind and a grim steadiness of purpose qualified
him for achieving that end. But a brooding disposition, a love of the mysterious rather than of the beautiful, and a deep-rooted mystical strain in his nature
drew him to art and literature. He read Scott and
Borrow, and romantic tendencies took definite possession of a mind unprotected by any classical education.
Ruskin and Preraphaelite art introduced him to Pre-
raphaelite verse. He fell a prey to the charm of Rossetti's 'sugared sonnets' (translations from the
Italian). Then came *Atalanta* and *Poems and Ballads* ;
this country solicitor was one of the many victims of
Dolores and *Anactoria* to whom reference has already
been made. And his legal soul was lost.

It was at least much imperilled. London drew him
like a magnet ; he was more often in the capital than
his occupations warranted. Whether for this or other
reasons his father's business declined. His brother—
a solicitor in London—died. Through a common
friend, Dr. Gordon Hake, he was introduced to
Rossetti. The dice were cast. He threw up everything
and settled in London (1872). He probably met
Swinburne at Madox Brown's house in the course of
1872, although the poet was not much in London in
that year. If we may follow Gosse, who purports to
give Watts' own version, his first attempt to gain the
acquaintance of Swinburne was 'so unsuccessful that the
door of hope seemed closed to him '. Neither should
we wonder : Watts was provincial and middle-class ;
Swinburne aristocratic and cosmopolitan. Moreover
Watts was approaching these great poets in an intensely
serious spirit of admiration, and expected to find them

as sad, sorrowful and sincere as their own verse ; Swinburne's boisterous humour and satirical tirades disconcerted him. It was some time before he rediscovered
the poet behind the Baudelairian *grand seigneur*. He
was at the time more attracted to the already diseased
and more serious personality of Rossetti. As to Swinburne, let us say frankly that at first he must have
found Watts a bore.

But he was drawn to him by inevitable forces which
far exceeded the superficial importance of first impressions. It is not correct to say that Watts had a genius
for friendships ; he had the gift to develop and improve
them. But a friendship must first be started, and Watts
had not, especially in those days, that easy wit, those
genial manners which make it possible to establish an
immediate intimacy. He was no Howell, though he
was worth twenty Howells. But he possessed two
saving gifts in the eyes of the artists and bohemians of
genius (full of genius, but short of money, always at a
loss to convert the one into the maximum of the
other) whom he knew : first he was a lawyer ; and
secondly he was a literary critic. He was already
Rossetti's legal adviser ; Swinburne was in the thick
of his quarrel with Hotten ; he was bound to have
recourse to Watts. By the end of October 1872 we
find them corresponding regularly together.

This will enable us to answer at least partly the
much-vexed question of the relations between Swinburne and Watts. How did the poet who had enjoyed
the friendships of Rossetti, Meredith, Morris, Burton,
Mazzini, choose to make his closest friend of a country
solicitor of undoubted ability but of questionable
genius ? How did the eternal rebel, whom even

Mazzini could not quite tame and who had exhausted the patience of an Admiral and a collegeful of Dons, let alone the British public and Press, come to obey that gruff voice from Huntingdonshire, to live with Watts, and to give up in his favour not all but a great deal of his independence ?   We can at least watch the first steps of their acquaintanceship.

The publication of *Songs before Sunrise* by Ellis had not marked the end of Swinburne's difficulties with Hotten. The poet, under the pressure of circumstances in August 1866, had become entangled with a publisher of doubtful character who was determined not to let him go scot-free. He had waived his claims to *Songs before Sunrise* but not to further works of Swinburne, in particular the *Bothwell* and several books on the Elizabethans which he had unwisely been allowed to advertise. It was Watts' task—and honour—to extricate Swinburne from his clutches.

For now the negotiations were not conducted casually by friends who could only spare a little time, like W. M. Rossetti ; Hotten was confronted with a lawyer, honest, as disinterested as could be, and one who had sworn in his soul that England's greatest lyric poet, a man of international reputation, should not for ever, through the mismanagement and dishonesty of others, be a financial failure. He had to be infinitely patient and wary ; for neither Hotten nor Swinburne were ordinary beings. In October 1872 Ellis was ready to become Swinburne's publisher ; the great difficulty was to obtain Hotten's consent in an amicable manner, offering, if necessary, to buy his stock. But *Songs before Sunrise* sold very slowly, and on November 9 Watts had to report to Swinburne that Ellis had 'politely declined' to buy Hotten's stock ; but he added that he had approached another publisher, King, who was willing to consider the matter if he could examine a detailed statement of Hotten's sales and stock. The problem was to obtain such a statement from Hotten, who seems to have remained several years without rendering Swinburne any accounts. After calling three times, Watts saw Hotten and was promised the document. But Hotten refused to let the poet write his *Essay on Chapman* for another firm. 'He is ignorant and vulgar', tactfully concluded Watts, ' but he knows you can write a capital essay.'

On December 5, Hotten's statement had not been sent, and Watts was contemplating legal action. King was still anxious to consider the matter. But Swinburne discovered that King had purchased the *Contemporary Review* and was the publisher of the Collected Works of Robert Buchanan ! He wrote to Watts a flaming letter expressing his ' surprise and disgust '. This nearly broke Watts' heart ; but he answered with inexhaustible tact and patience : ' I admire your indomitable pluck, but why descant [*sic*] King ? He is making a generous (between us a foolish) offer. The *Contemporary Review* was just a commercial affair. . . . Yet I understand your feeling'. With admirable diplomacy Watts dropped the King scheme (' we must fire him up ') and approached Chapman and Hall : the firm made very liberal terms and offered to bring out a cheap edition of the poems (uniform with the works of Carlyle). Swinburne was delighted at this ' turning of the tide after so many years of drifting and insecurity and ill-luck in all business matters '.

He wrote in a triumphant mood to his friend Powell :
' Apart from the profit and credit [arising from a 2*s.*
edition of his works] please imagine me stalking
triumphant through the land and displaying on every
Hearth in every Home of my country, naked and *not*
ashamed, the banner of immorality, atheism and
revolution ! ' Watts pursued successfully the negotiations with Chapman ; in his next letter the cool business instinct of the man is revealed with uncommon
intensity : ' You will get [from Chapman] the cash
you want. But don't show you need it. Mr. Chapman is not likely to take a mean advantage (he is a
gentleman). But it is wonderful how practical gentlemen are in business matters, as you may have observed
if you have ever bought a horse from a friend or sold
one to him. Imperceptibly to himself, Mr. Chapman
would be more anxious to deal liberally with you if he
thought we didn't care a damn whether he dealt with
us or not. He himself has lost a card or two, by
exhibiting his own anxiety to treat. As a man, I like
him the more, but as a trader, I respect him the less '.
There is something almost sinister in this last sentence.
Indeed, indeed the man who wrote it was no ordinary
legal adviser ; he had in him a strain of Ulysses and
Machiavelli ; how well he deserved that nickname of
' Watts the wise ' by which he was known among his
new friends !

Chapman went so far as to have a specimen page
of the cheap edition printed and submitted to Swinburne. But Hotten was still the great difficulty ; a
statement was extracted from him in January 1873,
but as soon as he heard that Swinburne intended to
leave him, he claimed that an ' oral contract ' between

them ' provided he should always print and sell the
books he now has on hand and that you cannot take
them out of his hands. He will litigate. He means
fight '. And Watts lamented ' This business is most
harassing '.

Watts conferred with Howell and W. M. Rossetti,
who had assisted in the negotiations of August 1866.
Swinburne declared that Hotten's claim as to an ' oral
contract ' was false ; but he did so with a reticence
which must have disconcerted Watts. The truth was
that Swinburne was half-afraid, because there was a
skeleton in his, or rather in Hotten's, cupboard.
Hotten, it has been said repeatedly, was a publisher
of dubious character ; he was responsible for books
dealing with flagellation etc. Swinburne had been im-
prudent enough to give him ' a list[1] drawn up in my
hand of scenes in school which he was to get sketched
for me on approval by a draughtsman of his acquaintance (I believe one Corcoran who did vignettes for one
or two of his books) in which list I had explained the
posture and actions of " swishing "'. This practice of
Swinburne to ' order ' drawings of scenes he previously
described in detail was with him quite a passion, and
it was partly this which endeared to him people like
Solomon and Howell, who were able to draw—which
he could not do himself. And he now feared that
Hotten might be induced to publish those ' descriptions ' in some ' History of Flagellation ' or
' Romance of the Rod '. ' But of course ', he added
in his letter to Howell, ' you would say nothing to
anyone, least of all men to Watts '.

[1] Those ' school lists ', together with other papers of the same character, were
once in the possession of Mr. Wise, who gave them to an Oxford friend.

Did Watts suspect anything ? It is not unlikely, though he did not let it appear. But Chapman had heard about Hotten's contentions, and also that the latter had a stock of 5,000 unsold volumes ! The publishers are an extremely shy and timorous race, rather akin to the hare—as depicted in La Fontaine's fable. Many have taken fright at less. He begged Watts to wait some weeks as Hotten was threatened with bankruptcy. Meanwhile ' Watts the wise ' lavished the wisest advice on Swinburne. : ' Don't sell *Bothwell* too cheaply. Publish your lyrics in an American paper first ' ; he was thus the means of opening for Swinburne an important source of profits on the American market.

Small wonder if Swinburne was grateful and suggested on March 28 that ' we might begin mutually to drop the Mr. in writing as friends '. In less than a year Watts had gained Swinburne's friendship, but he thoroughly deserved it by his endless labours, his mixture of diplomacy and sound advice, his capacity to combine flattery with business realities.

However, circumstances did not allow Watts' intervention to develop fully : he had in January 1873 filed a bill in Chancery against Hotten ; but in June Hotten died suddenly. His successor and former partner, Andrew Chatto, showed great anxiety to remain Swinburne's publisher and, as he was a man of unstained character, Swinburne, on Watts' advice, retained him, and the Chapman scheme came to nought.

It should not however be believed that, being now his friend, Watts' influence increased unceasingly, and that Swinburne was more and more swayed by him until, one day, the poet was kidnapped and locked up at the Pines. Swinburne retained his full independence, and Watts had again and again to be very careful. In June 1873 he had suggested that in the forthcoming volume of *Essays and Studies*, all papers on contemporary poets should be omitted. ' I am astonished at your suggestion ', replied Swinburne curtly ; ' the points on which I am undecided are those only on which I asked your advice in my last letter '. This drew a long epistle from Watts in which he humbly admitted that ' he had no more to say ' and that Swinburne ' certainly did not ask his advice upon it '. The studies on contemporary poets were duly included in the volume of 1875.

Again in 1877, in spite of Watts' heated objurgations, Swinburne, not perhaps without some impish delight at ' my friend Watts' horror at the inconceivable idea of my so " debasing myself " ' had *A Year's Letters* published anonymously in the *Tatler* ; he also sent, in the teeth of Watts' opposition, the manuscript of *Lesbia Brandon* to the printers in the same year. But, owing to Watts' sure gift of developing friendships, and to Swinburne's sense of gratefulness, the relations between the two men ripened into intimacy (in the letter to Watts written in 1877 from which quotation has already been made Swinburne went on to say ' thank something there are " spirits of another sort " . . . witness Jowett himself, Nichol, and (last in date among my closest friends but certainly not least in my love and trust and gratitude) yourself '). In July 1874 Swinburne had introduced Watts to the alleged source of his style and philosophy—the Marquis de Sade— ' to whom I owe (as what do I not owe ?) the means of expressing in some not wholly inadequate degree my sentiments towards God and Man ' ; although Watts refused to share his friend's enthusiasm, Swinburne was able, in the course of his letters, to make those references to the forbidden book for which he had a real genius.

In 1875 Watts had become one of the leading critics on the staff of the *Athenaeum*, and Swinburne, who had every reason to frown on Minto, was through his friend introduced to Norman MacColl, who welcomed in his columns most of his proffered contributions. In 1878, at the time when he returned from Glasgow, Swinburne seems to have been with Watts on the same intimate and facetious terms as with Nichol or W. M. Rossetti.

So much may be taken for granted, and no more. When in the summer of 1879 matters reached the alarming crisis which has been described, Watts had no legal claim to take charge of Swinburne, no assurance that his intervention would not be resented, and even, it seems, no special warrant from Lady Jane, though he knew from previous letters and conversations that she would only be too glad if he could relieve her of a mortal anxiety. At the beginning of June 1879 however he ventured to remove from his chambers in Great James Street a dying Swinburne, who had not taken any food for days and was in such a state of prostration that he was unable to object. Watts took him, not to The Pines which was not yet rented by him, but to his sister's house at Putney, Ivy Lodge. He at once advised Lady Jane who answered on June 10 : ' I am so glad Algernon is out of town. Bring him on Thursday. Tell me what I had best do about his treatment'. A few hours later

Swinburne who had only stayed a day or two at Putney, was safely back at Holmwood, and soon began to work happily at *Tristram, Mary Stuart* and his *Study of Shakespeare*. But this was no definite solution ; Holmwood was just about to be sold. If he was allowed to come back to London on his own, Swinburne would soon again be ' at death's door ', as the London Press had just been reporting with only too much truth. Watts considered that Rossetti was now a hopeless invalid, that Swinburne though ill was eminently curable, and might develop into a pleasant inmate ; he decided to share his home with him if it could be arranged. Lady Jane agreed. But how was Algernon to be persuaded ? An opportunity offered itself : the sale of the Admiral's library, out of which Swinburne was entitled to a sum not exceeding £2,000. The poet, we know, was again in financial straits ; Lady Jane made it clear that she was ready to let him have at once £1,000. But this arrangement must be conditional on ' his giving up his lodgings in London ' to live with Watts. ' This is absolutely necessary ', she added. Swinburne had no chance of saying no. Holmwood was sold ; Watts had already rented a house for his friend and himself, The Pines, Putney Hill ; on September 27th they moved in. Swinburne was quite reconciled to the idea, and found the view ' really very nice '. Auvergne, Tuscany, Normandy, Mentone, Cauterets were now but mere recollections ; he might as well be content with Putney and Wimbledon Commons. And the name of his new residence had to do duty for

> The smell and shade of old-world pine-forests
> Where the wet hill-winds weep.

CHAPTER VIII

'WHERE THE WET HILL-WINDS WEEP'
(1879–1909)

THAT Watts's intervention saved Swinburne there cannot be any doubt. From 1879 to the very last years of his life, no mention of ill-health occurs in the correspondence : bilious attacks, indigestion, lack of sleep or appetite, and even accidental falls and lily poisoning disappeared as by magic. One year (1880) during which Swinburne did not leave The Pines sufficed to achieve that miracle : regular hours and a gradual weaning from alcoholic excesses were the means used by Watts, but the miracle lies not in the nature of the means applied but in the fact that they proved applicable. In October 1880 Lady Jane Swinburne visited The Pines and was amazed at the change in the condition of her son : ' I am so glad to have seen my son well and happy ', she wrote to Watts. ' What a contrast to former days ! ' ; and she added, rather unexpectedly : ' The return to the religious faith of his youth I feel is so much more hopeful when that fatal tendency from which he has suffered so much is got the better of '. Swinburne was the first to realize that he owed Watts his life : he submitted, remembering his quarrels with landladies, his endless financial troubles and his near escape from death, to the prospect of remaining at The Pines to the end of his days. His friendship for Watts became, from the end of

1879, tinged with deep gratitude.[1] ' There is a friend that, as the wise man saith, Clings closer than a brother ' he wrote prophetically some two years later. Watts had done what no other of his intimate friends would or could do ; it was the first time perhaps that one of the numerous friendships of Swinburne resulted in direct practical good to himself. His gratitude to Watts was well deserved ; nor can it be wondered at that he treasured and rejoiced in

> That pearl most precious found in all the sea.

No one could seriously deny this. But the question is whether Swinburne did not have to pay too heavy a price for even that inestimable service ; whether Watts by the alleged evil influence he exerted on Swinburne's friendships, inspiration and reputation did not forfeit his right to the thanks of lovers of poetry. It is all very well to speak, as Edmund Gosse did, of Swinburne's ' captivity at The Pines ', his having been ' bullied by the old horror of Putney ', and ' Watts' rattlesnake fascination over him ' ; but Gosse had too sensitive a soul to speak dispassionately about one whom he suspected to have destroyed the most wonderful friendship of his life. Without being influenced by what he said or the fashion he set we must consider the facts carefully.

It has often been urged that Watts' ' intervention ' was a good thing in so far as Swinburne's *life* was concerned, a bad one in so far as he destroyed his *inspiration*, thereby lessening the poet's fame. The contrary

---

[1] ' I must say I do feel the want of a God (of faith and friendship) to whom I might offer sacrifices of thanksgiving for the gift of such a good friend as I have in you ' (To Watts, Autumn 1879). ' I cannot but keep thinking . . . how long since, how many years ago, I should have died as my poor brother has just died if instead of the worst of wives I had not found the best of friends ' (To Watts, August 1891).

view might just as well be taken : had Swinburne never gone to The Pines, we should in all probability have lost *Tristram, The Heptalogia, Balen, Mary Stuart,* several exquisite poems and some remarkable pages of prose, while Swinburne's slow agony and lonely death in ' the five old chambers ' of his London flat, ' which Poe would have delighted to describe ', would have been a fitting close to the elf-like existence of one whom the daily Press had already hailed on several occasions as ' Shelley the second '. And yet this view might also be erroneous : I am not sure that, despite all that has been written, those thirty years of semi-isolation at Putney, the ' clockwork regularity ' and unreal character of the poet's life, the picturesque contrast between his former and his later years, his poems and his actual ways, his own personality and that of Watts,—' the little old genius and his little old acolyte in their dull little villa '—I am not sure that those scenes, slightly comical, but tinged with wistful melancholy, witnessed as they were by dozens of critics and men of letters of the rising generation, did not on the whole rather brighten the aureole round Swinburne's head and increase interest in his personality.

It is clear that no definite conclusion can be reached, and it is far less futile to try to analyse the various points on which Watts' influence may have made itself felt, how far it succeeded in modifying natural tendencies, and how far it failed to do so. In the course of this demonstration two things will, I trust, appear which may as well be stated straightaway : first Watts, once he had saved Swinburne's life, does not seem to have had any set plan as to diverting the poet's inspiration in one special direction, although, being human and

somewhat wilful, his personal prejudices and idiosyn-
crasies were bound to affect his friend in isolated instances. Watts had only one set purpose, which arose
from his practical instincts : he was determined that
England's greatest living poet, after being too long the
dupe of unscrupulous friends and publishers, from
both a material and moral point of view, should be
turned from a financial failure into a commercial and
social success ; he thus set about putting his house in
order, forgetting perhaps that in matters of poetry
' souvent un beau désordre est un effet de l'art '. On
the other hand it must be borne in mind that, though
it had been possible for Watts, with Lady Jane's com-
plicity and all his friends' tacit approval, to take charge
of the diseased body of Swinburne, it was quite another
matter to change in a few months the powerful personality that had produced *Atalanta* and *Bothwell*,
Chastelard and *William Blake*. All that Watts could
do was to turn to account Swinburne's natural tendencies, to make them swerve slightly to right or left,
to discourage or excite some of his activities. But
Swinburne's inner poetic spirit was beyond his reach
and he may have known it ; though no longer exactly
the ' master of his fate ', Swinburne remained to a great
extent ' the captain of his soul '.

It was of course in the province of the poet's ' social '
life that Watts' ' tyranny ' was chiefly felt. Swinburne
was not allowed to go about town as before. There
were obvious reasons for this, but the embargo sub-
sisted even when by the end of 1880, after his recovery,
the necessity was no longer imperative. In particular
Watts was always very unwilling to allow Swinburne
to pay visits of some duration to his friends outside

London. In August 1883 he spent a few days with Jowett, and this seems to have been the only exception to Watts' new-laid rule.[1] But of course Swinburne was allowed to visit his mother and relations regularly. Lady Jane Swinburne resided in various parts of England after the sale of Holmwood, and thus we find her son staying for considerable periods at Bradford-on-Avon (1881, 1883, 1887), Cheltenham (1891), Alton (1887, 1892), Chestal (1894) and Solihull (1895, 1896). On the other hand, until 1890 the two friends went regularly to the sea-side once or twice a year, so that Swinburne might indulge his passion for swimming. He thus took Watts to Guernsey and Sark in September 1882.

> Once more I give my body and soul to thee,
> Who hast my soul for ever : cliff and sand
> Recede, and heart to heart once more are we . .

exclaimed Swinburne in his delight, after several months of enforced separation from the sea. But, though he found the islands as beautiful as ever, one disappointment awaited him : the elusive Hugo was not there. Fortunately, in October came a pressing invitation to attend the fiftieth anniversary of the first performance of *Le Roi s'Amuse*. Watts, who had no great admiration for Hugo, raised objections ; but Swinburne got Vacquerie to send him a peremptory letter : ' Certes vous aurez vos deux places, nous serons trop heureux de vous les offrir. J'ai lu tout à l'heure votre lettre à Victor Hugo qui en a été ravi et qui vous en remercie. Donc nous comptons sur vous

[1] In June, 1881, Watts refused, much to the indignation of the authorities, to let Swinburne attend the celebration of the Eton 9th Jubilee for which he had written an Ode. It is possible that the prospect of his spending the night at the college in the midst of old ' scholastic associations ' may not unreasonably have alarmed Watts.

et M. Théodore Watts'. Watts understood that if
he did not go, Swinburne would go alone, and he went.
The two friends were in Paris on the 20th of November. The wildest things have been said about the
meeting between Hugo and Swinburne : the form
of humour which consists in making very cheap jokes
about very great men, I do not profess to understand.
It is true that Hugo on this occasion was surrounded
by hundreds of worshippers and not easily accessible ;
it is true that Swinburne was now struck by deafness,
a hereditary infirmity in his family. But, beyond these
two facts, there do not seem to exist any grounds
for stating that the interview did not give the two
poets great pleasure : Swinburne dined at Hugo's
house on the 20th, and his host drank his health ; the
rehearsal and the performance of the play on the 21st
and 22nd were a great success : of course Swinburne
was unable to hear most of the words, but it does
not require much reflection to realize that he knew
Le Roi s'Amuse almost by heart and could afford to
follow the acting very well. The conversation he had
with Hugo in his box after the third act leaves us in
no reasonable doubt as to the fact that the ' Master '
was perfectly aware of Swinburne's identity. Although
Swinburne was not constantly in the company of Hugo,
he could not have felt neglected or ' out of it ' for
he was paraded as a lion by the then famous blue-
stocking Tola Dorian ; moreover he was introduced to
Leconte de Lisle and the two men, as might have been
expected, sympathized. An English newspaper correspondent wrote at the time :

Swinburne came to Paris to see *Le Roi s'Amuse* and to do
homage to the Master. During the past few days he has been

the lion of some exotic blue-stocking salons, and the journalist-poets, like Catulle Mendés, have written wonderful articles on his ' strange silhouette ', his ' measureless brow ', his ' pale lips ' and ' the striking mobility of the features of the bizarre artiste ' ; ' England was revolted by the audacity of this passionate, sensuous and subtle poet '.

All tends to prove that Swinburne was duly admired and honoured, and suffered, if anything, from an excess of popularity. The following brief account of his visit written no more than a fortnight after his return to The Pines should remove all doubt as to the success of his ' pilgrimage ' :

> You will probably (*The Times* announced the event in its largest type !) have seen that I have been to Paris for the second night (the first bearing date just 50 years before to a day) of *Le Roi s'Amuse*, and at last ' kissed hands ' at the only levée I shall ever go to. Victor Hugo received me with literally fatherly kindness. No words can express his charm of manner as a host. I dined at his house the day after my arrival in Paris. He is altogether miraculous, looks at least 20 years younger than his age—walks and talks to match—i.e. like a rather notably robust man of 60.
>
> He introduced me to the translatress of some of my verses into French—a Russian princess by birth and—*need* I add—a nihilist by creed and practice. She has a most lovely little daughter and a magnificent stud . . . Russian and Arabian horses. Fair owner : spirit, fire, grace.
>
> I met at her house the Frenchman I most wanted to meet outside the Master's own peculiar circle—Leconte de Lisle, the poet, Hellenist and free-thinker, a very noble and amiable old man . . .

Even after the hyperboles of so many odes, letters, sonnets, essays, hymns, the visit to Hugo does not seem to have been the anti-climax which so many expected.

But after 1882 Swinburne was not to leave the shores of England any more. He and Watts decided that English sea-side places were good enough for them, and that they would have none of those foreign holiday resorts ; Admiral Swinburne, who in former days did not altogether approve of his son's trips abroad, had said that ' sea-side amusements especially in their continental form did not appeal to me '. Here the aristocratic sailor and the middle-class lawyer felt at one. And Swinburne, echoing Watts, soon repeated that nothing in foreign lands could beat the particular English beauty-spot they had just visited.

Thus they went to Sidestrand, Norwich, in the summer of 1883 and again in 1884. Watts thought that even a holiday ought to be turned to practical account if possible, and he insisted on Swinburne undertaking what he had seldom attempted before—except in his early Preraphaelite days—poetry of a purely descriptive form. The result was *A Midsummer Holiday* (1884), a collection of fine ballads, each of which ends with a glowing tribute to friendship ; but a fatal discrepancy between matter and form appears here as in *By the North Sea* and most of the later descriptive verse of Swinburne. In September 1886 they went, after Swinburne's usual stay at Bradford, to Eastbourne and Beachy Head where the moving lines *To a Sea-mew* were written. In 1887, 1888 and 1889 they spent three successive summers at Lancing-on-Sea, near Cromer. It was on the latter occasion that Swinburne composed *A Swimmer's Dream*, a record of a swimmer's *emotions* far more successful than all that he had attempted in the way of pure *description* of nature.

After 1889 these seaside holidays ceased or at least became exceptional.[1] It is about this date that the retirement at The Pines becomes more severe, that Swinburne ' pronounces his vows ' and becomes more exclusively the ' book-monk of a suburban Thebaid ', as has been exquisitely said. Up till 1890 most of Swinburne's old friends had been allowed to see him from time to time. We find that in April 1880 he was still giving readings of his poems. True, Watts may have had certain preferences, and may have favoured his friend's intercourse with P. B. Marston at the expense of his relations with Gosse, but on the whole Swinburne kept up a large number of his former friendships. After 1890 most of those ties broke ; many friends had died,[2] he had quarrelled with some[3] ; the others he did not see any more : even the faithful Nichol, who had long enjoyed so much prestige, was discarded : ' I have seen much less of you than I hoped these last three years ', he complained in 1893 ; ' I suppose I am never to see you again '. It was then and after the death of his mother (1896) that Swinburne began to live more and more with his books and with his memories. In February 1904, after he had been ill several weeks with pneumonia, he wrote

[1] In 1904 Swinburne and Watts made another stay at Cromer.

[2] The deaths of Rossetti and Howell had for Swinburne unpleasant consequences : in the former instance Fanny Schott became the possessor of Swinburne's letters to Rossetti, and this correspondence which occasionally was of a highly indecent character had to be bought back from her. More compromising still were the poet's letters to Howell ; they fell into the hands of George Redway, the publisher, who exchanged them for the copyright of *A Word for the Navy* (1887). He sold his copyright to Chatto in 1896. Swinburne's correspondence with Howell was, after the poet's death, sold by Watts-Dunton with other letters and documents to Mr. Wise.

[3] As for instance Whistler ; see below.

pathetically to W. M. Rossetti : ' I am not yet allowed
to go out.   I went out once for a short drive and a
short walk (weeks ago—I am beginning to lose count
of time) with Watts-Dunton who thinks it was then
that I got a chill. . . . They have got me a really
beautiful type for the forthcoming edition of my poems
in six volumes : of course it will be sent to you—but
not to anyone else—or hardly.   Who is there to send
them to, for that matter ? '

He was not quite cut off from the world.   He kept
up a limited correspondence.   Watts-Dunton introduced to him people whom he had carefully selected.
Among the many ' tourists ' who were allowed to visit
the little 'museum' at The Pines, I would choose two
as particularly representative of the fascination exerted
by the name of Swinburne over the most widely
different members of the younger generation.   One
was drawn to Swinburne's poetry from the wealthy
circles of the London Produce Market : Mr. Thomas
James Wise has recorded[1] how ' like most young men
and young women in similar case I no sooner began to
read seriously the poetry of Swinburne than I became
fascinated with the rush and music of his verse and
felt its impulse and virility '—a testimony all the more
interesting as its sincerity is backed up by the unfailing
labours of Mr. Wise since Swinburne was 'revealed' to
him in 1880.   When he writes : ' The formation of
my Swinburne Library was not prompted by the mere
impulse of acquisition ', he confirms what we already
knew—namely that his many efforts as bibliographer
etc. of Swinburne had their source, not in any collec-
tor's whim, but in a heart-felt admiration for the poet

[1] *A Swinburne Library* by T. J. Wise, 1925 : Introduction.

ALGERNON CHARLES SWINBURNE, *ÆTAT 52*

Photo Elliott & Fr₃

who had fascinated him ' with the rush and music of
his verse '. We must now listen to the picturesque
narrative of his first visits to The Pines :

Three hundred and sixty-five days were included in the year
1886. One of those days was a red-letter day for me. . . . It was
with a thrill of delight that I was one day informed by Miss
Mathilde Blind that she had asked and obtained permission to
bring me to The Pines, and that upon the following Sunday
afternoon I was to call for her at her rooms in Manchester
Square. I kept the appointment, and we drove to Putney.
We were received by Watts-Dunton, and after a while I was by
him led upstairs and introduced to Swinburne. Never before
and never since have I found anticipation and realization so
entirely at variance. Largely as a result of the half-mythical,
almost legendary tales which Dr. Furnivall loved to relate of
Swinburne's sayings and doings in the pre-Putney days, I had
looked to encounter a small, unkempt, red-haired man, leaping
rather than walking across the room in a state of uncontrolled
excitement, and when conversing raising his voice to a scream.
In place of this curious monstrosity I found a quiet, well-
groomed gentleman, slightly below middle height. His hair
was grey with just a ruddy trace in it, and his manner of address
unassuming and polite. He received me with pleasant courtesy,
and leading me to a seat made me feel immediately and entirely
at ease. In answer to some questions with which I had prepared
myself he told me a little, though not much, about his own
books, and then brought out for my inspection his series of the
first editions of Shelley. To see these Shelleys was the professed
object of my visit to Putney. In about half an hour from the
moment I had been ushered into Swinburne's study the door
slowly opened ; Watts-Dunton stole silently into the room
and gently shepherded me away. I think I must have found
grace in Swinburne's sight, for at parting he expressed pleasure at
my visit, and asked me to come again on the following Sunday
afternoon at 3 o'clock to see his Plays.
On the following Sunday I accordingly went, and carefully
so arranged my journey across London that I should arrive at
Putney at the stipulated time. But by some mischance my
progress was delayed, and it was 3.15 when I knocked at the
door of The Pines. Watts-Dunton himself admitted me. He
was evidently nervous, and quietly reproved me for my lack of

punctuality. 'Swinburne has been expecting you for the last half-hour', he said, 'and is quite excited by your non-arrival'. I followed him upstairs, and upon the door being opened, a very different Swinburne from the poet of the previous Sunday met my view. His extensive collection of quarto plays were ranged in rows upon the table. Round his table he was walking rapidly, pausing at every few steps to change the order of some book. He was full of excitement, and after the briefest word of welcome dragged me to the further side of the table where his Chapmans were placed. During the whole of the hour or so the interview lasted he was hardly still for two consecutive minutes. For a moment he would pause to place a book in my hand, and begin to tell me of its points ; then stop suddenly, seize upon another volume, place it upon the one I already grasped, and commence to enlarge upon it. Then, before the story was half told, a third was thrust upon me, and a commencement was made by its owner of a relation of its beauty. And so we went on, until my lap was full. . . .

Such was the commencement of my intercourse with the circle at The Pines.

Those visits were of real importance, as they encouraged and rendered possible the task which Mr. Wise then set himself—namely the detailed bibliographical and literary history of all the published or unpublished works of Swinburne. As far as I know, no other modern writer in English literature has been favoured with such a continuous series of publications, extending over more than thirty years, and all tending to the ultimate elucidation of his life and works. Mr. Wise's *Catalogue* and *Bibliographies*, which are not mere dry lists and repertories, but constitute a *corpus* of carefully edited documents, forming an almost continuous, though occasionally technical, narrative, have given rise to the large number of international studies on Swinburne which have recently appeared or are still in preparation. But Mr. Wise's labours, apart from their scholarly value, strike me as not devoid of further significance and interest. Not many of us, especially if endowed with wealth, would be willing to expend considerable time, trouble and intellectual activity on the greater glory or at least the truer fame of a poet, however great or misjudged. I therefore made bold to ask Mr. Wise what it was which attracted him to Swinburne in such a way, and I have received the following brief but typical statement :

> I was fascinated by Swinburne the *Man* nearly as much as by his *Works*. At his best he was simply magnificent as a talker, particularly when discussing Landor, Shelley and the Plays. His criticism was clearly expressed, and not spoiled in the utterance by the hammer blows of too numerous adjectives and adverbs— a vice I feel assured he contracted mainly from Victor Hugo.

The second ' specimen ' I shall beg leave to select belongs to a somewhat later period. It was in 1895 that this promising artist, full of penetration and understanding, Mr. (now Sir) William Rothenstein succeeded by means of his youthful talent in persuading Watts to get Swinburne to sit for him. It is here essential to quote his own words[1] reflecting as they do the impression which Swinburne, once a favourite in the Preraphaelite circles, now created on artists of the younger generation :

August 4th.

Went with A. K. after lunch to-day to Putney, to see Watts; a little, round, rosy, wrinkled man, with a moustache like a walrus, and a polished dewlap, dressed in a sort of grey flannel frock-coat, which he had evidently hurriedly donned (a threadbare coat was on the sofa) as we came in, rose to greet us. He was very welcoming ; I was naturally interested to see the

[1] Sir William Rothenstein kindly communicated to me this extract from his private diary when it was still in manuscript. It has since been printed in *Memories and Men* (1931).

interior of The Pines. A room with a fine large window looking on to a long narrow garden, surrounded by ivy-grown walls, a little plaster statue in the middle, near which was a rather ugly painted yellow iron-cane seat. Round the walls hung large drawings by Rossetti, studies, stippled in chalk for the Pandora, and other works, a splendid drawing of Mrs. Morris, lying back with her hair luxuriously spread behind her head, her hands held up before her, and a drawing in chalk of Watts himself. Also a portrait of Rossetti by Ford Madox Brown, obviously very like, but rather thin and dirty in colour, and an interesting one of himself against a gold screen, two heads, charmingly painted by Knewstub, a water colour by Miss Siddall and two by Frederick Shields.

'Ah, you know Whistler—dear Jimmy', said Swinburne's companion, 'how clever he is, one of the most brilliant of men, I have known him intimately these 20 years. What genius ! Latterly owing to his quarrelsome nature, though I myself have had no difference with him—still, owing to his misunderstanding with my friends, I have ceased to see him. But what a talker ! Is he doing well now ? Some say yes, some no. Surely he was in the wrong over Sir William Eden. George Moore I am rather prejudiced against—but of course I don't know him and I have not read his books—but I trust Jimmy always for being in the wrong—he loves a quarrel'. . . . Before we left, he told me he had, with great difficulty, made Swinburne promise to sit to me—a rare thing for the poet to be gracious on that point ; 'we both dislike sitting', he said with a glance at his own portrait drawn 25 years ago by Rossetti. I am to return at the end of the week, to make a drawing of Swinburne.

August 10th.

Go to the Pines, Putney. Swinburne gets up as I enter, rather like Lionel Johnson in figure, the same chétif boy, narrow shoulders and nervous twitch of the hands, which, however, are strong and fine. A much fresher face than I would have imagined from accounts heard, a fine nose, a tiny glazed green eye, a curiously clear auburn moustache, and a beard of a splendid red. How young he looks, notwithstanding his years. He was so nervous, that of course I was embarrassed, and Watts being there we both talked at him, keeping our eyes off one another. Occasionally I would glance at his profile, less impressive, less 'like' than his full face. When at last the sitting began, no sitter ever gave me so much trouble. For besides always changing his pose, he is so deaf, that he could not hear me ; and after sitting a short time, a nervous restlessness seized on him, which held him the whole time. I felt a beast sitting there torturing him. Nor did I feel that I could do anything worthy of him. When he saw the drawing he was kind enough to say ' I must be like, for I see all my family in it'. While I was drawing he recited a burlesque of Nichol's, 'The Flea', he called it, and he talked a good deal of recent criticism—a bumper of newspaper cuttings were strewn over a couch near the window. He speaks with the accent of an Oxford Don, and with a certain gaiety, with gracious and rather old-fashioned manners. He behaves charmingly to old Watts. He had a new suit of clothes, as though especially for a portrait, which seemed to cause him as much discomfort as sitting still. He was like a schoolboy let out of school, when I said I would not bother him any longer. He then showed me a number of his treasures— odd views of different scenes, an early Burne-Jones drawing, photographs of people, including a fine one of Rossetti. Watts suggested I should make a drawing of this for Swinburne, but Swinburne asked if I could make one from a rather poor engraving of George Dyer, Charles Lamb's friend, for him instead. . . . And this of course I promised to do. . . . He praised Baudelaire as a poet, and said he liked Meredith immensely— as a man— . . .

Swinburne thus remained the object of many tributes of admiration and even sympathy. But now he was no longer treated cordially by men who were his equals in age and genius like Morris and Burne-Jones ; or with affectionate authority as in the case of Rossetti and Jowett ; nor even with that zealous admiration which he liked to describe among ' ses disciples à lui ' in the seventies ; he was shown with infinite precautions and warning, like a rare bibelot to a party of sightseers in some art-gallery, and when a stray sunbeam made the gold and enamel of his mind give a sudden flash, it was received with amazement and awe.

If we want to form an idea of the extent and limits of

Watts' influence over Swinburne in the later part of his life, we can perhaps do no better than turn to the poet's political views as expressed in his poems and correspondence. I have endeavoured to show in the preceding chapter what was Swinburne's embarrassment and how since the *Muscovite Crusade* (1876) he had been in a state of hesitation and confusion and had found it impossible to become reconciled either to the Liberals or Tories, Gladstone or Disraeli : his principles were upheld by personalities he abhorred ; and often the personalities he was attracted to held a doctrine opposed to all his past as a Mazzinian Radical. Watts realized that he must be extremely careful, as he had had the experience that Swinburne would not compromise where principles were at stake. Moreover, it seems that Watts' own views on politics were not of a very strict nature. On two things however he probably insisted : first Swinburne's political effusions, if there need be any, must be, when at all publishable, of an immediate and easy sale. This is doubtless why the poems of Swinburne no longer offered that aloofness and abstract character which is so typical of *Songs before Sunrise* ; his political sonnets, ballads etc. became far more topical than they had been and can for the most part be ascribed to a special occasion, which rendered them more directly interesting to contemporary readers, however obscure they may seem now. On the other hand Watts, partly from reasons of expediency, partly out of his own convictions as a staunch middle-class Englishman, was resolved to do all he could to prevent Swinburne from vilifying his own country and holding out as a model to England nations who were not fit to undo her shoe-laces.

In the field of foreign affairs he let him more or less have a free hand, though suppressing from time to time his most violent outbursts. Swinburne's interest in Italy was exhausted : he had nothing new to say in his poem to the memory of Mazzini, *After Nine Years* (1881). His interest in France was failing.[1] His rising distrust of Germany reached a climax when in 1881 the Kultur-Kampf came to an end and Bismarck bowed to the Pope (*Bismarck at Canossa*). One article of his political faith however remained unchanged from his boyish enthusiasm at the news of Balaklava to his death in 1909 : hostility to the absolute rulers of Russia. *The Launch of the Livadia* (1880) is a fine example of allegorical imprecation :

> All curses be about her, and all ill
> Go with her . . .

But the year 1881 offered a more splendid opportunity than the mere launching of an imperial yacht ; on March 1st Alexander II was murdered :

> By no dry death another king goes down
> The way of kings . . .

exclaimed the poet in *Dysthanatos* ; his curses had proved effective.

Swinburne never relented ; the persecutions of the Jews, Poles and Finns which marked the reign of Alexander III made his denunciation still more outspoken. Not even Watts could prevent him from printing *Russia : an Ode* in 1890, in which ' the duty

---

[1] The sonnet *Let us Go Hence* on the son of Napoleon III is merely a mechanical continuation to the series of invectives of the *Dirae* ; Watts obtained that it should be buried in the *Notes* to *Studies in Songs*. *The Fourteenth of July* in which he laments the refusal by the French Senate to grant an amnesty to the communal convicts simply repeats Hugo's similar attitude.

of tyrannicide', which had been a cherished dogma
of the Old Mortality in 1857, is reasserted with
youthful exuberance :

> Love grows hate for love's sake ; life takes death for guide.
> Life hath none but one red star—Tyrannicide . . .
> ' God or man be swift ; hope sickens with delay :
> Smite and send him howling down his father's way '.

The ill-starred Nicholas inherited the weight of Swinburne's wrath in 1894, as is shown in the fierce and
truly prophetic sonnet *Czar Louis XVI* (1905).

So measureless was Swinburne's hatred of Russia
that it extended to all those who were on friendly terms
with the government of the Czar. When in 1886 the
Franco-Russian entente became evident, Swinburne
wrote three sonnets, *The Russ and the Frenchman*, soon
followed (1887) by *Russo-Gallia* ; Watts withheld them
from publication but afterwards sold them to Mr.
Wise by whom, despite Sir Edmund Gosse's objurgations, they were quite sensibly preserved. There is
no reason why the variations of Swinburne's highly
sensitive nature should not be on record :

> Falsehood, thy name is France !

he exclaimed, remarking that Hugo's death had set
him free from former bonds :

> Quenched is the light that lit thee ; dead the lord
> Whose lyre outsang the storm, outshone the sword.
> At him too spit thy scorn ; he too was great.

It is only fair to add that Swinburne's new-fangled
Francophobia,[1] possibly not discouraged by Watts,

---

[1] ' Swinburne talked violently against the French, saying he had lost all interest in
them since France has become a Republic, as they are always ready to fly at our
throats and would crush us at any moment ' (Sir W. Rothenstein's Diary, 10
August, 1895).

had been nursed by the comments of the French Press on the *Pall Mall Gazette* articles of W. T. Stead exposing in 1885 the deficiencies of the English Criminal Law. It is well known that as a reply to the outbursts of the Parisian Press (which had not spared Swinburne's personality on this and previous occasions) the poet wrote his *Rondeaux Parisiens*. Those very fine vituperative pieces are open to one chief objection : the irony is at once so violent and so veiled that one is at times in doubt whether the author condemns French ' cant ' or actual English vices :

Love, purity, shame are unknown to the rascally Briton.
Mendacity, malice, rapacity—ever the same—
Are the marks of a nation accustomed to spurn and spit on
    Love, purity, shame ...
But at least we believed that their clime was a bridle and bit on
The passions—that Albion the virtuous was worthy her fame :
And we find that her virtues are cushions for vices to sit on
    Love, purity, shame.

For this, and for many other reasons, no English review would print the *Rondeaux* in 1886. But they illustrate as well as explain Swinburne's revulsion of feeling. His attitude to France remained moderately hostile until 1894, when the sonnet *Carnot* followed in 1899 by *After the Verdict* point to a revival in interest and sympathy, although the later sonnets *Lutetia* and *Meretrix Moribunda* show how bitter was the poet's resentment of the criticism of England which was then common in the French Press. But Germany now engrossed Swinburne's angry attention. The growth of her militarism, the absolute character of her institutions led him to consider her as a second Russia. When the two emperors in 1905 greeted each other

as ' Admirals of the Pacific and the Atlantic ' his indignation burst out in its usual violent manner :

> What are ye Germans, men by shame unstrung,
> That none has yet plucked out the swaggerer's tongue
> Which still this Bobadill-Parolles wags . . . ?

Those typical lines constitute nearly[1] the last utterance of Swinburne on the foreign affairs of Europe.

It was however with reference to home politics that
Swinburne's point of view was completely modified.
Up till now England had occupied very little place
in his works ; even in his writings of 1876 he was
concerned with the *foreign* policy of England, the brilliant policy of *prestige* and colonial expansion pursued
by Disraeli. As regards home affairs Swinburne described himself as late as 1880 as an ' English Republican ', a worshipper of Milton and Cromwell—
and as such preserved an attitude of unconcern and
even scornful discontent about the *régime* and institutions of which he disapproved. With infinite diplomacy Watts undertook to mend all this. Already in
1877 Swinburne, in the sonnets *The White Czar*, had
spontaneously replied to ' some insolent lines addressed
by a Russian poet to the Empress of India '. Watts
pointed out to his friend how bitterly the Queen, who
represented the country, was attacked in the foreign
Press ; he added that she was after all the successor
of Elizabeth and Cromwell. Swinburne, on account
of his Mazzinian distrust of kings, however democratic
they might appear, and also perhaps in part owing to
the old hereditary feeling of devotion to the Stuarts,

See *Memorial Verses on the Death of Karl Blind* (1907):
. . . When Bismarck and his William lie
Low even as he they warred on—damned too deep to die.

detested the Hanoverian family. Although he had printed nothing against Queen Victoria, his unpublished parodies—*La Fille du Policeman*, *Sœur de la Reine*—treat her with scant respect, and his correspondence before 1872 contains references to her couched in most unequivocal language. But Watts rediscovered the patriotic string which could be heard in *Modern Hellenism* (1857) and the *Death of Sir John Franklin* (1860) and set it throbbing once more. Circumstances came to his help ; on March 2nd 1882, scarcely a year after the murder of Alexander II, a madman, named Roderick MacLean, fired what was possibly a blank cartridge at Queen Victoria ; Swinburne was all the more stirred by the news as the attempted murder had taken place at Windsor and MacLean had been arrested with the help of indignant Eton boys ! I am not sure that he did not wish he might have been one of them ! He remembered his early enthusiasm for Balaklava. He remembered the Queen's visit while he was still an Etonian in 1851 ; he remembered the lines he had written for Gloriana :

> 'Tis Gloriana now her palace seeks
> And in that single voice wide Albion speaks . . .

Those early memories, the contrast between the character and fate of the two rulers, Watts' persistent sermons, were too much for him. In a sonnet (*Euonymos*) he paid public homage to ' the calm crowned head that all revere ' and proclaimed that

> No braver soul drew bright and queenly breath
> Since England wept upon Elizabeth. [1]

[1] Here the change in Swinburne's attitude was patent, glaring ; for this was the seventh attempt on the life of the Queen ; in particular in 1872 an Irish boy had threatened her with a pistol and demanded the release of Fenian prisoners. But Swinburne had no thanksgiving to offer on *that* occasion.

All over England the outrage was causing an endless display of loyalty and reverence ; thus, for the first time perhaps, Swinburne was, in a political poem, at one with the mass of public opinion. And Watts beamed and rubbed his hands.

Nor was this all : when five years later, in 1887, Swinburne wrote a song for the Jubilee, he was prevailed upon to introduce several lines of praise to the 'blameless Queen ', and it was not Watts' fault if he did not add more : ' Indeed Watts wished me to say, and thinks I should have said more about the Queen than the little word I did say ' (To Isabel Swinburne, June 1st, 1887). When Tennyson died in 1892 it is not impossible that wild ambitions haunted the mind of Theodore Watts ; there was no greater poet than Swinburne alive, none who was more particularly qualified for the duty of celebrating in verse of high quality a definite occasion, and he had shown that he could be a national poet. A great many people thought that he was the obvious man to succeed Tennyson. But the past was not to be forgotten ; for political and religious reasons Swinburne could not be offered the post of Laureate. There was only one thing more impossible than to overlook him, and that was to appoint him. Moreover, had he been asked, we may feel sure that the ' still small voice in him ' would have urged him to refuse,[1] as he later was to refuse an honorary degree and a state pension ; for he felt that, by keeping out of all official recognition, he remained a greater figure. But it was no small praise for Watts that he should have reconciled the author of *Songs*

---

[1] ' May I die a Poet Laureate ! ' was with him a favourite exclamation of emphatic denial.

before Sunrise to the dynasty, and rendered him conceivable as a laureate.

It was however much easier to secure an expression of qualified respect for the ruler of the empire than to define clearly Swinburne's relation to the politics of the country. His position as we know was delicate ; he could not very well, on account of his volume of 1871, keep aloof ; the authority of his name was claimed by various parties on various occasions. And yet he found it impossible to embrace bodily the views of one party in particular. His hostility to Gladstone he was careful not to make public until 1885 : for after all Gladstone was head of the party which ought to have been nearest to his heart. The *Note on the Muscovite Crusade* contained a not unkindly reference to him. Swinburne had developed, in spite of the 'Irish particles in his blood', a keen dislike of the National Land League and of Parnell ; to such an extent that early in 1883 he took the trouble to write a letter in French to the *Rappel* correcting some statements in an article on *La Question Irlandaise* : 'J'ose croire que vous ne serez pas trop prompt ', he wrote, ' à me soupçonner en lisant ce qui va suivre de cette espèce de patriotisme étroit et faussé, de ce chauvinisme anglais que j'ai toujours dénoncé et combattu de mon mieux'. And he proceeded to show how X . . . (Parnell) 'encourageait de Sade au nom de la liberté'. But at the time Gladstone was precisely doing his utmost to crush the Home Rulers, and Swinburne could not but approve of his attitude. In fact the poet indirectly supported him when by the end of 1883 the opposition of the House of Lords to the Reform Bill, which was to be passed in 1885, became obvious. It is possible that Tennyson's acceptance of a peerage was resented at The Pines, but it is useless to try and explain away in that way the vituperative poems against the Upper House which the poet published in *A Midsummer Holiday* :

> Is a vote a coat ? Will franchise feed you,
> Or words be a roof against the rain ?

he makes the worthy peers exclaim. But soon irony yields to a fierce indignation :

> They are worthy to reign on their brothers,
> To contemn them as clods and as carles,
> Who are Graces by grace of such mothers
> As brightened the bed of King Charles.

Contrary to what Edmund Gosse would have us believe we must conclude that Swinburne's democratic tendencies, as already vented in *A Marching Song* (1870), ran away with him, much to the dismay of Watts. But in such instances Swinburne was irrepressible.

It was in 1885 that he definitely made up his mind about Gladstone. No one could be more keenly attracted than he was to the heroic, manly figure of General Gordon ; no one could feel more indignant at the first undecided, then callous, attitude (alleged or real) of the Prime Minister during the siege and massacres of Khartoum. All the chivalrous and soldierly elements in his patrician nature rebelled. He began a fine poem on Gordon [1] which to this day remains unpublished. It will be seen that his admiration for the hero

---

[1] Now in Mr. Wise's collection.

> Beloved and blest of children, heaven-born head,
> Nailed up and spat on like the head of Christ,
> Crowned by the nails and hallowed quick and dead
> By scorn and spittle, filth and falsehood, shed
> Upon thee whom we saw self-sacrificed . . .

was only matched by his scorn of those whom he held
as responsible for the fall of Khartoum :

> Irresolute, instable as water—yea
> And false as water—how shall ye escape
> The dark damnation that men's judgments lay
> On them that tempt and comfort and betray ?
> What tho' your fame set herds of fools agape ?

His hate of Gladstone then grew keener and keener,
and he vented it in satires which Watts kept carefully
locked up :

> The conqueror tongue, the warrior tongue is king.
> Forsaken, silent, Gordon dies and gives
> Example : loud and shameless Gladstone lives,
> No faction unembraced or unbetrayed,
> No chance unwelcomed and no vote unweighed . .
> He feigns a viler faith than late he feigned
> And licks the patriot hand that once he chained.
> Their wrongs he learns, by heart if not by rote,
> And all Kilmainham thunders from his throat.

The last lines show clearly that it was Gladstone's
change of attitude to Parnell which proved the last
straw for the back of Swinburne's indignation. What
the negotiations of Kilmainham (1882) had fore-
shadowed, Gladstone's speeches of 1886 proved beyond doubt : he had become a Home Ruler. But this
immediately caused the Liberal split and the creation
of Chamberlain's Unionist party. Swinburne heard

the news with immense relief and jubilation, and began
to sight a harbour on the seas of his endless political
troubles ; this third party had been as it were cut ready-
made for him.   It had none of the disadvantages of
the Tory and Liberal factions.   He cast his lot with
them and became a staunch Unionist.

Nor was his support purely platonic ; he put his
name and talent at the service of the new cause ; just
before the general election, in June 1886, he published *The Commonweal, a Song for Unionists*, in which
he did his best to make Parnell and Gladstone ridicu-
lous and hateful :

What are these that howl and hiss across the strait of westward
    water ?
What is he who floods our ears with speech in flood ?
See the long tongue lick the dripping hand that smokes and reeks
    of slaughter.
See the man of words embrace the man of blood.

And he concluded, as he had done in very different
circumstances in 1867, with a direct appeal to public
opinion :

Yet an hour is here for answer : now, if here be yet a nation,
    Answer England, man by man, from sea to sea !

England answered : the Unionists had a majority of
125, and Swinburne could claim a share in their
victory.

But he did not rest on his laurels ; in the course of
1887 he went on fighting for the Cause of Union,
sending letters to the Press (*Unionism and Crime—A
Retrospect*, etc.) to make his position clear and point
out that Mazzini would have dissociated himself from

the Parnellites, that the maker of Italian Unity would have been a champion of Unionism. The weak point in his argument was that Mazzini's Secret Societies bore a strong likeness to those of the Fenians, that his methods were not always unlike theirs. But he would not admit this. However it was chiefly in verse that he tilted at Gladstone and Parnell. In *The Question* (1887) he supported in a striking manner the Crimes Act which was being introduced to suppress Irish law-lessness. In the *Ballade of Truthful Charles* (Charles Parnell, the ' crownless king of Ireland') and *A Logical Ballade of Home Rule* (1889) he helped to discredit further the cause of Irish independence. But it is chiefly to the poem *The Jubilee* (1887) that we must turn if we want to understand the crisis through which Swinburne passed. He begins by a frank admission that the high hopes which had arisen years ago were not fulfilled ; in the following stanza all the disap-pointment which followed *Songs before Sunrise* is revealed :

> As from some Alpine watch-tower's portal
> Night, living yet, looks forth for dawn,
> So from time's mistier mountain-lawn
> The spirit of man, in trust immortal,
> Yearns toward a hope withdrawn . . .

And the only compensation which the watcher can find for this ' hope withdrawn ' is England, or rather the Commonweal :

> A commonweal arrayed and crowned
> With gold and purple, girt with steel
> At need, that foes must fear or feel,
> We find her, as our fathers found,
> Earth's lordliest commonweal.

All nations may have fallen short of the poet's ideal, but England, the commonweal, that community of four nations, comes nearest to it :

> Heard not of others, or misheard
>   Of many a land for many a year
>   The watchword Freedom fails not here . . .

It is no longer from Italy, or from France that the Universal Republic will arise and spread ; the poet strained his eyes in vain to perceive far off what was close at hand :

> The forces of the dark dissolve,
>   The doorways of the dark are broken :
>   The word that casts out night is spoken . . .
> And whence the springs of things evolve
>   Light born of night bears token.
>
> She loving light for light's sake only
>   And truth for only truth's, and song
>   For songs' sake and the sea's, how long
> Hath she not borne the world her lonely
>   Witness of right and wrong ?

Thus and not otherwise did Swinburne prophesy of Italy in 1868 ; and he has here recaptured in no small measure the fiery rhythm and inspiration of the *Songs*. The hymn closes triumphantly :

> With just and sacred jubilation
>   Let earth sound answer to the sea
>   For witness, blown on winds as free,
> How England, how her crowning nation
>   Acclaims this jubilee.

From the great Mazzinian shipwreck, Swinburne had been rescued at last. After years of weary tossing he

found himself cast on the shore of his native land and
Watts loudly applauded.[1]

Of Swinburne's other poems, little need be said from
the biographical point of view. During the years 1880–
1882 Swinburne concentrated on some major works
which ill-health and idleness had prevented him from
concluding before. In that sense we are indebted to
Watts for *Mary Stuart* (1881) and *Tristram* (1882),
but in that sense only. Both poems were conceptions of
Swinburne's early youth, and had been begun years
ago. *Mary Stuart* which had been planned, started
and lost in manuscript several times, shows more concentration and outline than *Bothwell*, but, in spite of
the pathetic close, does not reproduce the romantic
glamour of *Chastelard*. Despite Mary Beaton's final
statement we did *not* hear

> that very cry go up
> Far off long since to God, who answers here.

It was a very different sort of cry. Swinburne's long
and painstaking study of his subject, as evidenced in *The
Character of Mary Queen of Scots* (January 1882) and
Mary Queen of Scots (Encyclopaedia Britannica, 1883),
had given him a detachment, more scientific than
dramatic, which prevented him from instilling into
his work the breath of life. But, now the task was over,
he forgot all he had learnt, he bade history and documents farewell and his normal attitude to the Queen
was restored. She became once more the ' red star of
boyhood's fiery thought ' ; and the flesh of Chastelard

---

[1] Swinburne's political utterances were henceforth logical and continuous : see
The Armada (1880), *England* and *The Union* (1893), *Trafalgar Day, Cromwell*
(1895), *The Battle of the Nile* (1898) and the poems on the Boer War (1899–1902).
Thus is explained the imperialist tone of his later poems, his belief in the ' mission '
of the English race, considered as ' elect '.

tingled again with pleasure at the mere thought of suffering for her sake :

> Was ever heart so deadly dear
> So cruel ?

Watts did probably tone down some of the most ardent amatory passages in *Tristram* : Swinburne was thus led to substitute in the story of Tristram's relations with Iseult of Brittany the symbol of the hawthorn branch for that of the mud-stain, and he could write to W. M. Rossetti : ' I think I have treated the legend of Tristram and his virgin wife with all delicacy consistent with straightforwardness : so I trust there is nothing which could really " alarm " your sister in that poem.' In spite of this, the general impression given by the epic is that of a glorification of sensuous love ; in fact, although Swinburne had consulted endless medieval sources one cannot help thinking that the treatment is a little too gorgeous and refined for the simple Celtic legend. The atmosphere of the poem, with its flesh-painting effects and somewhat anachronic rhapsodies on Liberty and Fate, is rather that of the Renaissance ; it has not the true Pre-raphaelite ring, and one regrets a little the awkward unfinished ballad which Swinburne composed at Oxford. He was probably aware of this for the *Tale of Balen* (1894) exhibits the very opposite qualities : he has here returned to the more sober style and monotonous metre[1] of his early poems ; with unfailing instinct he has recaptured the essential feature of the medieval theme—the sense of unjust oppressive doom heroically endured :

[1] For the metre of *Balen* see Tennyson's *Lady of Shalott*.

Aloud and dark as hell or hate
Round Balen's head the wind of fate
Blew storm and cloud from death's wide gate,
But joy as grief in him was great
    To face God's doom and live or die,
Sorrowing for ill wrought unaware,
Rejoicing in desire to dare
All ill that innocence might bear
    With changeless heart and eye.

Balen is to *Tristram* what *Erechtheus* is to *Atalanta*.

From the *Tristram* volume of 1882 onwards a large portion of Swinburne's collections of verse contain poems devoted to the praise and description of babies. This love of Swinburne for very young children was genuine, and can be traced back to such an early date as 1864 when he noticed in the Uffizi Palace at Florence Andrea del Sarto's studies of

> round-limbed babies in red chalk outline, with full blown laughter in their mouths and eyes ; such flowers of flesh and live fruits of man, as only a great love and liking for new-born children could have helped him to render.

This purely animal delight in the company of rosy young creatures which sprang from complex feelings[1] was encouraged, flattered and developed out of all proportion by Watts and Lady Jane Swinburne. The former used this as hold on Swinburne's affections, for the poet had become passionately devoted to Herbert Mason, Watts' nephew, for whom he wrote *A Dark Month*; as for Lady Jane she hoped that 'it might lead

[1] See the *Whippingham Papers*, published anonymously in 1888. Also *The Children of the Chapel* (1864), the unpublished *Flogging Block* in Mr. Wise's collection, and especially the following illuminating sentence from *Lesbia Brandon* : ' Towards all beasts and babies he had always a physical tenderness ; a quality purely of the nerves, *not incompatible with cruelty*, nor grounded on any moral emotion or conviction '. (Italics mine.)

to the return of the faith of his youth in some hidden way'. But both were conscious that Swinburne went too far and she added : 'I hope you will guard the child from Algernon's harmful views. It is difficult to tell him not to overdo as you suggest. True he spoils his writings by not knowing where to stop.' Swinburne's effusions on infants have been compared with Blake's or Hugo's ; but they are never redeemed by the depth of emotion or the philosophic insight which distinguish those two writers ; they are at best vivid descriptions of the poet's delight at the sight of a healthy child.

Even Swinburne's mother recognized that he did not know where to stop. This became chiefly true after 1882 when, having got rid of his two major works, *Tristram* and *Mary Stuart*, his regained health and increased leisure allowed him to scatter his inspiration in scores of topical poems, articles and studies which even Watts had sometimes difficulty in selling, so numerous were they ; his output became amazing. From 1882 to 1909 he made 223 contributions to various reviews, magazines and newspapers and published well over twenty volumes. This fatal tendency was greatly encouraged by Watts' unfailing habit of proclaiming Swinburne's last work, whatever its value, one of the best he had ever composed. It is impossible, even from a strictly biographical point of view to do justice to all of them. But there is one last class of poems about which a few more words must be said. After 1880 the pessimism which had been a marked feature of Swinburne's inspiration tended to grow lighter ; not unnaturally, owing to a more regular and comfortable mode of existence, his view of life

became tinged with a mild form of optimism. This
was due largely to Watts, whose constant friendship
and deep mystical tendencies finally succeeded in
making Swinburne believe that immortality of the soul
in some wise was to be thought probable. Swinburne
had always held that this was not impossible : ' On
the question of what is called the immortality of the
soul—i.e. the survival or renascence of conscious and
individual personality after death—I have always
thought such transmigration of consciousness an open
field for speculation or belief . . . ' (To W. M.
Rossetti, 19 October 1875.) He now went further
and asserted : ' I do now, on the whole, strongly
incline to believe in the survival of life—individual
and conscious life—after the dissolution of the body '.
(To W. B. Scott, April 17, 1882.) This view is
reflected in many poems of the later period, in particular in the collection *A Century of Roundels*, which
contains, in a metrical form which appears slight and
artificial, the lyrical expression of many earnest feelings
and ideas :

> Death, if thou wilt, fain would I plead with thee ;
> Canst thou not spare, of all our hopes have built,
> One shelter where our spirits fain would be,
>   Death, if thou wilt ?

Such an attitude of semi-hopeful doubt is typical of
Swinburne's later verse. This evolution, however
striking it may seem, should not surprise us entirely ;
there always was in Swinburne's verse, despite the
belief in the blind power of fate, a virile acceptance of
the conditions of life, something strenuous, indomitable
and almost joyful, which intimated that for the poet

life possessed a definite meaning and perhaps an
ulterior end.

We must not, however, go one step further than
this : to all theistic religions, and more particularly
to Christianity, Swinburne remained to the end of his
days irrevocably averse. It is possible to be here very
dogmatic, for we possess a remarkable document in
a letter written to W. M. Rossetti as late as January
25, 1904 to acknowledge an edition of his sister's
poems : ' Good Satan ! what a fearful warning against
the criminal lunacy of theolatry ! It is horrible to
think of such a woman—and of so many otherwise
noble and beautiful natures—spiritually infected etc.'
And again ' J. M. Neale was a burning and a shining
light in that particular uppermost " high " branch of
the Anglican Church to which our mothers and sisters
belonged. In them that creed certainly was compatible
with an adorably beautiful type of character—which yet,
I cannot but think, might have been better in some
ways with a saner and wider outlook on life and death'.
(February 12, 1904.) On September 16, 1906 he
described himself half-humorously to the same correspondent as ' an humble antitheist '. To the end, in
Swinburne's verse, prose and correspondence, flashes
of the old fiery personality (or to change the metaphor, ' echoes of the still small voice' as he himself put
it) are visible and audible, which makes the reading of
his later works a task often tedious, but never quite
thankless : in the very thin-spun play *The Sisters* (1891)
there are wonderful autobiographical passages and
ample evidence of the old familiar sadistic conception
of the world which had not been expressed since
Atalanta and *Anactoria*.

Of his later prose there will be here very little to say ; contrary to what happened in the preceding period, its quality is inferior on the whole to that of the verse composed within the same dates. After 1881 the controversy which had been raging between Swinburne and Furnivall, president of the New Shakespeare Society, came to an end, and Watts did not permit him to enter into any other prolonged polemics—except of a political character. The two articles—*Whitmania* (1887) and *Mr. Whistler's Lecture on Art* (1888) reveal all the old power for invective and sustained irony ; it has been urged that they were both suggested, if not dictated, by Watts. He may have egged Swinburne on ; but the poet's dislike of Whitman's most glaring defects can be traced back to a much earlier date[1] ; as for Whistler, Swinburne is chiefly concerned with a fresh development of the painter's talent—his imitation of Japanese art. Watts may with his usual cleverness and tenacity, have developed some elements of Swinburne's former judgments at the expense of others ; he had no power to reverse them.

Miscellanies and *Studies in Poetry* contain some interesting essays, though many, written as they were for the Encyclopaedia Britannica (*Landor, Keats*, etc.), are impersonal and perfunctory. It is hard to discover in them a definite trend or evolution of the poet's thoughts and tastes in one particular direction. Swinburne became gradually less interested in contemporary subjects, and more immersed in the study of Elizabethan and Jacobean plays. The digressions which had adorned his volumes on Chapman and Shakespeare

---

[1] 1866. See my article, '*Swinburne et Whitman*', *Revue Anglo-Americaine*, October, 1931.

disappeared from his later works. So engrossed was he
in the mere delight of reading the text of those numberless dramas that he lost all sense of proportion : the
minor dramatists became as interesting to him as the
greater figures ;   insufficient difference was made
between masterpieces and works of the most mediocre
nature. He wrote in 1882 : ' My own impression is
that every English play in existence down to 1640
must be worth reprinting on extrinsic if not on intrinsic ground.' He wrote and rewrote much, read
and reread still more ; and with each year he seemed to
become less critical : the Elizabethans who had stood
him in such good stead in his youth seemed eventually
doomed to blunt and spoil completely a fine artistic
taste which had been uncommonly sound and sure,
despite its fantastic expression, and could on many
occasions become subtle and delicate.

In the *Dedicatory Epistle* to the Collected Edition of
his Poetical Works in 1904, however, we witness a
remarkable revival of Swinburne's critical faculties.
Although some of his judgments may appear unduly
severe, others perverse, that uncommon capacity of
lucid self-analysis, which we have already had occasion
to notice, is here more apparent, more truly remarkable
than ever.

This critical retrospect of 1904 should be considered
as Swinburne's literary testament : it is alleged by
Mrs. Disney Leith that Swinburne was ' utterly
unbusinesslike ' and that this accounted for the
regrettable omissions from which his relations suffered
when his Will was known in 1909. But of his intellectual wealth he had taken due and final stock by the
Midsummer of 1904. There is in that *Epistle* an

aloofness and detachment which suggest that, from an artistic point of view at least, the author considered that his career was at an end.

In fact, he seems to have become less and less concerned in what was taking place around him. In 1905 Watts (who had added the name of Dunton to comply with the terms of a family legacy in 1897) married Miss Clara Reich. Swinburne had met her during a short stay at Cromer in the preceding summer, and had been delighted with her company—' charming it was, and charming it will be ', he wrote to his surviving sister. ' But the time of the great event is not yet arranged. It will not be till I can get off a book I am now upon. Can you suggest any wedding present ? '

To Mrs. Watts-Dunton's vivid and colourful impressions we owe a more detailed account of the very last years of Swinburne's life than would otherwise have been accessible. Some of the particulars she mentions have appeared trifling to some reviewers ; I have found none uninteresting. She has described minutely the poet's time-table as it had become settled in a sort of mechanical regularity, or kingly etiquette, towards the end of his life ; Swinburne would breakfast at 10, alone in his library, enjoying his daily paper; we already know from the analysis of his later works with what close attention he followed day by day the political situation in England and abroad. About 11, he would go across Putney and Wimbledon Commons on a long walk, which lasted well over two hours and was marked by unfailing visits at some recognized shops or other stopping-places, such as the Rose and Crown Inn, where his glass of beer was ready for him. About

2.30, after his lunch, he retired for a prolonged siesta
till 4. From 4 to 6 he was at work in his library.
About 6 began those readings from Dickens or the
Old Dramatists to which Watts submitted as a compensation for the readings from Swinburne's own
poetry to a few select friends which had long ago been
discouraged. After his evening meal which took place
about 8, Swinburne went back to his library and had
more opportunities for work. It will be seen, however,
that not much of the day was devoted to original
composition, and that from 1880 to 1900, when
Swinburne's output was most considerable, he must,
for all his gift of improvisation, have given more time
to his work as poet and critic.

Although six years his senior, and by now a very
old man with his own particular ailments and a somewhat sedentary disposition, Watts-Dunton was still
watching over him carefully. At the end of March
1909 Watts-Dunton suffered from a serious attack of
influenza and was confined to his room. Swinburne
was left to himself, and in the course of his wanderings over the Common caught a chill to which he did
not pay immediate attention. Since his illness of 1903–
1904 his chest was weak. He soon developed lung
trouble. One morning he failed to get up and lay in
his bed, very quiet, refusing to take any food. Just
as in his lonely London rooms exactly thirty years ago,
he waited silently for death ; not perhaps with a clear
consciousness that the end was near, but certainly without any strong desire to regain his health. His mother
had died in 1896 ; two of his sisters in 1899 and 1903.
His youngest sister Isabel was the only survivor, and
her religious opinions had somewhat estranged her

from him. He had recently complained to W. M. Rossetti that most of his friends were gone. Apart from his affection for Watts-Dunton, there were but few ties, intellectual or sentimental, which still linked him with this world—except his love for poetry ; and, in that field, he knew that his work was done. It was some time before Watts-Dunton in his own weakened state realized the seriousness of his friend's condition. By April 1st Swinburne was very ill. Soon Sir Douglas Powell was called in consultation. But all efforts were of no avail. Swinburne died of double pneumonia on April 10th at 10 a.m., in his seventy-third year.

He was buried in Bonchurch Churchyard on April 15th. Watts-Dunton was unable to attend. The poet's sister Isabel, Sir John Swinburne and Mrs. Disney Leith, his cousins, were present. Isabel had waged a fierce war with Watts-Dunton, in order that the burial service should be read over the grave. But Watts, despite his weakness, was adamant. He replied to Isabel on April 14 :

In order not to wound his family, he was content when your dear mother died to listen to what he always deeply disliked, the burial service ; but up to his last moment he cherished the deepest animosity against the creed which he felt had severed him from his most beloved ties. Up to now I have kept from you this bitter fact, but now I recall a promise I made to him that the burial service should never be read over his grave.

God knows I would not of my own impulse have told you what I am telling, for I have no such strong feelings. But I could not rest if I broke the sacred promise. If I should break it, I should be miserable all my life. If he had made a slight matter of his antagonism against Christianity as so many free-thinkers do it would have been different, but with him it increased with his years and at the last (if I must say what I am sorry to say) it was bitterer than ever.

Cannot those broad-minded clergymen friends of yours do
something to relieve the matter ? While I was tossing on my
bed the promise flashed into my brain like lightning. This is
what I meant by the late discovery. Pray send me word by
your messenger boy what you have done in this matter.

A compromise was reached : the rector of
Bonchurch read the lines of the burial service as the
coffin left the hearse. It may be said, however, that the
dead man's desires were respected in their essentials.

When Swinburne's Will was read at the beginning
of May it was found that Watts-Dunton was the sole
inheritor of all he possessed [1] : he had thus paid his
debt of gratitude to his friend, not only for saving his
life in 1879 and looking after him ever after, but also
for the frequent and important professional services he
had rendered him between 1872 and 1879. However, not unnaturally, the family resented the fact that
the names of none of his relatives were even mentioned
in his Will, and considered it as ' a public slight '.
Watts' relations with Isabel Swinburne, which had at
one time been intimate, cooled off considerably.

At the end of this chapter which closes the poet's
life, we are again inevitably confronted with the question which has already eluded us at its opening : if
Swinburne had not known Watts, if he had been left
to die in 1879–80, would his fame have suffered or
gained by it ? It remains unanswerable. But it can
now be seen that, although occasionally subjected to
external influences, Swinburne remained true to himself

---

[1] The pictures and works of art remained at The Pines. A few books were sold.
Watts-Dunton made over the manuscripts of the poet to various collectors ; a great
many letters and manuscripts were thus scattered in divers libraries, but Mr. T. J.
Wise, thanks to his unfailing patience and generosity, secured the most important
documents and practically all unpublished manuscripts.

to the end. What is even more important still is that
in 1879 he had not fully or clearly expressed some
of his views and tendencies. In this long after-life at
the Pines he had ample time and opportunities for
revising, explaining and supplementing what he had
written. Had he not done so he would, as Keats,
Shelley or Chénier, have become the prey of unscrupulous, or, which comes to the same thing, imaginative
critics. Now, after *Tristram*, after *The Commonweal*,
after *Miscellanies* it would be very difficult to ignore
or misinterpret some features of the poet's personality.
In the days before he lived with Watts, Swinburne had
been free but irresponsible ; he had expressed his views
and principles in works which were often of superior
artistic merit, but, none the less, misleading and ambiguous. At the Pines he had ample time to review
and reconsider the activities of his dead self ; we know
that he was living in the past ; we may rest assured
that he often thought, with sympathy no doubt, but
also growing detachment, of that fascinating fairy-poet
(Shelley the second ?) who had passed away some time
in 1879 or perhaps in 1872. What he now wrote or
did was only a commentary or *scholia* to the early part
of his career. The thirty years at the Pines read like
the critical notes, often tedious or even painful, sometimes illuminating, which a soured and secluded, but
remarkably well-informed scholar appended to the life
and works of Algernon Charles Swinburne.

BIBLIOGRAPHICAL NOTE

I. *List of Swinburne's Works*

[This list makes no pretence at completeness : it aims at mentioning not the first appearance of all and sundry contributions to reviews, newspapers, etc., but only the collections of verse and prose, and, here and there, isolated poems or articles whose precise individual date offers a special interest. In the case of *Poems and Ballads, First Series*, of *Songs before Sunrise* and of *Songs of Two Nations*, it has been thought worth attempting to date individual poems. Works which appeared separately in book-form are marked with a *].

William Congreve [unsigned] 1857; Undergraduate Papers [5 contributions] 1858; *The Queen Mother and Rosamond 1860; Articles on Les Misérables [unsigned] 1862; Les Fleurs du Mal [unsigned] 1862; *The Children of the Chapel 1864; *Atalanta in Calydon 1865; *Chastelard 1865; *Byron 1866: *Laus Veneris 1866.

*Poems and Ballads 1866 : The Leper, Rondel (*Kissing her hair*), Song in time of Order, Song in time of Revolution, Before Parting, The Sundew, At Eleusis, August, A Christmas Carol, Saint-Dorothy, The Two Dreams, Aholibah, After Death, May Janet, The Sea-Swallows, The Year of Love—*before* 1862 ; Ballad of Life, Ballad of Death, Laus Veneris, Hymn to Proserpine, Ilicet, A Match, Faustine, A Cameo, Stage Love, Ballad of Burdens, Les Noyades, Masque of Queen Bersabe—1862 ; Triumph of Time, Anactoria, Hermaphroditus—1863 ; Itylus, Rococo, In Memory of W. S. Landor—1864 ; Before the Mirror, Dolores, Hesperia, Félise, Hendecasyllabics, Dedication—1865.

*Notes on Poems and Reviews 1866 ; *A Song of Italy 1867 ; An Appeal to England 1867 ; Matthew Arnold's New Poems 1867 ; *William Blake 1868 ; Ave Atque Vale 1868 ; *Ode on the Proclamation of the French Republic 1870 ; *The First Act of Bothwell 1871 ; Prelude to Tristram and Iseult 1871 ; Simeon Solomon's Vision of Love 1871.

Songs before Sunrise 1871 : Ode on the Insurrection in Candia, The Halt before Rome, Siena, An Appeal—1867 ; Blessed Among Women, The Litany of Nations, The Song of the Standard, Mentana : first Anniversary, A Watch in the Night—1868 ; Dedication, Quia Multum Amavit, Super Flumina Babylonis, Before a Crucifix, Christmas Antiphones, A New Year's Message, Cor Cordium —1869 ; Hertha, The Eve of Revolution, the Hymn of Man, Prelude, Monotones, Tenebrae, To Walt Whitman, Mater Dolorosa, Mater Triumphalis, Armand Barbès, Tiresias, Perinde ac Cadaver, A Year's Burden, Epilogue—1870.

*Under the Microscope 1872 ; Le Tombeau de Théophile Gautier 1872 ; *Bothwell 1874 ; A Letter to R. W. Emerson 1874 ; *George Chapman 1875.

Songs of Two Nations 1875 : A Song of Italy 1867 ; Ode on the Proclamation of the French Republic 1870 ; The Burden of Austria 1866 ; Intercession, Mentana : Second Anniversary, A Counsel, The Saviour of Society 1869 ; The Moderates, Mentana : Third Anniversary—1870 ; The Descent into Hell 1873.

*Essays and Studies 1875 ; The Devil's Due [signed Thomas Maitland] 1875 ; *Erechtheus 1876 ; *Joseph and his Brethren 1876; *Note on the Muscovite Crusade 1876 ; Nocturne 1876 ; Articles of Herbert Harvey 1877 ; *A Note on Charlotte Brontë 1877 ; The Sailing of the Swallow 1877 ; A Year's Letters 1877 ; Lesbia Brandon 1877 ; *Poems and Ballads, Second Series 1878 ; *A Study of Shakespeare 1880 ; *Songs of the Springtides 1880 ; *Studies in Songs 1880 ; *The Heptalogia 1880 ; *Mary Stuart 1881 ; *Tristram of Lyonesse and other Poems 1882; *A Century of Roundels 1883; *Les Cenci 1883 ; *A Midsummer Holiday 1884 ; Wordsworth and Byron 1884 ; *Marino Faliero 1885 ; *Miscellanies 1886 ; *A Study of Victor Hugo 1886 ; A Word for the Navy 1887 ; The Jubilee 1887 ; Whitmania 1887 ; *Gathered Songs 1887 ; *Locrine 1887 ; *The Whippingham Papers [anonymous] 1888 ; *A Study of Ben Johnson 1889 ; A Logical Ballad of Home Rule 1889 ; *Poems and Ballads, Third Series 1889 ; The Ballade of Truthful Charles 1889 ; Russia : an Ode 1890 ; *The Sisters 1892 ; The New Terror 1892 ; *Astrophel and other Poems 1894 ; *Studies in Prose and Poetry 1894 ; Robert Burns 1896 ; *The Tale of Balen 1896 ; *Rosamund, Queen of the Lombards 1899 ; Charles Dickens 1902 ; *A Channel Passage and other Poems 1904 ; *Chatto's Collected edition of the Poems and Plays [11 volumes with Dedicatory Epistle] 1904 ;

*Love's Cross-Currents [A Year's Letters] 1905 ; Czar Louis XVI 1905 ; *The Duke of Gandia 1908 ; *The Age of Shakespeare 1908 ; *Three Plays of Shakespeare 1909.

Posthumous Works : *Shakespeare 1909 ; Letters to the Press 1912 ; The Death of Sir John Franklin 1916 ; Early Letters to John Nichol 1917 ; *Posthumous Poems 1917 ; *The Boyhood of A. C. Swinburne 1917 ; Rondeaux Parisiens 1917 ; Letters to Victor Hugo 1917 ; Queen Yseult 1918 ; *The Letters of A. C. Swinburne [Rickett and Hake] 1918 ; *The Letters of A. C. Swinburne [Gosse and Wise, 2 volumes] 1918 ; The Italian Mother 1918 ; *Contemporaries of Shakespeare 1919 ; William the Ranter on William the Canter 1919 ; Letters to R. H. Horne, 1920 ; Autobiographical Notes 1920 ; *Ballads of the English Border 1925 ; *Bonchurch Collected edition of the Works of Swinburne (20 Volumes) 1926–1927.

II. *Works on Swinburne*

The only complete biography of Swinburne is that published by Edmund Gosse in 1917 (new edition in the Bonchurch Edition 1927). Most of the biographical material available is to be found in Mr. T. J. Wise's works :

A Bibliography of Swinburne (2 volumes 1918–19) ; A Swinburne Library (1925) ; Catalogue of the Ashley Library (10 Volumes 1922–1931). See also the volumes of letters mentioned in the preceding section and my *Jeunesse de Swinburne* Volume I (1928), which deals only with the years 1837–1867.

Among the manuscript sources one should mention the unpublished manuscripts and correspondence in the collection of Mr. T. J. Wise ; the letters of Swinburne to G. Powell in the library of Aberystwyth University ; and a few letters to Karl Blind in the manuscript department of the British Museum.

All other books on Swinburne are only partly biographical and should be consulted rather for their interpretation of facts which are already known, than for the presentment of new facts. Students of Swinburne's biography should not, however, fail to read : W. M. Rossetti's Poems and Ballads : A Criticism (1866), P. E. Thomas' A. C. Swinburne (1912), T. E. Welby's Study of Swinburne (1914 and 1926), E. V. Lucas' At the Pines (1916), Adah Isaac Menken : A Fragment of an Autobiography (1917), Coulson Kernahan's Swinburne as I knew him

(1919), P. de Reul's L'œuvre de Swinburne (1922), Clara Watts-Dunton's Home Life of Swinburne (1922), A. Galimberti's Aedo d'Italia (1925), H. Nicolson's Swinburne (1926), Max Beerbohm's And Even Now [No. 2, The Pines] (1926), A. S. Chew's Swinburne (1929), W. R. Rutland's Swinburne : a nineteenth century Hellene (1931), and many memoirs, biographies and letters by contemporaries and friends of Swinburne.

INDEX